MEMOIRS

OF

JOSEPH FOUCHÉ

Napoleon

From the painting by Robert Le Fevre

Courtiers and Favourites of Royalty

Memoirs of the Court of France
With Contemporary and Modern Illustrations
Collected from the
French National Archives

BY

LEON VALLÉE

LIBRARIAN AT THE BIBLIOTHÈQUE NATIONALE

Memoirs
of
Fouché

IN TWO VOLUMES
VOL. I

University Press of the Pacific
Honolulu, Hawaii

Memoirs of Joseph Fouché
(Volume One)

Collected by
Leon Vallée

ISBN: 1-4102-0359-X

Copyright © 2002 by University Press of the Pacific

Reprinted from the 1903 edition

University Press of the Pacific
Honolulu, Hawaii
http://www.universitypressofthepacific.com

In order to make original editions of historical works
available to scholars at an economical price, this
facsimile of the original edition of 1903 is
reproduced from the best available copy and has
been digitally enhanced to improve legibility, but the
text remains unaltered to retain historical
authenticity.

FOUCHE

UNDER the Revolution, the first Empire, and the Restoration, Fouché played one of the most important parts. He is one of their curious visages. But if he has traced his name in ineffaceable characters on all the pages of the history of his epochs, it must be recognised that the judgment passed on this politician is generally pretty severe.

A brilliant pupil of the Oratory, — a religious order which took as active a part in the theological squabbles of the Church as in the affairs of the temporal order, — Fouché devoted himself first to teaching, and we find him professor in the Oratory at Nantes when the Revolution breaks out. He is ablaze for the new ideas, and plunges into the political movement with the zeal of a convinced and ardent spirit. The department of Loire Inférieure having elected him deputy to the Convention, he takes his seat on the benches of the Mountain. When the Assembly tries Louis XVI., Fouché delivers one of the most vehement speeches, and votes for the King's death without appeal or respite. A little later he is among the number of those who overthrow the Girondins.

Sent on a mission into the Nièvre to put the law of suspects into execution, he places himself at the head of the anti-Catholic movement, suppresses the religious emblems which exist in the public places, and writes over the gates of the cemeteries, " Death is an eternal sleep." At the same time he rifles the churches of their gold and silver vessels and all their precious objects, which he sends to the Convention that they may be employed in the defence of the fatherland.

The Assembly next intrusts him with the formidable task of re-establishing republican authority at Lyons, where the chiefs of the rebellion have made common cause with the foreigner and the royalists. In his repression, Fouché shows himself pitiless: the blood of the Lyonnais flows in streams.

When he returns to Paris, Fouché resumes his place in the Convention, where he loses no time in engaging in the strife with Robespierre, against whom he gathers the old Dantonists and Hebertists, and whose resounding fall he initiates by organizing the coalition of the 9th Thermidor.

As prudent as ambitious, as sagacious as devoid of scruple, he has one foot in every camp. In touch with everything, he watches everything, scents to-morrow's success, and always ranges himself on the side where the wind of the day is blowing. He has already been with the Mountain, with the Jacobins, with the Thermidiorans, with Babeuf, and yet is still not at the end of his political incarnations.

He goes as ambassador to the Cisalpine Republic and to Holland. Then, when he returns to Paris, he obtains, August 1, 1799, the ministry of police. This time Fouché is at the summit of his desires; he is in his element; he has in his hand a terrible weapon, which he manages for the best good of his personal interests without the least remorse, with the finest cynicism.

From this instant he shows himself the enemy of the enfranchised, hastens to shut up the popular societies, suppresses eleven papers at a blow, arrests journalists. In compensation, he takes rigorous measures against the Chouans of La Vendée and Brittany; but he manages to mitigate the severity of the law in their favour, because he determines to spare the royalist faction, of which he may have need some day.

At this moment the Parisian world is thronging Josephine's drawing-rooms. Fouché is not content with frequenting them assiduously. He already renders services of all kinds to the future Empress, whom he succeeds in attaching by personal interest, and from whom he draws useful information as to high police matters. Then, when Bonaparte, back from Egypt, prepares his *coup d'état* of the 18th Brumaire, Fouché does not hesitate to betray the Directory, to paralyze the Dubois-Crancé ministry, which had suspicions, and to impose silence on his agents. He does more yet: the day the conspiracy is sprung, he sharply takes the side of Bonaparte, whom he seconds by every means in his power.

In payment for this treason, Fouché preserves the post of minister of police. He affects great moderation toward the republicans, while he adopts measures favourable to the *émigrés*, of whom many owe him the restitution of their confiscated and not yet sold estates. In short, Fouché prepares the country to submit to the coming yoke of absolutism.

He would be thenceforth very happy had he not to keep himself constantly on his guard, be incessantly on the alert to please a chief who cares very little for him, and who, extremely suspicious by nature, has him watched by counter-police. In this struggle of stratagem and address, Fouché, who by good fortune has the disposal of great pecuniary resources, is wonderfully tutored by Josephine, by Bourrienne the private secretary of Napoleon, and by innumerable agents hidden among all parties. This permits him to remain of good courage, and make himself indispensable.

But the gloomy First Consul hates indispensable people; so, in September 1802, he suppresses the ministry of police, which he consolidates with that of justice. As compensation and indemnity, Fouché is appointed senator, with the titular senatorial district of Aix, and receives out of the police-fund reserve the sum of 1,200,000 francs. For some months Fouché remains at Pontcarré, or at his house in the rue de Bac; up to the time (July 10, 1804) when, by a decree, Napoleon re-establishes the ministry of police, augments its functions, and confides the post to Fouché, who radically reorganises its numerous services, and makes the imperial police the most powerful and the best informed in Europe.

Fouché is now the first personage in France next to the Emperor; he governs the country efficiently when his master is at the head of armies beyond the frontiers. His influence is preponderant in everything. When it is a question of creating a new nobility, entirely honorary, that shall replace the old *noblesse* abolished by the revolution, Fouché supports the proposition. He becomes successively count, then Duke of Otranto.

Nevertheless one day, in consequence of a false manœuvre, he falls into disgrace, and is dismissed by Napoleon, who in full council reproaches him with "making war and peace without his participation." He retires to Ferrières; then, as the Emperor makes requisition for his correspondence and important papers, he refuses to sur-

render them, and flies to Italy to escape the consequences
of the imperial anger. In 1811, after a compromise, he
obtains the favour of returning to France, and continues
to intrigue, for intrigue with him is life. 1814 arrives.
Fouché offers himself to Louis XVIII. as minister; and
if he refuses the post at the last moment, it is simply
because he comprehends that the new monarchy is going
to founder.

In fact, Napoleon returns from the Isle of Elba, re-enters
the Tuileries, and recalls Fouché to the ministry of police.
The latter resumes the headship of his old functions; but
as he has no confidence in the duration of the Napoleonic
reign, he negotiates underhand with the Bourbons. Finally, after Waterloo, he wrings his abdication from the
Emperor, and has himself elected by the Chamber as
president of the provisional government. This time he
counts securely on becoming the sole master of the country. His illusion is short: he speedily realises that the
Bourbons intend to turn it over to the allies. He does not
hesitate an instant: he enters into the Restoration league.
So, a few days later, by King's Decree, he resumes possession of the ministry of police. In vain does he exert
himself to make ideas of moderation prevail with the
government. Overpowered, he is compelled to share in
measures of proscription, and the election of the " Undiscoverable Chamber " [1] overturns him from power.

He sets out for Saxony as ambassador; but he has
hardly installed himself at Dresden when the Chamber

---

[1] The " Undiscoverable Chamber " was the epithet given by Louis XVIII.
to the Chamber of 1815, in his joy at finding it so much more eagerly royalist
than he had expected; his meaning was, that no one would have supposed
such deputies could be discovered in France.

votes the law excluding the regicides from amnesty, and condemning to perpetual banishment whoever signed the "additional act,"[1] or took part in the government during the "Hundred Days." Fouché is instantly dismissed. He lives a few years more on a foreign soil, and dies of consumption at Trieste, December 25, 1820.

Such, in brief, is the career, so curious and so full, of the great policeman, whose life is only a group of contrasts. The plain professor of aforetime dies the owner of a colossal fortune; the savage republican of the Convention becomes one of the principal upholders of the empire; the proletarian is made a duke; the Terrorist marries a girl of the old nobility, Mademoiselle de Castellane; the regicide serves the royalty he has overturned; and the man before whose power a whole people has long bent, the man who seemed impregnable to human catastrophes, ends his days in the sadness of exile.

LÉON VALLÉE.

[1] The "Additional Act" was the name given by Napoleon to his ordinance on returning from Elba in 1815, by which a liberal representative government was constituted in France.

AUTHOR'S PREFACE

THESE Memoirs have neither been produced by party spirit, hatred, nor a desire for vengeance, and still less that they might afford food for scandal and malignity. I respect all that is deserving of honour in the opinions of men. Let me be read, and my intentions, my views, my sentiments, and the political motives by which I was guided in the exercise of the highest duties, will then be appreciated; let me be read, and it will then be seen if, in the councils of the Republic and of Napoleon, I have not been the constant opponent of the extravagant measures of the government; let me be read, and it will be apparent whether or not I have displayed some courage in my warnings and remonstrances; in short, by perusing me, the conviction will follow, that I owed it as a duty to myself to write what I have written.

The only means of rendering these Memoirs

advantageous to my own character, and useful to the history of those eventful times, was to rest them solely upon the pure and simple basis of truth; to this I have been induced, both by disposition and conviction; my situation also made it an imperative law to me, for was it not natural that I should thus charm away the *ennui* attendant upon fallen power?

Under whatever form, the Revolution had accustomed me to an extreme activity of mind and memory; irritated by solitude, this activity required some outlet. It has been, therefore, with a species of pleasure and delight that I have written this first part of my recollections.[1] I have, it is true, retouched them, but no material change has been made, not even during the anguish of my last misfortune, for what greater misfortune can there be than to wander in banishment, an exile from one's country!

France, thou that wast so dear to me, never shall I see thee more! Alas! at what a cost have I purchased power and grandeur? Those who were once

[1] This preface was prefixed to the first part, which was published at Paris separately.

my friends will no longer offer me their hand. **It is**
clear they wish to condemn me even to the silence
of the future. Vain hope! I shall find means to
disappoint the expectations of those who are already
anticipating the spoils of my reminiscences and revelations, of those who are preparing to lay snares for
my children. If my children are too young to be
on their guard against the artifices of the designing,
I will ensure their preservation by seeking, far from
the crowd of selfish and ungrateful men, a discreet
and faithful friend. But what do I say? This
other self I have already found, and it is to his
discretion and fidelity that I confide these Memoirs.
I constitute him the sole judge after my decease of
the propriety of their publication. He is in possession
of my ideas upon the subject, and I am convinced
he will only place my work in the hands of an
honourable man, one who is equally superior to base
intrigue and sordid speculation. This is assuredly
my only and best guarantee that these Memoirs
shall remain free from the interpolations and gar-
blings of the enemies to truth and sincerity.

In the same spirit of candour I am now preparing
the second part of them. I do not blind myself

to the fact that I have to treat of a period of peculiar delicacy, of one presenting innumerable and serious difficulties, whether we consider the times, the personages, or the calamities which it embraces. But truth, when not deformed by the malignancy of the passions, will ever command the attention of mankind.

EDITOR'S PREFACE

A PERUSAL of the author's preface will show that I might indulge some degree of self-satisfaction in the fulfilment of his intentions relative to the publication of these Memoirs. Pecuniary advantages had no share in the selection of myself as editor, and I dare affirm that in accepting the office I was actuated by equal disinterestedness. To all persons but myself, such a publication would have been a great *desideratum*, and they would only have considered it as a source of profit, perhaps after all ideal. On the contrary, I only saw in it a duty; this I have fulfilled, but not without hesitation : I will even confess that it became necessary to strengthen my own opinion by that of others. The title of the work, and the subjects of which it treats, appeared but too well calculated to create uneasiness in my mind. I was anxious neither to trespass against the laws, shock public decorum, nor offend the government of my country. Not daring then to confide in my own judgment, I consulted a gentleman of considerable experience, and his assurances have removed my apprehensions. If I requested him to favour me with a few notes, it was rather to confirm my own opinions than to present a contrast between the text and the commentaries Although these notes were far from being numerous, they had, however, nearly deprived me of the publication of these posthumous Memoirs. At length the person commissioned to fulfil the author's intentions yielded to the force of my reasons, and I am now enabled to announce to the public that no time shall be lost in bringing out the second part of the Memoirs of the Duke of Otranto. As to the intenseness of their interest, and their authenticity, I shall merely say with the author—READ.

CONTENTS OF VOL. I

LIST OF ILLUSTRATIONS
VOLUME I.

BIOGRAPHICAL NOTICE

JOSEPH FOUCHÉ, Duke of Otranto, born at Nantes
on the 29th of May, 1763, was one of the most remarkable men of the Revolution, and at the same time
one of the most difficult to appreciate. His life may be
divided into three very distinct epochs. In the first
he is simply a student and teacher at the school of the
Oratory; in the second he appears to us during some
years as the *Sëide*[1] of crime and anarchy; and in the
third one only sees the man of power pursuing with
perseverance and some dignity the self-imposed task of
remedying the evils that he and his accomplices had
brought upon France. In these two latter phases of
his public life he did right and wrong with ability and
calculation *à propos*. Through all these variations the
man showed himself privately as of good and simple
manners, sensible of friendship and the domestic affec-
tions, always full of *aménité*, and treating frivolity with
consideration. Whilst not pretending to an extraordinary amount of seriousness, he proved master of

---

[1] A character in the tragedy of "Mahomet," by Voltaire.
["Sectateur devoué, capable de commettre un crime par zèle
religieux."—*Littré.*]

himself not only in the lightest affairs of life, but also in the most serious crises.

His ability was best displayed in controlling events whilst appearing to submit to them, because he knew how to apppreciate them. No less discretion did he show in the selection of the men he employed.

The account of his life during the first of our three periods is very simple. Son of a captain in the merchant service at Nantes, Fouché was at the age of nine years confided to the care of the fathers of the Oratory, who had a college in that town. At the commencement his success in his studies was small. To a mind slow to develop itself he joined a gaiety of temperament which the masters mistook for want of aptitude. His intelligence showed itself rebellious to the generally accepted rules of grammar and of Latin and French versification.

He was about to be classed as a wretched scholar, when one of the tutors noticed that he preferred the most serious books, amongst others the *Pensées de Pascal*. Everything was done by this sensible instructor to cultivate agreeably the disposition of one who departed from the usual groove.

Fouché was intended for the navy, but his delicate appearance caused his father to give way to the representations of the Oratorians, and the favourite pupil of M. Durif, the tutor, was consecrated to the public instruction in this learned association. Having made some progress in mathematics, he was sent to the Institute of Paris. Here the first books put into his hands were Jansenius' commentaries on the Gospels and the catechism of the Council of Trent. Fouché avowed to his confessor what a dislike he had to these books, and the wise director conducted him to the library, where he permitted the young man to choose his own books. Fouché passed with distinction in philosophy and mathematics. All those who knew him at this peaceful time of his life give him credit for the regularity of his manners and zeal for his work. During the time that Fouché was at Arras he became acquainted with Robespierre, and when the latter was elected to the Constituent Assembly lent him several hundred francs for his journey and his establishment in Paris.

When Fouché was twenty-five he was appointed inspector of studies at the college of Nantes, when the ardour with which he embraced the new ideas threw him into the political storm. Not having taken orders he married, and founded the Popular Society of Nantes. He was not eloquent, but he distinguished himself by his manner of exaggeration, which at that time led to popularity. His election as deputy of the Loire-Inférieure in September, 1792, showed that he had calculated shrewdly.

During the first few months of the session of the Convention he was little remarked; he was biding his time, however. His acquaintance with Robespierre was renewed, but the disparity of their characters and

the diversity of their political views were not long in
causing a misunderstanding between them. Fouché
was too much of an egoist to submit to Robespierre, and
joined the Danton faction. From his first arrival in Paris
he frequented the Jacobin club, and appeared to have
a good understanding with Marat. At first he also
seemed to join Condorcet and Vergniaud; but already
the fight had commenced between the Girondists and
the Mountain, and Fouché was too well advised to join
the former party. Members of both parties were still
in the habit of meeting each other. Coming from
Fouché's house on one occasion, where they had
just dined, Robespierre was vehemently attacking Vergniaud, when Fouché, addressing the former, remarked,
"With such violence you may certainly gain the passions, but never esteem or confidence." Robespierre
never pardoned this remark, but the author, having become a person of importance, was pleased to repeat it.

At the trial of the King, Fouché was as violent in
his denunciation of royalty as was any member of the
Mountain whose revolutionary reputation was well established. He voted for death without appeal or respite.
As member of the Committee of Public Instruction,
Fouché at the sittings of 14th of February and 8th of
March, 1795, caused a decree to be issued for the sale
as national property of all the establishments of public
instruction except the colleges. On the Committee of
Finances he was not idle. He caused a decree to be
issued by which all property which had been kept in

hand by the fiscal authorities for any reason what-soever should be taken possession of by the government. All notaries and other officials were to give an account of all property conveyed by them since 1st of January, 1793, under a penalty of 20,000 francs. Ten years' imprisonment was threatened to any official conserving the property of an *emigré*.

Soon after, upon the proposition of Marat, Fouché was sent to the department of the Aube, where recruiting had been difficult, and was successful in raising a young and numerous militia simply by his persuasion. Sent afterwards to Nièvre to put into practice the decrees of the Convention with regard to religious service, he only took four days to accomplish his purpose. He made atheism the order of the day, decreeing that the dead should be buried in twenty-four, or at the latest forty-eight, hours, and the only inscription over them should be, *Death is eternal sleep*.

He caused all the churches to be pillaged, and sent the valuables to the Convention; for this he received high praise. In one of his messages was included this phrase: "You will see with pleasure two beautiful crosses of ornamented silver, and a ducal crown in red. The gold and silver have done more harm to the Republic than have the fire and iron of the ferocious Austrians and cowardly English." Chaumette, who was in the department at the time, sent a most laudatory letter to the Convention concerning Fouché.

The Convention were so well satisfied with Fouché's

conduct in the Nièvre that they sent him with Collot·
d'Herbois to Lyons in November, 1793, to put into
execution against that town the decree of destruction.
This decree was carried out in all its horrors. It was
at the time that this terrible work was being carried
out that Danton was executed.

Fouché returned to Paris, and was elected president
of the Society of Jacobins on 6th of June, 1794. This
growing popularity offended Robespierre, who had not
forgotten the incident at the "Fête of the Supreme
Being," when Fouché had predicted to him his approaching fall. Fouché was summoned to appear before the Jacobin society on the charge of persecution
of the patriots. He declined to attend, but requested
the society to defer its judgment until the report of the
committees had been published. An individual from
Lyons, having made certain charges against Fouché,
the latter was expelled the society. He had a narrow
escape from Robespierre's vengeance, his head being
demanded. Tallien pursued him mercilessly. Denunciations continued to arrive from all the places where
Fouché had been in power, and especially from Lyons.
The inhabitants of Gannat also demanded his head,
making the most terrible charges against him. The
denunciations were overwhelming. His orders to the
administrators of the departments were sent to the
Convention. Laurenceot, the representative of Nevers,
accused him of not having rendered any account of the
taxes, which amounted to more than two million francs

in the commune of Nevers alone. In an attempt to turn aside these attacks, Fouché attempted to again make friends with Tallien and the Thermidorians, whom he had not approached since Robespierre's fall. He found them willing, but weak. The result of this universal *déchainement* was that Fouché was arrested, but he was soon released. He then lived partly in disgrace, until intrusted by the Directory with a mission to the frontier of Spain.

About this time Fouché made the acquaintance of Barras. Fouché, being in the secret of the Babeuf conspiracy, disclosed it to Barras, and was in, return offered employment. He preferred, however, to have a share of the army contracting, and thus build up an immense fortune. At the 18th Fructidor (September 4th, 1797), Fouché again rendered Barras and his party assistance by his timely warning and counsel. Barras now rewarded Fouché, as desired by him, by sending him as ambassador to the Cisalpine Republic. In consequence of Fouché's conduct there, the Directory caused him to be replaced. Relying on Barras' influence, he was tardy in leaving Milan, but was obliged at last to return to Paris. Fouché was the gainer by this arrangement, he being accorded an indemnity for displacement, the power of his opponents (Merlin and Rewbel) being then on the decline.

Fouché was next sent as ambassador to Holland, but had hardly arrived there when he was appointed minister of police (July 31st, 1799). Fouché on his appointment at once rose to the occasion and grasped the situation, having for some time coveted the position.

Fouché's first actions tended to give offence to his old friends the demagogues, who flattered themselves that they would find nothing but complaisance in the pro-consul of the Commune *affranchie*. He obtained *carte blanche* from the Directory, which enabled him to limit the license of the journals as well as the audacity of the popular societies. Fouché saw that to show weakness would be to lose all, and, therefore, when attacked by the Manège Society, their club was closed. He also closed the Jacobins' Hall. The laws against the relatives of the *emigrés* were mitigated ; and by this means he gained some royalist agents, and was enabled to finish more quickly the civil war. Shortly afterwards he was bold enough to suppress, at a single blow, eleven of the most important journals of the Jacobins and Royalists. Fouché was attacked by Briot in the Council of the Ancients, the latter declaring that Fouché was preparing a *coup d'état*, and after having recalled the atrocities of the missions of the deputy of Nantes, demanded the suppression of the ministry of police. On the morrow the Directory inserted in its journals a eulogy of their minister.

Briot would not own himself beaten ; but returned to the charge. The situation was becoming strained. Joubert had been killed at Novi, and thus all the plans of the Directory had been reversed, as they had looked to Joubert for support. They were casting about for a successor to him when Bonaparte disembarked on the coast of Provence. Fouché was already in indirect communication with the new dictator. Judging from the state of affairs that the Directory could not sustain itself, he took care not to hinder the conspiracy of Bonaparte. There is no doubt that though he was ready to agree if it were successful, he was none the less ready to strike if it failed. All precautions were taken. Had Bonaparte failed, his head and those of his accomplices would have been in jeopardy. Fouché told the intimates of Bonaparte that the latter should lose no time, for if the Jacobins were allowed to rally, and he were decreed, all would be lost. Fouché kept himself so well informed of all that transpired at Saint-Cloud that, when the orders were brought from Bonaparte not to allow the fugitive deputies to return, those who brought the orders found themselves anticipated. Fouché hoped by this action to win the favour of the new victor. He used his power with discretion, doing his best to calm the fears of the nervous and restoring to liberty those who had been arrested. By acting in this way he came into conflict with Sieyès— "le haineux Sieyès qui ne rêvait que proscriptions." Finally, Fouché was successful, and his administration was such that the general police earned a character for justice and moderation. He was also successful in obtaining better treatment for those of the *emigrés* who had been shipwrecked at Calais; and when he found that the ameliorating orders were not properly carried out, he did not rest until he had obtained the release of the unfortunate *emigrés*, who were commanded to quit the territory of the Republic.

One result of the improved state of affairs was that the priests who had been expelled were allowed to return and exercise their calling. Under the Directory the *filles publiques* had been made use of as spies, thus obtaining indefinite license. The scenes in the Rue St. Honoré and the Palace Egalité were scandalous every evening. By Fouché's orders these women were arrested. They demanded their release on the ground that they were police agents. This demand being sent to Fouché, he answered that their arrest had been appreciated by the public, and that he could not order their release, also saying that the good they did was counterbalanced by the evil, and that it would be a disgrace to the law if such agents were necessary. Confirmed as consul with Cambacérès and Lebrun, Bonaparte took care to keep Fouché near him; not that his confidence in the latter was so great—on the contrary, but the extent and power of the revolutionary secrets of which the minister had made himself master rendered his services indispensable. His presence in power rallied to the First Consul the revolutionary interests which had been alarmed at the dangers with which the Republic was threatened. Fouché also rendered himself useful by efficacious measures relative to the troubles in the departments of the West. During all this time he did not neglect to increase his own fortune by permitting gambling, and became one of the richest men in France. It is said that he was paid 3,000 francs a day by one establishment alone for his goodwill. This immense revenue enabled him to make presents to members of the Court and to the Bonaparte family, who were able to furnish him with information. It is thus that he continued to have as pensioners Bourrienne and Josephine, and to the latter he is said to have given 1,000 francs a day. Lucien and Joseph Bonaparte were inimical to Fouché, and did all they could to disparage him to their brother, who, having a *penchant* for the details of police, organised several rival systems. So commenced a play of ruse against ruse between Fouché and his emulators. Informed by Bourrienne or Josephine, he often caused the Court police to fall into the snare they themselves had laid for him. Fouché was amused at this little war, seeing that he always obtained the advantage; but he showed so much mystery in the means he took to combat the plot against the Consul's life, that sometimes Bonaparte thought his police had the advantage of those of the minister. The latter had smothered, just before its execution, a project of this kind formed by Juvenot and about twenty Jacobins. While these were under arrest, news came of a fresh plot to murder the Consul at the opera. During the time that Fouché had the plotters under supervision, one of them, a cashiered officer named Harrel, revealed it spontaneously to Bourrienne. He, by desire of Bonaparte, did not

mention it to Fouché, and acted in concert with the
commander of the guard of the Consuls in order to
follow the progress of the plot. Bourrienne, through
the agency of the denouncer Harrel, furnished the
conjurés with the money necessary to purchase the
arms. The gunsmith refused to supply arms without
the authority of the police. Thereupon Fouché gave
his permission. The First Consul, thinking to take his
minister unawares, reproached him bitterly. Fouché
endured his reproaches with his accustomed calm, his
answer being to cause the man from whom he obtained
his first information to appear. This was Barère, then
charged with the political part of the journals written
under the ministerial influence. Fouché and Bonaparte
now united to allow this affair to proceed to a certain
extent. Bonaparte went to the opera, and the police
agents arrested Diana, Ceracchi, and their accomplices.

This affair caused an unpleasantness between Bonaparte and Fouché, which was soon augmented by the
courtiers inimical to the latter. After the explosion of
the infernal machine, the courtiers openly accused the
Jacobins and their protector Fouché. Different accounts
are given of the scene that occurred on the morrow of
this attempt. Bonaparte is said to have approached
Fouché with the question, " Well, do you still say this
was the work of the Royalists ? " " Yes, I will say it,"
remarked Fouché. Bourrienne states that Bonaparte
remarked that he did not rely upon the police of
Fouché, but kept his own police. One of the zealous

courtiers of the consular power, Rœderer, approached Josephine and said, " The days of the First Consul should not be left at the disposition of a man surrounded by scoundrels." Josephine answered, "The most dangerous men are those who wish to give Bonaparte ideas of an hereditary dynasty, of divorce, and of marriage with a princess." The explanation of this is that a pamphlet had just appeared, entitled " Parallel of Cromwell, Monk, and Bonaparte," the aim of which was to re-establish the hereditary monarchy. It was Lucien, minister of the interior, who had caused this pamphlet to be distributed. Fouché hastened to Malmaison and placed the pamphlet before Bonaparte, with a report on the inconvenience of an initiative so badly disguised. Bonaparte pretended to be annoyed, and demanded why he had allowed such a dangerous publication to appear. When told that the delinquent was his brother Lucien, " Then," said he, " your duty as minister of police was to arrest him." This appeared the more strange to Fouché, seeing that he had seen proofs of the pamphlet with corrections in Bonaparte's own hand. Lucien and Bonaparte quarrelled concerning this affair, the former being dismissed ; and so, to all appearances, Fouché had triumphed. Bonaparte appeared to be grateful to him for the precautions taken to insure his safety.

Bonaparte insisted upon the proscription of some of the Jacobins, although Fouché contended that it was not they but the Royalists who were the authors of the 3rd Nivôse. When Bourrienne ventured to plead also for the revocation of the proscription, agreeing with Fouché that the Jacobins were not the guilty parties, "Bah!" said Bonaparte, "at any rate, I have got rid of them."

It was about this time that the Abbé de Montesquiou, on the part of Louis XVIII. and the Duchess de Guiche, charged with a mission from the Count d'Artois, succeeded, firstly, in placing before Bonaparte a letter, in which the King demanded his crown from this second Monk, and secondly, in procuring an interview with Josephine, who was the friend of the *emigrés*. Fouché was informed by Josephine of what was taking place, and was annoyed that he had not received any orders from Bonaparte with regard to it. He then represented to the latter that he was the man of the Revolution and could be only that. This, with other representations, made a deep impression upon Bonaparte, and the duchess received orders to quit.

After the peace of Amiens, Bonaparte caused his secret agents to propose for him the consulate for life. Fouché opposed this, and soon found that a certain reserve was shown towards him, and that mysterious conferences were held at the house of Cambacérès. Always well served by his spies, Fouché informed his numerous friends in the senate, the result being that this body only prolonged the power of the First Consul for ten years (2nd of May, 1802). Bonaparte exhibited great irritation at this, but the other consuls decreed that the voice of the people should be taken. Bonaparte was elected for life, and proceeded to the Luxembourg with a magnificent *cortège*, but he was much annoyed at the silence of the people on the way, and complained of it to Fouché, who replied that he had not been ordered to provide an enthusiasm. At this interview Bonaparte finally turned his back on Fouché, which was supposed to predict the latter's near disgrace. Since the treaties of Luneville and Amiens the First Consul had been annoyed by the English journals representing him as under the tutelage of Talleyrand with regard to foreign affairs, and Fouché for the affairs of the interior. The latter wearied Bonaparte by his persistent counsels and his general opposition to this budding tyrant. Fouché had taken advantage of his position to interfere not only with affairs of state, but also with those of the family of Bonaparte and the Court. He often represented himself as being the repairer of the errors of the executive, and thus sang his own praises at the expense of the chief of the state. What Bonaparte forgave still less was that Fouché sought not only to be useful, but to render himself necessary. The First Consul looked upon the police force organised by Fouché as being a power outside the government, and at a critical time very likely to be dangerous, seeing the versatile character of the minister. Often when the latter was publicly attacked by Bonaparte with regard to his conduct of affairs, Fouché kept silence, not caring to excuse himself by divulging that which was then secret. This silence irritated Bonaparte, although he understood the motive of it. The enemies of Fouché, with Bonaparte's brothers at their head, took advantage of this feeling. Bonaparte hesitated for some time, but finally, after working with Fouché in the forenoon, as usual, charged Cambacérès with the mission that he dared not carry out himself. Anxious to attenuate the disagreeableness of the disgrace as much as possible to a man who, though dismissed, retained a deal of influence, Bonaparte thus wrote to the senate: "The citizen Fouché has responded by his talents, by his activity, and by his attachment to the government to all that has been required of him. Placed in the midst of the senate, should other circumstances redemand a minister of police, the government will not be able to find one more worthy of its confidence."

Fouché was appointed chief of the senatorship of Aix, which added a revenue of 30,000 francs to the 36,000 that he received as senator. In presenting his report to the First Consul at the final interview, Bonaparte remarked that there was a reserve of 2,400,000 francs, and he gave half of this sum to Fouché. Fouché was thus enabled to retire to private life in comfort. His enemies were disconcerted at this. Amongst those who assisted most at the fall of Fouché was Regnaud de Saint-Jean-d'Angély, who afterwards said, "Fouché conspires against the Emperor even when he is still. Each of his dreams is a plot. I shall distrust him even after his death."

Josephine saw with regret the dismissal of this minister, with whom she had an understanding, imagining that he would be able to turn Bonaparte's thoughts from the idea of a divorce. The duties of the minister of police were united to those of the minister of justice in the hands of Régnier under the title of chief justice. During the summer of 1802 Fouché spent some peaceable days on his estate at Pontcarré. He came but rarely to Paris, where he received at his superb hotel in the Rue du Bac all the distinguished personages of the Revolution, keeping up a political activity inseparable from his existence. In the month of November he was called upon to transact some business with the deputies from the Swiss cantons. He was, therefore, on the eve of taking again the reins of power, which the incapacity of his successor and new plots caused Bonaparte to repent ever having taken from him. The ex-minister several times said of Régnier, "He is too gullible and too foolish to manage the police well; he will allow the First Consul to fall into the first snare." This was what did happen, so that the enemies of Fouché have stated that it was he who fomented the conspiracy of Georges and Pichegru. The First Consul hastened to call upon Fouché for advice. The issue of the above-mentioned conspiracy was the assassination of the Duke d'Enghien, of which Fouché remarked, "It is much worse than a crime; it is a fault." At the time of Moreau's arrest, Fouché opposed the arrest of his wife, an act of violence which might have aroused the people. The ex-minister obtained a promise of clemency from Bonaparte, and prevailing upon Moreau to ostracise himself, gained the thanks of Bonaparte.

Fouché now saw that it was necessary to agree to the crowning of Bonaparte, as he was the only man able to control events. Fouché's assistance was now considered more necessary than ever, and by a decree of the 10th of July, the ministry of police was re-established. By a thoroughly complete system, Fouché managed to relieve himself of the details of business, and reserved to himself alone the direction of the superior police. In the cabinet of the minister were collected all the foreign papers which were prohibited elsewhere. By this means he held the most important threads of foreign politics, and, with the Emperor, was able to control or balance the minister of foreign affairs.

The police of Fouché acquired such a reputation that he was able to count amongst his agents many persons of high rank—some diplomatists, senators, councillors of state, some of the great lords who had emigrated, and people of letters. He caused it to be imagined that where three or four persons were gathered together, someone was present to report. Informed of all, he was able to advise Bonaparte of any public sufferings, and was able to prevent many evils and to resist the passions and violences of the Emperor. During the absence of Bonaparte, Fouché maintained a profound peace at home, which surprised even the conflicting parties themselves. One of the causes of his success was that he never failed in his engagements, and when he had promised his support to anyone, he always kept his word. The most surprising conquest that he made was over the Royalist chiefs, whom he had caused to be arrested because of letters being found implicating them. Fouché would entertain himself for hours together among them, and they were known to admit that, though they had been vanquished, they had never before been subjugated.

The letter that Fouché addressed to the bishops was a remarkable one. It is too lengthy to insert here, but in it he claimed a connection between his functions and theirs.

Fouché saw that public opinion would not be entirely favourable to Bonaparte, unless the latter destroyed by his presence and his personal efforts the unpleasant feeling engendered by, among other incidents, that of the assassination of the Duke d'Enghien. He, therefore, counselled Bonaparte to travel, and the journey to the camp at Boulogne, to Aix-la-Chapelle, and to Mayence was the result. Fouché was not responsible for the fate of Wright in the Temple, he not having supervision of that prison.

The brilliant campaign of Austerlitz and the peace of Presburg had reinstated Napoleon in public favour. Frankly, Fouché was able to congratulate him upon the amelioration of public opinion. " Sire," said he, " Austerlitz has shaken the old aristocracy. The Faubourg

St. Germain no longer conspires." Bonaparte was en-
chanted, and avowed that in all his battles and perils
he always had in view the opinion of Paris and of the
Faubourg St. Germain. Thus the old nobility came
in crowds to the Tuileries. Fouché was now accused
by the old Republicans of protecting the Royalists;
but he did not change his general rule of attempting
to unite all parties in a common interest.

After the peace of Presburg (25th of December,
1805) Bonaparte thought of creating a new nobility,
and consulted Fouché on the subject, who had no
objection, and was decorated with the eagle of the
Legion of Honour. He was afterwards created count,
as were also all the members of the senate. In
March, 1806, he was admitted to the first rank as
Duke of Otranto, with a large endowment on the
state of Naples. This high position never dazzled
Fouché, and he was one of the few who always told
the truth to the Emperor. He was totally opposed
to the continental campaign, of which the first decree
from Berlin in 1806 declared Bonaparte to be at war
with all the commerce of Europe. He knew with how
much blood and with what efforts the doubtful victory
of Eylau had been bought. Paris even did not ignore
it; and when Bonaparte wrote to Fouché complaining
of his inertia and negligence, the latter sent him letters
from the army which had reached him. After the
peace of Tilsit Bonaparte entertained designs upon
Spain, and Fouché had the good sense to attempt to

dissuade him. "Go to Portugal, if you wish," said he, "that is truly an English colony; but the Bourbons of Spain are and always will be your humble prefects, and you have no cause to complain of them." But Bonaparte ridiculed the fears expressed that he would find himself between two fires, saying that he was sure of Alexander. When the knowledge of the invasion of Spain was made public, the reprobation of it was general.

About this time the son of Hortense died, and with his death Bonaparte saw the hope of perpetuating his dynasty vanish. This loss prompted Fouché and all those whose political existence depended upon Bonaparte to think seriously, and he submitted his reflections to Bonaparte in a memorial the subject of which was the dissolution of his marriage with Josephine and union with one suited to his high position. Prompted by an excess of zeal or by impatient ambition, Fouché, after having consulted certain senators, warned Josephine. Bonaparte soon learnt from Josephine of this false step of Fouché and censured it, but would not send him away (*le chasser*).

Finding himself opposed in the *corps legislatif*, Bonaparte complained of it to Fouché, who advised him to dissolve that body, saying that if Louis XVI. had acted thus he would still have been reigning. "But, Duke of Otranto," said Bonaparte, "I believe you are one of those who sent him to the scaffold." "Yes," said Fouché coolly, "and it is the first service that I rendered your Majesty."

The result of the battle of Essling caused great inquietude in Paris.   Fouché now seemed at the zenith
of his power.   The English had landed at Walcheren,
and all Belgium bid fair to fall into the power of an
enemy who was able to advance to the frontiers of
France. when Fouché organised an army, calling upon
Bernadotte to command it, and forced the English to re-
embark.   But in this instance Fouché gave Bonaparte
offence, firstly, by giving the command to a general in
disgrace, and secondly, by a letter addressed to all
the mayors : " Let us prove to all Europe that if the
genius of Bonaparte can give glory to France by his
victories, his presence is not necessary to repulse our
enemies."   Fouché now did his utmost to curb Bona
parte's ambition, saying that after having resuscitated
the empire of Charlemagne, he ought to think of
making it durable.

Fouché at this time found himself constantly in opposition to Bonaparte.   A rival police, called the gendarmerie, were organised and the command given to Savary,
which was a great vexation (*déboire*) for the minister.

It was against the advice of Fouché that the Pope
was dispossessed of his estates.   At the marriage of
the Emperor many cardinals absented themselves.
Bonaparte wished to arrest them, and had an altercation on the subject with Fouché.   Finally it was
agreed that the delinquents should be banished to
different small towns of France, and compelled to habit
themselves in black as simple priests.

Bonaparte wished Holland to bear all the charges of the continental system. This was opposed by his brother Louis, and Fouché was accused of encouraging the opposition. Bonaparte, wishing for peace, authorised Fouché to concert with the King, his brother, an arrangement with the Court of St. James. Fouché ambitiously thought to make a private arrangement with the English minister of foreign affairs, and engaged Ouvrard as the go-between. Affairs were progressing favourably, when Bonaparte himself opened negotiations through a house of commerce in Amsterdam. Thus resulted a double negotiation and a conflict of propositions which annoyed the English minister, and the envoys were sent home. Bonaparte was furious at this, and ordered Ouvrard to be arrested. He also took the portfolio of police from Fouché and bestowed it on Savary, after having accused the former of making peace and war without his authority. Fouché was appointed governor of Rome, the Emperor softening the blow by a very flattering letter. Fouché pretended to be very humble, and offered to explain Savary's duties to him, even begging him to stay at the same hotel under the pretext of putting in order the papers he wished to transmit to him. Savary had the simplicity to believe all this, and at the end of three weeks had some insignificant papers handed to him, the rest having been burnt. Fouché knew well that it was never intended that he should be allowed to go to Rome; but, pretending to be duped, he had all his household got up in the style of that of a governor-general, and his equipages bore in large letters, "Equipages of the Governor-general of Rome." When he requested his orders and permission for a final interview, he was told to go to his country seat and await instructions. There he amused himself until waited upon by ambassadors from Bonaparte, who requested him to deliver up autograph letters and papers not found at the ministry. He refused, and Bonaparte uttered threats, of which Fouché was soon informed. He then went to Florence, but receiving alarming news from Paris, thought of going to the United States. He chartered a vessel, but sea-sickness was too much for him; and although an English captain promised him an antidote and offered to convey him to England, he declined to again trust himself on the ocean. Acting upon advice, he submitted to the Emperor, offering to give up any letters if a receipt were given him and permission to go to Aix. There he was received with extraordinary honour, for a minister in disgrace, and regularly received news from the political world of Paris.

Bonaparte was now preparing his expedition to Russia, and Fouché was permitted to present to him a memorial against the campaign. Nothing could be done to disenchant Bonaparte. The abdication of Louis Bonaparte caused Fouché to consider the fall of Napoleon possible. He thereupon thought of a project for taking the regency from Maria Louisa.

Metternich, with the idea of saving France from invasion, discussed certain affairs which he was enabled to
re-open at a later period. After his defeat at Leipsic,
Bonaparte, fearing the presence of Fouché in Paris,
ordered him to Rome, of which he was yet the titular
governor. In January, 1814, he addressed a letter to
the Emperor, advising him to concentrate his armies
between the Alps, the Pyrenees and the Rhine, and to
declare to Europe that he would not pass his natural
frontiers, this being the only way by which he could
ensure a veritable peace. Some time after he received
orders to evacuate the Roman states. This he did,
but not before obtaining from the King of Naples
arrears of 190,000 francs for his emoluments as
governor-general of Rome, &c. Fouché went to Rome,
but his discourses hostile to Bonaparte causing him to
be suspected, he left. He dared not approach Paris,
but at Avignon he addressed the authorities, informing
them of the approaching fall of the imperial government. At the news of the events of the 31st of March,
he hastened to Paris, hoping to participate in the new
direction of affairs, and arrived there on the same day
as the Count d'Artois. On the 23rd of April he wrote
to Bonaparte, advising him to leave Elba and go to
the United States. This letter coming to the knowledge of Louis XVIII. caused him to consider the
advisability of including Fouché in the ministry. The
conduct of the new government all agreed was un-
satisfactory, and Fouché at last saw that Bonaparte's

return was possible. At the last moment Louis XVIII.
authorised Monsieur to offer him the portfolio of the
minister of police, but in an interview that they had
Fouché told him that it was too late, that Bonaparte
was bound to return, and that the latter would wish
him to accept that position. He offered to be the
private correspondent of Louis XVIII., his excuse being
that, even if he were serving two masters, he would
be best serving France. He is said to have predicted
that Bonaparte would not last three months, and to
have written to the Duke d'Aumont, "You save the
monarch, and I will save the monarchy."

The day following the interview with Monsieur, the
new prefect of police, Bourrienne, received orders to
arrest Fouché, the carrying out of which order would
have afforded him much pleasure, as by so doing he
would have greatly obliged his friend Savary, who
hoped that if Fouché were removed he would receive
the portfolio of police on the return ot Bonaparte.
Fouché, informed as usual, was able to escape the
snare laid for him. Fouché's purpose was to again
proclaim the Republic with Bonaparte as generalissimo,
but the military party were too strong for any such
arrangement. During this crisis Fouché played his
part so well that he was able to appear both as the
patron of the Republicans and the protector of the
Royalists, leaving Bonaparte only the power of
the bayonets. Thus in the famous declaration of the
Council of State there occurred this phrase, inspired

by Fouché, which gave a contradiction to all the doctrines of the Empire: "The sovereignty rests only in the people; it is the only source of power." By establishing lieutenants of police in all parts of the kingdom, Fouché was able to brave without fear the tottering Emperor. Bonaparte more than once considered the advisability of ridding himself of Fouché. Once he was inclined to have him shot, but was dissuaded by Carnot. It is said that Bonaparte told Fouché that he knew that he had sold himself to the enemy, and that he ought to shoot him, but he would leave that task to others, and would prove to him that he was not able to influence his destiny in the slightest. After Waterloo Fouché forced the situation by the advice that he gave to the different parties. He advised the Bonapartists to demand the dissolution of the Chamber, and then warned the opposite party to be on the alert to oppose it. Bonaparte was compelled to abdicate, as is well known.

Too enlightened to think that it was now possible to proclaim a republic, Fouché would have been in favour of the Orleans branch of the royal family, but was content if it became necessary to accept the elder branch, on certain conditions being agreed to.

Fouché was engaged at this time in various negotiations, and in a famous letter to the Duke of Wellington he inferred that the Duke of Orleans would be a suitable occupant of the throne. But the latter did not seem to have that ambition, and retired to his

d

villa at Twickenham. It is stated that Wellington declined to treat with the French nation except upon the understanding that Louis XVIII. would be re-established.

Fouché has been accused of throwing obstacles in Bonaparte's way, preventing him making his escape, and in such a manner that he was likely to be captured by the English. After Wellington's determination concerning Louis XVIII., it was necessary for those who formed the provisional government either to come to terms or to fight. All agreed that the capital was not in a state to stand a siege. Fouché was desirous that the treaty about to be entered into should not have the appearance of a humiliating capitulation. The French army was to take up its position behind the Loire. Fouché and his friends were enabled to arrange matters as they wished. It is said that Fouché and Talleyrand gave reciprocal guarantees—Fouché to Talleyrand on behalf of Bonaparte, and Talleyrand to Fouché with regard to Louis XVIII. Certain conditions were agreed to by the provisional government to be demanded of the King if he returned. Among them were these : That the tricolour should be preserved, two chambers maintained, and all enjoying honours and pensions should continue to receive them as heretofore.

Fouché and his colleagues soon learnt that the allied powers considered that the authority exercised by the chambers was illegitimate, and that all they were expected to do was to proclaim Louis XVIII. king and then dissolve. Carnot was inclined to protest, but Fouché saw the futility of it. Louis XVIII. then re-entered Paris, and Fouché and Talleyrand again became members of the ministry. This displeased Carnot, and a disagreeable scene took place between the latter and Fouché.

In spite of his election to the chamber by three departments, Fouché resigned in September, 1815, not agreeing with the royalist reaction which had set in. He was appointed ambassador to Dresden, but was affected by the law of the 12th of January, 1816, and lost his position and right to dwell in France. He retired to Prague, and became a naturalised Austrian in 1818. He then went to Trieste, where he died on 25th of December, 1820. He left a fortune of fourteen million francs.

Fouché was twice married, on the second occasion (August, 1815), after having been a widower two years, to Mdlle. de Castellane, whom he had known at Aix when exiled there in 1810. Louis XVIII. and the princes signed the marriage contract.

Letter of Fouché (Feb. 1793) wherein he declaims
against the egotism of certain Republicans

From the Bibliothèque Nationale of Paris "Manuscrits français, nouvelles
acquisitions, No. 31, page 75."

Photographed under the direction of Leon Vallée
especially for this work

Citoyen, ... devoir ... que ceux qui veulent ... s'attacher au bien commun; ... MO ... pour Connétable toutes les ... d'égalité, ils sont nos seuls ennemis vraiment Redoutables, ... seuls peuvent nous ôter ... puisqu'ils ... peuvent assurer notre liberté, nos républiques ... nous laisser la vie. adieu, ... de amis, que les sentiments de liberté & d'égalité se ... dans les cœurs, & ne ... jamais de ... que pour celui qui fournira plus de bras, & plus de sang à la patrie.

p.s. j'ai remis au comité colonial toutes les pièces que vous m'avez adressées, ... les citoyens Fournier, Verneuil & Gervais ... tout le zèle que je mettrai à presser le rapport de leur affaire.

p.s. Vous me demandez si ... m'a communiqué quelqu'une de vos lettres? ... mon silence est une preuve que je n'en ai ... reçu aucune, je ne laisse jamais les lettres de mes frères sans réponse

MEMOIRS

OF

JOSEPH FOUCHÉ

DUKE OF OTRANTO

THE man who, in turbulent and revolutionary
times, was solely indebted for the honours and power
with which he was invested, and, in short, for his distinguished fortune, to his own prudence and abilities;
who, at first elected a national representative, was,
upon the re-establishment of order, an ambassador,
three times a minister, a senator, a duke, and one of
the principal directors of state affairs; this man would
be wanting to himself if, to answer the calumnies of
libellers, he descended to apology or captious refuta-
tions: he must adopt other means.

This man, then, is myself. Raised by the Revolution, it is only to a counter one, which I foresaw, and
might myself have brought about, but against which
at the critical moment I was unprepared, that I owe
my downfall.

This fall has exposed me, defenceless, to the
clamours of malignity and the insults of ingratitude;
me, who for a long time invested with a mysterious
and terrible power, never wielded it but to calm the

passions, disunite factions, and prevent conspiracies;
me, who was never-ceasingly employed in moderating
and tempering power, in conciliating and amalgama-
ting the jarring elements and conflicting interests
which divided France. No one dares deny that such
was my conduct so long as I exercised any influence
in the government or in the councils of the state.
What have I, an exile, to oppose to these furious
enemies, to this rabble which now persecute me,
after having grovelled at my feet? Shall I answer
them with the cold declamations of the school, or
with refined and academic periods? Certainly not;
I will confound them by facts and proofs, by a true
exposition of my labours, of my thoughts, both as a
minister and a statesman; by the faithful recital of
the political events, and the singular circumstances
through which I steered in times of turbulence and
violence. This is the object I propose to myself.

From truth I think I have nothing to dread; and
even if it were so, I would speak it. The time for
its consummation has arrived: I will speak it, cost
what it may, so that when the tomb covers my mortal
remains, my name shall be bequeathed to the judgment
of history. It is, however, just that I should appear
before its tribunal with these Memoirs in my hand.

And first, let me not be considered responsible
either for the Revolution, its consequences, or even
its direction. I was a cipher; I possessed no authority when its first shocks, overturning France,
shook Europe to its foundations. Besides, what was
this Revolution? It is notorious that, previous to the
year 1789, presentiments of the destruction of empires

had created uneasiness in the monarchy. Empires themselves are not exempted from that universal law which subjects all mundane things to change and decomposition. Has there ever been one whose historical duration has exceeded a certain number of ages? At most their greatest longevity may be fixed at twelve or fourteen centuries, whence it may be inferred that a monarchy which had already lasted thirteen hundred years without undergoing any violent change, was not far from a catastrophe. Of what consequence is it, if, rising from its ashes and reorganised, it has subjected Europe to the yoke and terror of its arms? Should its power again escape, again will it decline and perish. Let us not inquire what may be the new metamorphoses to which it is destined. The geographical configuration of France ensures us a distinguished part in the ages yet to come. Gaul, when conquered by the masters of the world, remained subjected only for three hundred years. Other invaders are now forging, in the north, the chains which shall enslave Europe. The Revolution erected a bulwark which arrested them for a time—it is being demolished piecemeal; but though destroyed, it will again be raised, for the present age is powerful; it carries along with it men, parties, and governments.

You who exclaim so furiously against the wonders of the Revolution; you who directed it without daring to face it; you have experienced it, and perhaps may experience it once more.

Who provoked it, and whence did we first see it rise? From the saloons of the great, from the

cabinets of the ministers. It was invited, provoked
by the parliaments and by those about the King—by
young colonels, by court mistresses, by pensioned men
of letters, whose persons were protected, and sentiments
re-echoed by duchesses.

I have seen the nation blush at the depravity of
the higher classes, the licentiousness of the clergy, the
ignorant blunders of the ministers, and at the picture
of the disgusting dissoluteness of the great modern
Babylon.

Was it not those that were considered the flowers
of France, who, for forty years, established and supported the adoration of Voltaire and Rousseau? Was
it not among the higher classes that the mania of
democratical independence, transplanted from the
United States into the French soil, first took root?
Dreams of a republic were already afloat, while corruption was at its height in the monarchy! Even
the example of a monarch exemplary and strict in his
morals could not arrest the torrent. During this de-
moralisation of the upper classes, the nation increased
in knowledge and intellect. By continually hearing
emancipation represented as a duty, it at length believed it as such. History itself can here attest that
the nation was unacquainted with the arts which
prepared the catastrophe. It might have been made
to have advanced with the times; the King, and all
men of intellect, desired it. But the corruption and
avarice of the great, the errors of the magistrates and
of the court, and the mistakes of the ministry, dug
the pit of destruction. It was, besides, so easy to
urge to extremities a petulant and inflammable nation,

one which, on the slightest provocation, would rush
into excesses ! Who fired the train ? Did the Archbishop of Sens, did Necker[1] the Swiss, Mirabeau, La
Fayette, D'Orleans, Adrian Duport, Chauderlos Laclos,
the Staëls, the Larochefoucaulds, the Beauveaus, the
Montmorencys,[2] the Uvailles, the Lameths, the La
Tour du Pins, the Lefrancs de Pompignan, and so
many other promoters of the triumphs in 1789 over
the royal authority—did these belong to the *tiers-état?*
But for the meetings of the Palais Royal and Mont
Rouge, the Breton Club had been harmless. There
would have been no 14th of July if on the 12th the
troops and generals of the King had done their duty.
Besenval was a creature of the Queen ; and Besenval,
at the decisive moment, in spite of the King's orders,
sounded a retreat, instead of advancing against the

[1] For short biographical sketches of the principal personages
mentioned in these Memoirs, see Alphabetical Appendix at end
of volume.

[2] This name so truly French, and already so illustrious from
its historical celebrity, has become, if possible, still more respectable, since the Duke Matthieu de Montmorency, to whose
conduct Fouché here alludes, has done honour to himself by a
public avowal of his fault. The sincerity and nobleness of his
conduct as a minister and a statesman have likewise gained
him universal esteem. M. Fouché cannot injure the reputation
of so respectable a character. The great protector of the old
noblesse under the imperial *régime*, Fouché recriminates here,
in order to reproach that very noblesse with its participation
in the Revolution ; it is among the revolutionists a forced re-
crimination. What he says may be true in some respects ; but
a small minority of an order is not the whole of it ; there will
also always be an immense distance between the follies, impru-
dences, and faults of 1789, and the dreadful crimes of 1793.
Fouché's subtle manner of reasoning, in order to exculpate
himself, does not appear to us historically conclusive.—*Note by
the Editor.*

insurgents. Marshal Broglio himself was paralysed by his staff. These are incontrovertible facts.

It is well known by what arts the common people were roused to insurrection. The sovereignty of the people was proclaimed by the defection of the army and the court. Is it surprising that the factious and the heads of parties (*meneurs*) should have got the Revolution into their hands ? The impulse of innovations and the exaltation of ideas did the rest.

The Revolution was commenced by a prince who might have mastered it, changing the dynasty, but his cowardice permitted it to proceed at random and without an object. In the midst of this distress some generous hearts, some enthusiastic minds, joined with a few freethinkers (*esprits forts*), sincerely imagined that a social regeneration was practicable, and, trusting to protestations and oaths, employed themselves in its accomplishment.

It was under these circumstances that we, obscure men of the *tiers-état*, and inhabitants of the provinces, were attracted and seduced by the dreams of liberty, by the intoxicating fiction of the restoration of the state. We pursued a chimera with the fever of the public good; we had, at that time, no secret objects, no ambition, no views of sordid interest.

Opposition, however, soon inflaming the passions, party spirit gave rise to implacable animosities. Everything was carried to extremity. The multitude was the sole mover. For the same reason that Louis XIV. had said, "I am the state," the people said, "We are the sovereign; the state is the nation;" and the nation proceeded quite alone.

And here let us remark a fact which will serve as a key to the events which will follow, for these events bear upon the wonderful. The dissentient royalists and the counter-revolutionists, for want of available materials for a civil war, finding themselves shut out from honours, had recourse to emigration—the resource of the weak. Finding no support at home, they ran to seek it abroad. Following the example of all nations under similar circumstances, the nation desired that the estates of the emigrants should be held as a guarantee for the motives which had induced them to arm themselves against her, and to wish to arm all Europe. But how could the right of proprietorship, the foundation of the monarchy, be touched, without sapping its own basis? Sequestration led to spoliation; and from that moment the whole fell to ruin, for the mutation of property is synonymous with the subversion of the established order of things. It is not I who said, "Property must go into other hands!" This sentence was more agrarian than all that the Gracchi could have uttered, and no Scipio Nasica was to be found.

From that moment the Revolution was nothing but a scene of ruin and destruction. The terrible sanction of war was wanting to it, and the European cabinets, of their own accord, opened the Temple of Janus. From the commencement of this great contest, the Revolution, full of youth and ardour, triumphed over the old system, over the despicable coalition, and over the wretched and discordant operations of its armies.

Another fact must also be adduced, in order to draw from it an important inference. The first coalition was repulsed, beaten, and humiliated. But let us suppose that it had triumphed over the patriotic confederacy of France; that the advance of the Prussians into Champagne had met with no serious obstacle as far even as the capital; and that the Revolution had been disorganised even in its very birthplace: admitting this hypothesis, France would certainly have shared the fate of Poland, by a dismemberment and by the degradation of its sovereign; for such was at that time the political theme of the cabinets and the spirit of their co-partnership diplomacy. The *progress of knowledge* had not yet introduced the discovery of the European confederacy, of military occupation, with subsidies. By preserving France the patriots of 1792 not only rescued her from the hands of foreigners, but laboured, though unintentionally, for the restoration of the monarchy. This is incontestable.

Much outcry has been made against the excesses of this sanguinary Revolution. Could it remain calm and temperate when surrounded by enemies and exposed to invasion? Numbers deceived themselves, but few were criminal. The cause of the 10th of August is alone to be ascribed to the advance of the combined Austrians and Prussians. Had they marched later it would have been of little consequence. The suicide of France was not yet near at hand.

Undoubtedly, the Revolution was violent, and even cruel in its progress; all this is historically known, nor shall I dwell upon it, such not being the object of this work. It is of myself I wish to speak, or rather of the events in which I was concerned as a minister of state. It was necessary that I should introduce the subject, and describe the character of the

times. Let not the generality of my readers suppose
that I shall tediously recite my private life as a private
individual or obscure citizen. Of what advantage
would it be to know the first steps of my career?
Minutiæ such as these can only interest the famished
compilers of contemporaneous biography, or the simple-
tons who read them; they have nothing to do in
common with history, and it is to that which I aspire.

My being the son of the owner of a privateer, and
of having been at first destined for the sea, can be
of little consequence: my family was respectable. It
can likewise afford but little interest to know that I
was brought up among the Pères de l'Oratoire, that
I was one myself, that I devoted myself to teaching,
and that the Revolution found me prefect of the
college of Nantes; it may, at least, be inferred that
I was neither an ignoramus nor a fool. It is likewise
entirely false that I was ever a priest, or had taken
orders. I make this remark to show that I was perfectly at liberty to become a freethinker or a phi-
losopher, without being guilty of apostasy: certain it
is that I quitted the oratory before I exercised any
public functions, and that, under the sanction of the
law, I married at Nantes, with the intention of
exercising the profession of a lawyer, which was much
more consonant to my own inclinations and to the
state of society. Besides, I was morally what the
age was, with the advantage of being so neither from
imitation nor infatuation, but from reflection and
disposition. With such principles, is it no subject
of self-congratulation to have been nominated by
my fellow-citizens, without the employment either of

artifice or intrigue, a representative of the people at
the National Convention ?

It is in this political defile that the deserters of
the Court wait to attack me. There are no exaggerations, no excesses, no crimes, either when in office or
in the tribune, with which they have not loaded my
historical responsibility, taking words for actions, and
forced speeches for principles ; neither taking into the
account time, place, nor circumstance ; and making
no allowance for a universal delirium, for the republican
fever, of which twenty millions of Frenchmen felt the
paroxysms.

My first introduction into the government was in
the Committee of Public Instruction, where I connected
myself with Condorcet, and through him with Vergniaud. A circumstance relating to one of the most
important crises of my life must here be mentioned.
By a singular chance, I had been acquainted with
Maximilian Robespierre at the time I was professor
of philosophy in the town of Arras, and had even
afforded him pecuniary assistance to enable him to
settle in Paris, when he was appointed deputy to the
National Assembly. When we again met at the Convention, we at first saw each other frequently, but
the differences of our opinions, and, perhaps, the still
greater dissimilarity of our characters, soon caused a
separation.

One day, at the conclusion of a dinner given at
my house, Robespierre began to declaim with much
violence against the Girondins, particularly abusing
Vergniaud, who was present. I was much attached
to Vergniaud, who was a great orator and a man of

Girondists on their Way to Execution

unaffected manners. I went round to him, and advancing towards Robespierre, said to him, "Such violence may assuredly enlist the passions on your side, but will never obtain for you esteem and confidence." Robespierre, offended, left the room, and it will shortly be seen how far this malignant man carried his animosity against me.

I had, however, no share in the political system of the Gironde party, of which Vergniaud was the reputed head. I conceived that the effect of this system would be to disunite France by raising the greater portion of it in circles (*zones*) and provinces against Paris. In this I foresaw great danger, being convinced that there was no safety for the state but in the unity and indivisibility of the body politic. This was what induced me to enter a faction whose excesses I inwardly detested, and whose violences marked the progress of the Revolution. What horrors waited on the names of Morality and Justice! But it must be admitted, we were not sailing in peaceful seas.

The Revolution was at its height; we were without rudder, without government, ruled by only one assembly, a species of monstrous dictatorship, the offspring of confusion, and which alternately presented a counterpart of the anarchy of Athens and the despotism of the Ottomans.

It is here, then, that the Revolution and the counter-revolution are politically at issue. Is the question to be decided by the jurisprudence which regulates the decisions of criminal tribunals or the correctional police? The Convention, notwithstanding

its atrocities, its excesses and its furious decrees, or
perhaps by those very decrees, saved the country
beyond its integral limits.   This is an incontestable
fact, and for that reason I do not deny my participation in its labours.   Each of its members, when
accused before the tribunal of history, may confine
himself to the limits of Scipio's defence, and say with
that great man, "I have saved the republic; let us
repair to the Capitol to thank the gods!"

There was, however, one vote which is unjustifiable;
I will even own, without a blush, that it sometimes
awakens remorse within me.   But I call the God of
Truth to witness, that it was far less against the
monarch that I aimed the blow (for he was good and
just) than against the kingly office, at that time
incompatible with the new order of things.   I will
also add, for concealment is no longer of avail, that
it then appeared to me, as to so many others, that
we could not inspire the representatives and the mass
of the people with an energy sufficient to surmount
the difficulties of the crisis but by abandoning everything like moderation, breaking through all restraint
and indulging the extremity of revolutionary excess.
Such was the reason of state which appeared to us
to require this frightful sacrifice.   In politics even
atrocity itself may sometimes produce a salutary effect.

The world would not now call us to account if
the tree of liberty, having taken strong and firm root,
had resisted the axe wielded even by those who had
planted it with their own hands.   That Brutus was
more happy in erecting the noble edifice which he
besprinkled with his children's blood, I can readily

conceive; it was far easier for him to have placed the fasces of the monarchy in the hands of the aristocracy already organised. The representatives of 1793, by sacrificing the representative of royalty, the father of the monarchy, for the purpose of founding a republic, had no choice in the means of accomplishing their object. The level of equality was already so violently established in the nation, that the authority was necessarily intrusted to a floating democracy : it could only work upon a moving sand. After having condemned myself as judge and accused, let me, at least, be allowed to avail myself, in the exercise of my Conventional duties, of some extenuating circumstances. Being dispatched upon a mission into the department, forced to employ the language of the times, and to yield to the fatality of circumstances, I found myself compelled to put in execution the law against suspected persons. This law ordered the imprisonment, *en masse*, of priests and nobles. The following is what I wrote, the following is what I dared to publish, in a proclamation issued by me on the 25th of August, 1793 :

" The law wills that suspected persons should be removed from social intercourse ; this law is commanded by the interests of the state ; but to take for the basis of your opinions vague accusations, proceeding from the vilest passions, would be to favour a tyranny as repugnant to my own heart as it is to natural equity. The sword must not be wielded at hazard. The law decrees severe punishments, and not proscriptions, as immoral as they are barbarous."

It required at that time some courage to mitigate as much as was in one's power the rigour of the

Conventional decrees. I was not so fortunate in my missions as collective commissioner (*commissariat collectif*), because the power of decision was not intrusted to myself alone. Throughout my missions, the actions which may be considered as deserving of censure will be found far less than the everyday phrases expressed in the language of the times, and which in a period of greater tranquillity still inspire a kind of dread; besides, this language was, so to speak, official and peculiar. Let not also my situation at this period be mistaken. I was the delegate of a violent assembly, and I have already proved that I eluded or softened down several of its severe measures. In other respects these pretended pro-consulates reduced the commissioned deputy to nothing more than a man-machine, the wandering commissary of the Committees of Public Safety and of General Security. I was never a member of these government committees; therefore I never held, during the Reign of Terror, the helm of power; on the contrary, as will shortly be seen, I was myself a sufferer by it. This will prove how much my responsibility was confined.

But let us unwind the thread of these events. Like that of Ariadne, it will conduct us out of the labyrinth, and we can then attain the object of these Memoirs, the sphere of which will increase in importance.

The paroxysm of revolution and of terror was at hand. The guillotine was the only instrument of government. Suspicion and distrust preyed upon every heart; fear cowered over all. Even those who held in their hands the instrument of terror were at times menaced with it. One man alone in the Convention appeared to enjoy an inexpugnable popularity: this was

Robespierre, a man full of pride and cunning; an envious, malignant, and vindictive being, who was never
satiated with the blood of his colleagues; and who,
by his capacity, steadiness, the clearness of his head,
and the obstinacy of his character, surmounted circumstances the most appalling.   Availing himself of his
preponderance in the Committee of Public Safety, he
openly aspired, not only to the tyranny of the decem-
viri, but to the despotism of the dictatorship of Marius
and Sylla.   One step more would have given him the
masterdom of the Revolution, which it was his audacious ambition to govern at his will; but thirty victims
more were to be sacrificed, and he had marked them
in the Convention.   He well knew that I understood
him; and I therefore was honoured by being inscribed
upon his tablets at the head of those doomed to
destruction.   I was still on a mission when he accused
me of oppressing the patriots and tampering with the
aristocracy.   Being recalled to Paris, I dared to call
upon him from the tribune to make good his accusation.   He caused me to be expelled from the Jacobins,
of whom he was the high priest; this was for me
equivalent to a decree of proscription.[1]   I did not trifle

---

[1] After the death of Danton, of Camille Desmoulins, and
other deputies who were seized during the night at their habita-
tions by a mere order of the committees, delivered over to
the revolutionary tribunal, tried and condemned without being
able to defend themselves, Legendre, the friend of Danton,
Courtois, Tallien, and above thirty other deputies, never slept
at home ; they wandered about during the night from one to
another, fearful of sharing the same fate as Danton.   Fouché
was more than two months without having any fixed residence.
It was thus that Robespierre made those tremble who seemed to
oppose his views to the dictatorship.—*Note by the Editor.*

in contending for my head, nor in long and secret deliberations with such of my colleagues as were threatened with my own fate.   I merely said to them—
among others to Legendre, Tallien, Dubois de Crancé,
Daunou, and Chénier — " You are on the list, you
are on the list as well as myself; I am certain
of it ! "   Tallien, Barras, Bourdon de l'Oise, and
Dubois de Crancé evinced some energy.   Tallien contended for two lives, of which one was then dearer
to him than his own : he therefore resolved upon
assassinating the future dictator, even in the Convention itself.   But what a hazardous chance was this !
Robespierre's popularity would have survived him, and
we should have been immolated to his manes.   I therefore dissuaded Tallien from an isolated enterprise
which would have destroyed the man but preserved his
system.

Convinced that other means must be resorted
to, I went straight to those who shared with Robespierre the government of terror, and whom I knew to
be envious or fearful of his immense popularity.   I revealed to Collot d'Herbois, to Carnot, to Billaud de
Varennes, the designs of the modern Appius ; and I
presented to each of them separately so lively and so
true a picture of the danger of their situation, I urged
them with so much ability and success, that I insinuated into their breasts more than mistrust—the
courage of henceforth opposing the tyrant in any
further decimating of the Convention.   " Count the
votes," said I to them, " in your committee, and you
will see that when you are determined he will be reduced to a powerless minority of a Couthon and a

Saint-Just. Refuse him your votes, and reduce him to stand alone by your *vis inertiæ*."

But what contrivances, what expedients were necessary to avoid exasperating the Jacobin club, the Seides, and the partisans of Robespierre! Sure of having succeeded, I had the courage to defy him on the 20th Prairial (8th of June, 1794)—a day on which, actuated with the ridiculous idea of solemnly acknowledging the existence of the Supreme Being, he dared to proclaim himself both his *will* and *agent*, in presence of all the people assembled at the Tuileries. As he was ascending the steps of his lofty tribune, whence he was to proclaim his manifesto in favour of God, I predicted to him aloud (twenty of my colleagues heard it) that his fall was near. Five days after, in full committee, he demanded my head and that of eight of my friends, reserving to himself the destruction of twenty more at a later period. How great was his astonishment, and what was his rage, upon finding amongst the members of the committee an invincible opposition to his sanguinary designs against the national representation! It has already been too much mutilated, said they to him, and it is high time to put a stop to a proscription which at last will include ourselves.

Finding himself in a minority, he withdrew, choked with rage and disappointment, swearing never to set foot again in the committee so long as his will should be opposed. He immediately sent for Saint-Just, who was with the army, rallied Couthon under his sanguinary banner, and by his influence over the revolutionary tribunal, still made the Convention and all those who were operated on by fear to tremble. Being confident of the support of the Jacobin club, of Henriot, the commander of the national guard, and of all the revolutionary committees of the capital, he flattered himself that he had still adherents fully sufficient to carry him through. By thus keeping himself at a distance from the seat of power, he was desirous of throwing upon his adversaries the general execration, of making them appear as the sole perpetrators of so many murders, and of delivering them up to the vengeance of a people which now began to murmur at the shedding of so much blood. But, cowardly, mistrustful, and timid, he was incapable of action, and permitted five weeks to pass away between this secret secession and the crisis which was silently approaching.

I did not overlook his situation; and seeing him reduced to a single faction, I secretly urged such of his enemies as still adhered to the committee, at least to remove the artillery from Paris, who were all devoted to Robespierre and the commune, and to deprive Henriot of his command, or at least to suspend him. The first measure I obtained, thanks to the firmness of Carnot, who alleged the necessity of sending reinforcements of artillery to the army. As to depriving Henriot of his command, that appeared too hazardous; Henriot remained, and was near losing all; or rather, to speak the truth, it was he who on the 9th Thermidor (27th of July) ruined the cause of Robespierre, the triumph of which was for a short time in his power. But what could be expected from a *ci-devant* drunken and stupid footman.

What follows is too well known for me to enlarge

Robespierre

Engraved by Florenza after picture by A. Lacauchie

upon it. It is notorious how Maximilian the First
perished ; a man whom certain authors have been
very anxious of comparing to the Gracchi, to whom
he bore not the slightest resemblance, either in
eloquence or elevation of mind. I confess that, in
the delirium of victory, I said to those who favoured
his ambitious views, " You do him much honour ; he
had neither plan nor design : far from disposing of
futurity, he was drawn along, and did but obey an
impulse he could neither oppose nor govern." But
at that time I was too near a spectator of events
justly to appreciate their history.

The sudden overthrow of the dreadful system
which suspended the nation between life and death,
was doubtless a grand epoch of liberty ; but in this
world good is ever mixed with evil. What took place
after Robespierre's fall ? That which we have seen to
have been the case after a fall still more memorable.
Those who were the most abject before the decemvir
could, after his death, find no expression strong enough
to express their detestation of him.

It was soon a subject of regret that so happy an
event had not been made to contribute to the public
good, instead of serving as a pretext to glut the hatred
and vengeance of those who had been sufferers by the
Revolution. To terror succeeded anarchy, and to
anarchy reaction and vengeance. The Revolution was
blasted both in its principles and end; the patriots
were for a long time exposed to the fury of the
Sicaires, enlisted in companies of the Sun and of
Jesus. I had escaped the proscription of Robespierre,
but I could not escape those of the reactionists. They

pursued me even into the Convention, whence, by dint of recriminations and false accusations, they caused my expulsion by a most iniquitous decree; I was for almost a year the victim of every species of insult and odious persecution. It was then I began to reflect upon man, and upon the character of factions. I was compelled to wait—for with us there is nothing but extremes — I was compelled to wait till the cup was full, till the excesses of reaction had placed in jeopardy the Revolution itself and the Convention *en masse*. Then, and not till then, it saw the abyss which yawned at its feet. The crisis was awful—it was existence or non-existence. The Convention took up arms; the persecution of the patriots was stopped, and the cannon of one day (13th Vendémiaire)[1] restored order among the crowd of counter-revolutionists, who had imprudently risen without chiefs and without any centre of object and action.

The cannon of Vendémiaire, directed by Bonaparte, having in some degree restored me to liberty and honour, I confess that I was the more interested in the destiny of this young general, who was clearing for himself a road by which he was soon to arrive at the most astonishing renown of modern times.

I had still, however, to contend with the severities of a destiny which did not yet seem inclined to bend and be propitious to me. The establishment of the Directorial *régime*, after this last convulsion, was nothing more than the attempt of a multifarious government, appointed as the directors of a democratical republic of forty millions of souls; for the Rhine and the Alps

[1] Napoleon's whiff of grapeshot (Carlyle), 5th of October, 1795.

already formed our natural barrier. This was, indeed, an attempt of the utmost boldness, in presence of the armies of a coalition, formed by inimical governments and disturbers of the common peace. The war, it is true, constituted our strength; but it was attended with reverses, and it was as yet uncertain which of the two systems, the ancient or modern, would triumpn. More seemed to be expected from the capacity of the men intrusted with the direction of affairs than from the force of events and effervescence of recent passions : too many vices discovered themselves. Our interior was also not easily to be managed. It was with difficulty that the Directorial government endeavoured to open itself a safe road between two active and hostile factions —that of the demagogues, who only considered our temporary magistrates as oligarchs easily to be replaced, and that of the auxiliary royalists abroad, who, unable to strike a decisive blow, fanned in the southern and western provinces the embers of civil war. The Directory, however, like every new government, which almost always possess the advantage of being gifted with activity and energy, procured fresh resources, and brought back victory to the armies, stifling at the same time intestine war. But it was, perhaps, too much alarmed at the proceedings of the demagogues; first, because their principal rendezvous was in Paris, under the eyes of the Directory itself; and secondly, because the discontented patriots constituted their sole power. This difficulty, which might have been easily avoided, caused a deviation in the policy of the Directory. It abandoned the revolutionists, an order of men to which it owed its existence, and preferred favouring those chameleons, devoid of character and integrity—the instruments of power so long as it can make itself respected, and its enemies the moment it begins to totter. Five men who in the Convention had been remarkable for the energy of their votes, upon being invested with supreme authority were seen to repel their ancient colleagues, to caress the *métis*[1] and the royalists, and adopt a system totally opposed to the condition of their existence.

Thus, under the republican government, of which I was a founder, I was, if not proscribed, at least in complete disgrace, obtaining neither employment, respect, nor credit, and sharing this unaccountable dislike for nearly three years with a great number o my former colleagues, men of approved abilities and patriotism. If I at length made my way, it was by the assistance of a particular circumstance, and of a change of system brought about by the force of circumstances. This deserves being particularised.

Of all the members of the Directory, Barras was the only one who was accessible to his former but now cast off colleagues; he had, and deserved, the reputation of possessing an amiability, candour, and generosity peculiar to the people of the south. Without being well versed in politics, he had resolution and a certain tact. The exaggerated reflections upon his manners and his moral principles was precisely what drew around him a court which swarmed with intriguers, male and female. He was at this time Carnot's rival; and only maintained himself in the public opinion by the idea that, in case of need, he would be seen on horseback, braving, as

[1] Mongrels.

on the 13th of Vendémiaire, every hostile effort; he also affected being the premier of the Republic—going to the chase, having his packs of hounds, his courtiers, and mistresses. I had known him both before and after the catastrophe of Robespierre, and I had remarked that the justice of my reflections and presentiments had had its effect upon him. I had a secret interview with him, through the medium of Lombard-Taradeau, one of his commensals and confidants. This was during the first difficulties of the Directory, at that time struggling with the Babeuf faction. I imparted my ideas to Barras; he himself desired me to draw them up in a memorial; this I did, and transmitted it to him. The position of the Directory was therein politically considered, and its dangers enumerated with the greatest precision. I characterised the faction Babeuf, which had dropped the mask before me, and showed him that, while raving about the agrarian law, its real object was to surprise and seize by assault the Directory and the supreme power, which would again have plunged us into demagogy with terror and bloodshed. My memorial had its effect; the evil was eradicated. Barras then offered me a second-rate place, which I refused, being unwilling to obtain employment by mere drudgery; he assured me that he had not sufficient interest to promote me, that his efforts to overcome the prejudices of his colleagues against me had been ineffectual. A coolness succeeded, and all was deferred.

In the interval an opportunity presented itself of rendering myself independent as far as fortune was concerned. I had sacrificed my profession and my

existence to the Revolution, and by an effect of the
most unjust prejudices the field of advancement was
closed against me. My friends pressed me to follow
the example of several of my former colleagues, who,
finding themselves in the same case with myself, had
obtained, by the influence of the directors, shares in
the government contracts (*fournitures*). A company
was formed; I was admitted into it, and by the influence of Barras, I obtained a share of the contracts.[1]

I thus commenced making my fortune, after the
example of Voltaire, and I contributed to that of my
partners, who distinguished themselves by the punctu-
ality with which they fulfilled the clauses of their
contract with the Republic. I was myself the director,
and in this new sphere found myself enabled to assist
more than once many worthy but neglected patriots.
Affairs, however, still grew worse in the interior. The
Directory confounded the mass of the revolutionists
with demagogues and anarchists, and these latter were
not punished without the former coming in for their
share. Public opinion was permitted to take the most
erroneous direction. The reins of government were in
the hands of the republicans, and they had opposed
to them the passions and prejudices of an impetuous
but superficial nation, which obstinately persisted in
viewing citizens zealous in the cause of liberty as

[1] There is always a certain degree of artifice even in what
Fouché allows. Let us, however, give him credit for having
spoken the truth as much as it was possible for him to do; it
is not a little to have obtained his avowal of having commenced
his fortune by jobbing in the contracts. It will be seen likewise,
in the course of his Memoirs, whence he drew his immense riches
at a later period.—*Note by the Editor.*

sanguinary men and terrorists.   The Directory itself, carried away by the torrent of prejudice, could not continue in the prudent track which had hitherto preserved and strengthened it.   Public opinion was daily more and more falsified and perverted by servile writers, by reviewers in the pay of the emigrants and of foreign powers, openly recommending the destruction of the new institution: their principal object was to vilify the republicans and the heads of the state.   By permitting itself to be thus disgraced and dishonoured, the Directory, whose members were divided amongst themselves by a spirit of rivalry and ambition, lost all the advantages which a representative government affords those who have ability enough to direct it.   What was the consequence?   At the very moment our armies were everywhere victorious—when, masters of the Rhine, we were achieving the conquest of Italy in the name of the Revolution and the Republic—the republican spirit languished in the interior, and the result of the elections terminated in favour of the counter-revolutionists and the royalists.   A great schism became inevitable as soon as the majority of the two councils declared against the majority of the Directory.   A kind of triumvirate had been formed, composed of Barras, Rewbel, and Reveillère-Lepaux: three men inadequate to their duties in so important a crisis.   They at length perceived that the only support of their authority was the cannon and the bayonet, so that, at the risk of arousing the ambition of the generals, they were compelled to call in the armies to their assistance: another serious danger, but one which, not being so immediate, was the less anticipated.

It was then that Bonaparte, the conqueror of
Lombardy and the vanquisher of Austria, formed a
club in each division of his army, invited the soldiers
to discuss the politics of the day, and represented to
them the two councils as traitors sold to the enemies
of France, and, after having made his army swear upon
the altar of their country to exterminate the *brigands
modérés*, sent abundance of threatening addresses into
all the departments, as well as into the capital. In
the north, the army did not confine itself to delibera-
tion and the signing of addresses.   Hoche, general-in-
chief of the army of Sambre-et-Meuse, dispatched arms
and ammunition on the road to Paris, and marched
his troops upon the neighbouring towns.   For some
secret reasons this movement was suddenly suspended ;
either because there was not a perfect understanding
upon the mode of attacking the two councils, or, as I
have great cause to believe, the object was to procure
the conqueror of Italy a more exclusive influence in
the direction of affairs.   It is certain that the interests
of Bonaparte were at that time represented by Barras
in the Directorial triumvirate, and that the gold of
Italy flowed like a new Pactolus into the Luxembourg.
Women took an active part in affairs ; they at this
time conducted all political intrigues.

On the 4th of September (18th Fructidor), a military
movement placed the capital in subjection.   This bold
manœuvre was executed by Augereau, Bonaparte's lieu-
tenant, expressly sent for the purpose.   As in all convulsions in which the soldiers intermeddle, the toga
succumbed beneath the bayonet.   Two directors, fifty-
three deputies, and a great number of authors and

printers of periodical journals who had perverted public opinion, were banished without any form of trial. The elections of forty-nine departments were declared null, and the administrative authorities were suspended, previous to being reorganised in the spirit of the new revolution.

In this manner the royalists were vanquished and dispersed without fighting, by the mere effect of a military demonstration; in this manner the popular societies were reorganised; thus it was that a stop was put to the reaction upon the republicans; and thus the appellation of republican and patriot was no longer a cause for exclusion from employments and honours. As to the Directory, in which Merlin de Douai and François de Neufchâteau replaced Carnot and Barthélemy, who were both included in the number of the exiles, it at first acquired some appearance of energy and power; but in reality it was only a fictitious power, incapable of resisting troubles or reverses.

Thus the only remedy for evil was violence; an example the more dangerous, as it compromised the future.

Previously to the 18th Fructidor, a day which seemed destined to decide the fate of the Revolution, I had not remained idle. The advice I gave the director Barras, my suggestions, my prophetic conversations, had contributed in no small degree to impart to the Directorial triumvirate that watchfulness and stimulus of which its gropings and irresolutions had stood so much in need. Was it not natural that an event so favourable to the interests of the Revolution ought also to turn to the advantage of the

persons who had founded and preserved it by their
intelligence and their energy?[1] Hitherto the path of
the patriots had been strewn with thorns : it was
time that the tree of liberty should produce fairer fruit
for those who were to gather and taste it ; it was
time that the high employments of the state should
devolve upon men of superior abilities.

To conceal nothing, however, we were much embarrassed by the coalition, by the scourge of civil war,
and by the still more dangerous manœuvres of the
chameleons of the interior.   On the other hand, by
our energy and the force of circumstances, we were
masters of the state and of every branch of power.
The only question now was the insuring entire possession according to the scale of intellect and capacity.
All other theory at the conclusion of a revolution is
but folly or impudent hypocrisy; this doctrine finds its
place in the hearts of those even who dare not avow
it.   As a man of ability, I declared these trivial truths,
till then regarded as a state secret.[2]   My reasons were
appreciated ; the application of them alone caused embarrassment.   Intrigue did much, a salutary impulse
the rest.

A soft shower of military secretaryships, portfolios,
commissariats, legations, embassies, secret agencies and
commanderies of divisions soon came, like the manna
from heaven, to refresh my ancient colleagues, both

---

[1] An invaluable confession, explaining at once the *motives of
every revolution*, past, present and to come.—*Note by the Editor.*
[2] As far as I know, none of the heads of the Revolution
have as yet said so much.   Fouché is truly open and undisguised in his avowals.—*Note by the Editor.*

in the civil and military departments. The patriots, so long neglected, were now provided for. I was one of the first in seniority, and my worth was well known. I, however, resolutely refused the subaltern favours which were offered me; I was determined to accept of none but an employment of consequence sufficient to introduce me at once into the career of the highest political affairs. I had the patience to wait; and indeed waited long, but not in vain. This once Barras overcame the prejudices of his colleagues, and I was nominated, in the month of September, 1798, not without many previous conferences, &c., ambassador of the French Republic to the Cisalpine Republic. It is well known that for this new and analogous creation we were indebted to the victorious arms and acute policy of Bonaparte. Austria, however, was to be indemnified by the sacrifice of Venice.

By the treaty of peace of Campo Formio (a village of Frioul, near Udine) Austria had ceded the Pays Bas to France; and Milan, Mantua, and Modena to the Cisalpine Republic. She had reserved to herself the greatest part of the Venetian states, with the exception of the Ionian Islands, which France retained. It was easily seen that this was only a fresh stimulus for us, and the revolutionising of all Italy was already a subject of conversation. In the meantime the treaty of Campo Formio served to consolidate the new republic, the extent of which ensured its being respected. It was composed of Austrian Lombardy, of the Modenese, of Massa and Carrara, the Bolognese, the Ferrari, Romania, Bergamasque, Bressan, Cremasque, and other possessions of the Venetian state on the Continent.

Already matured, it demanded its emancipation; that is to say, that instead of languishing under the severe guardianship of the French Directory, it might live under the protection and influence of the great nation. In fact, we were more in want of valiant and sincere allies than of submissive vassals. Such was my opinion, and likewise those of the Director Barras and of General Brune, at that time commander-in-chief of the army of Italy, and who had just removed his head-quarters from Berne to Milan. But another director, whose system of policy and diplomacy was decidedly opposite, insisted that all, both friends and foes, were to be subjected by power and violence. This was Rewbel of Colmar, a harsh and vain man. He conceived there was much dignity in his view of the subject. He shared the weight of important affairs with his colleague, Merlin de Douai, an excellent juris-consult, but a very inferior statesman. Both these gave the law to the Directory, for Treilhard and Reveillère-Lepaux were but novices. If Barras, who remained *per se*, sometimes obtained an advantage over them, it was by dexterity and the good opinion they entertained of him. They thought him a man of sufficient nerve to be always ready for a *coup de main.*

But we had now recovered from the intoxication of victory. My initiation into state affairs took place at so important a crisis that it will be necessary to give a sketch of its prominent features, especially as it is a preliminary absolutely indispensable for the comprehending of what follows. In less than a year the peace of Campo Formio, which had so much deceived the credulous, was already sapped to its base. Without compunction we had made terrible use of the right of the stronger in Helvetia, at Rome, and in the East. Not finding kings, we had made war upon the shepherds of Switzerland, and had even attacked the Mamelukes. It was the expedition into Egypt in particular which gave the deepest wound. The origin of that expedition is sufficiently curious to be noted here. Bonaparte held a multifarious government in horror, and despised the Directory, which he called the five kings in routine (*cinq rois à terme*). Intoxicated with glory upon his return from Italy, welcomed with almost frantic joy by the French, he meditated seizing upon the supreme government; but his party had not as yet sufficiently established itself. He perceived—and I use his own expressions — that *the pear was not yet ripe.* On its side, the Directory, who feared him, found that the nominal command of the English expedition kept him too near Paris; and he himself was not much inclined to seek his destruction against the cliffs of Albion. To say the truth, it was scarcely known what to do with him. Open disgrace would have insulted public opinion and increased his reputation and his strength.

An expedient was thus being sought for, when the old bishop of Autun, a man distinguished for his shrewdness and address, and who had just introduced into foreign affairs the intriguing daughter of Necker, conceived the brilliant plan of ostracism into Egypt. He first hinted the idea to Rewbel, then to Merlin, taking upon himself the acquiescence of Barras. His plan was nothing but an old idea which he had found amongst the rubbish of the bureau, and which he had furbished up for the occasion. It was converted into a state affair. The expedient appeared the more fortunate, as it at once removed the bold and forward general, subjecting him at the same time to hazardous chance.

The conqueror of Italy at first mention entered unhesitatingly, and with the greatest ardour, into the idea of an expedition which not only could not fail to add to his renown, but would also ensure to him distant possessions, which he flattered he should govern either as a sultan or a prophet. But soon cooling, whether he perceived the snare, or whether he still aimed at supreme power, he drew back; but it was in vain for him to struggle, to raise obstacle upon obstacle—all were removed; and when he found himself reduced to the alternative of a disgrace, or of remaining at the head of an army which might revolutionise the East, he deferred his designs upon Paris, and set sail with the flower of our troops.

The expedition commenced with a kind of miracle, the sudden taking of Malta, but this was succeeded by the fatal catastrophe of the destruction of our squadron in the waters of the Nile. The face of affairs immediately changed. England, in its turn, was in the delirium of triumph. In conjunction with Russia she set on foot a new general war, of which the government of the Two Sicilies was the ostensible cause. The torch of war was lighted at Palermo and Naples by hatred; at Constantinople by a violation of the rights of peace and of nations. The Turk alone had justice on his side.

So many untoward circumstances coming fast upon

each other produced a deep impression upon Paris ;
it seemed that the political horizon again became
cloudy. Open preparations were made for war, and
everything assumed a threatening aspect. The rich
had already been subjected to a forced and progressive
loan of forty-eight millions, with which levies were
enabled to be raised. From this time may be dated
the idea and establishment of the military conscrip-
tion, an immense lever which had been borrowed from
Austria, perfected and proposed to the councils by
Jourdan, and immediately adopted by the placing in
active service two hundred thousand conscripts. The
armies of Italy and Germany were reinforced. All the
preliminaries of war burst forth at once—insurrection
in Escaut and the Deux Néthes, at the gates of
Malines and Brussels ; troubles in the Mantuan territory and at Voghera ; Piedmont on the eve of a convulsion ; Geneva and Milan torn by the contending
factions and inflamed by the republican fever with
which our Revolution had inoculated them.

It was when surrounded by this gloomy prospect
that I set forward on my embassy to Milan. I arrived
at the very moment when General Brune was about
to effect, in the Cisalpine government, without an
essential alteration, a change of individuals, the key
to which change was in my possession. The object
was to remove the power into the hands of men
possessing greater energy and firmness, and to commence the emancipation of the young republic, in order
that it might communicate the impulse to the whole
of Italy. We premeditated this *coup-de-main* with the
hope of forcing into acquiescence the majority of the

Directory, which held its sittings at the Luxembourg.[1]
I concerted measures with Brune, I encouraged the
most ardent of the Lombardian patriots, and we decided that the movement should be put in execution,
and that there should be neither proscriptions nor
violence. On the morning of the 20th of October a
military demonstration was made; the gates of Milan
were closed; the directors and the deputies were at
their posts. There, by the simple impulse of opinion,
under the protection of the French troops, and at the
suggestion of the general-in-chief, fifty-two Cisalpine
representatives send in their resignations, and are replaced by others. At the same time the three directors, Adelasio, Luosi, and Soprensi, chosen by the

---

[1] Fouché does not give us sufficient information respecting
this plan of revolutionising all in the exterior, a plan at that
time disapproved by the majority of the Directory, and of which
General Augereau was one of the first victims.   Commander-
in-chief of the army of Germany, after the 18th Fructidor, he
was about to revolutionise Suabia, when he was recalled and
disgraced. Bonaparte had part in this, and was furious when
they were already desirous of demolishing his work, the peace
of Campo Formio. After his departure for Egypt, Brune and
Joubert will be seen to share the disgrace of Augereau, on the
same account.   This plan, which was renewed by the *propa-
gandum* in 1792, appears to have had no other defender in the
Directory but Barras: this was but a weak support.   Rewbel
and Merlin would not proceed precipitately in the affair; already
alarmed at their excesses in Egypt and Switzerland, they persisted in cradling themselves in a situation which was neither
that of peace nor war. It must be owned that the bold attempt
of universal revolutionising, which they only dared to attempt
by halves, gave to the revolutionists of France a great power
of choice in the operations of the campaign of 1799, which
rushed upon them from within and without.   The Revolution
stopped, and assumed a more masculine character.—*Note by the
Editor.*

ex-ambassador Trouvé, and confirmed by the French Directory, are likewise invited to resign, and were replaced by three other directors, Brunetti, Sabatti, and Sinancini. Citizen Porro, a Lombardian patriot, full of zeal and intelligence, was appointed minister of police. This repetition of our 18th Fructidor, so easily effected, was confirmed by the primary assemblies; thus we rendered homage to the sovereignty of the people, by obtaining its sanction to the measures adopted for its welfare. Soprensi, the ex-director, with twenty-two deputies, came to place their protests in my hands; all my endeavours to obtain their acquiescence to the measure were useless. It became necessary to issue an order for removing Soprensi by force from the apartments he occupied at the directorial palace; and I was compelled to receive from him a fresh protest, the purport of which was that he denied the general-in-chief the right which he had arrogated over the Cisalpine authorities. Here the opposition ended—we surmounted every difficulty without noise or violence. It may be supposed that the couriers were not idle; the ex-deputies and the malcontents had recourse to the Directory of Paris, to which they appealed.

I, on my part, dispatched an account of the changes of the 20th of October, dwelling particularly upon the experienced judgment of the general-in-chief, the justice of his views, the example which France had itself given on the 18th Fructidor, and the still more recent one, when the Directory found itself under the necessity of nullifying the elections of several departments, in order to remove several obnoxious or

dangerous deputies. I then launched into more important considerations, invoking the terms and the
spirit of the alliance entered in between the French
and Cisalpine republics, a treaty approved by the
council of ancients on the 7th of March preceding.
In this treaty the new republic was explicitly acknowledged as a free and independent power, upon these
conditions only, that she should take part in all our
wars; that she should set on foot all her forces at
the requisition of the French Directory; that she
should support twenty-five thousand of the French
troops, by providing an annual fund of ten millions
for that object; and, finally, that all her armaments
should be under the command of our generals. I
guaranteed the strict and faithful execution of this
treaty, protesting that the government and the welfare
of this nation would find a more certain pledge, and a
still firmer support, in the energy and sincerity of the
men to whom the power had just been intrusted;
finally, I brought forward my instructions, which
authorised me to reform, without tumult or violence,
the vices of the new Cisalpine government, the excessive and expensive numbers of the members of the
legislative body, the administrations of the departments, &c., and which recommended me to take care
that the form of the republican government was not
oppressive to the people. From that I proceeded to
guarantee also the existence of immense resources; the
legislative body of Milan having authorised the Directory to sell thirty millions of national domains, in
which was included the property of the bishops. The
dispatch of General Brune, the general-in-chief, per-

fectly coincided with mine; but all was useless. Pride and vanity, as well as the lowest intrigues, and even foreign insinuations, were opposed to us. Besides, the matter was now to solve one of the highest questions of immediate policy, of the adoption or rejection of the system of the unity of Italy divided into republics, effected by the sudden overthrow of the old corrupted governments, already tottering and incapable of supporting themselves, a system which we do honour to ourselves for having made to triumph. This nervous and decisive policy was not to the taste of the wary minister who at that time directed our foreign affairs (Talleyrand); he employed roundabout means to ruin our plan, and he succeeded. Rewbel and Merlin, whose vanity was brought into play, exclaimed loudly against the affair of Milan; we had only on our side the isolated vote of Barras, which was soon neutralised. A decree made, *ab irato*, on the 25th of October, formally disavowed the changes effected by General Brune. At the same time the Directory signified to me its disapprobation, informing me that it would have much satisfaction in seeing all the ex-directors and deputies reinstated in their places.

I could easily have exculpated myself in this affair, in which I was thought not to have taken a direct part, having arrived at my post at the commencement of the preparations, of which, in strictness, I could neither know the origin nor object. Such would have been the conduct of a man anxious to preserve his situation at the expense of his opinion and honour. I adopted a more candid and firmer mode of procedure. I protested warmly against the disapprobation

of the Directory; I pointed out to them the danger of
retrograding; besides, the will of the people had been
declared in the primary assemblies, so that it was
impossible to undo what had been done without the
risk of being guilty of the most blamable frivolity and
inconsistency. I also insisted how impolitic it would
be to displease the Cisalpine patriots, and to risk
exasperating that republic at the very moment when
the hostilities, on the eve of commencing against
Naples, could not fail of being the prelude to a
general war. I announced to them that thirty
thousand Austrians were assembling on the Adige;
but I was preaching to the winds. Brune, upon receiving the decree of the Directory which annulled
the depositions made on the 20th of October, received
instructions to leave the army of Italy, and to proceed
to command in Holland. He was fortunately replaced
by the brave, modest, and honourable Joubert, particularly qualified to calm and repair all. Milan was
in a state of fermentation, and the two rival factions
found themselves again opposed to each other—the
one full of hope at being re-established, and the other
resolved to make a firm stand—when a new decree
from the Directory reached me, bearing date the 7th
of November. It refused to acknowledge the will
of the people, and ordered me to break off all relations with the Cisalpine directory till that authority
had been reorganised such as it was previous to the
20th of October. The Directory likewise ordered a
new convocation of the primary assemblies. I was
much hurt at this contempt of the republican principles, upon which my first proceedings had been

founded. The servile, vexatious system by which a republic, our ally, was to be governed, appeared to me the height of imbecility. In the midst of the serious circumstances in which the Italian peninsula was about to be placed, it was nothing less than degrading men and reducing them to the situation of mere machines; it was besides diametrically opposite to the stipulations and the spirit of the treaty of alliance. I explained myself—I did more: I in some degree vindicated the majesty of the two nations by addressing to the Cisalpine directory a message, of which the following are the principal heads:

"Vain, citizen directors, is the attempt to infer that your political existence is transitory, because it has been accompanied by an act justly disapproved of and strongly condemned by my government. (Here a palliative was necessary.) Your fellow-citizens, by giving it their sanction in your primary assemblies, have given you a moral power for which you will henceforth become responsible to the Cisalpine people.

"Proudly, then, assert its independence and your own; hold with firmness the reins of government which are intrusted to you, without being embarrassed by the perfidious suggestions of calumny; make your authority respected by a powerful and well-organised police; oppose the malignity of the passions by displaying a majesty of character, and confound all the machinations of your enemies by an inflexible justice.

"We desire always to give peace to the world; but if vanity and the thirst of blood cause arms to be wielded against your independence, woe to the traitors! Their dust shall be spurned by the feet of free men.

"Citizen directors! elevate your minds with events; be superior to them if you wish to command them; be not uneasy about the future; the solidity of republics consists in the nature of things; victory and liberty shall pervade the world.

"Temper the ardent activity of your fellow-citizens, in order to render it productive. . . . Let them learn that energy is not delirium, and that to be free is not to be licensed to do evil."

But the Italian character was little capable of appreciating these precepts. I everywhere sought for a firmness tempered by constancy, and, with few exceptions, I found nothing but wavering and pusillanimous hearts.

Enraged at such language, addressed to the Cisalpine Republic, our routine sovereigns (*souverains à terme*) sitting in the Luxembourg, dispatched in all haste to Milan the citizen Rivaud in quality of commissioner-extraordinary: he was the bearer of a decree ordering me to quit Italy. I paid no attention to it, persuaded that the Directory had not the right to prevent me living as a private individual at Milan. A sympathetic conformity of opinions and ideas with Joubert, who had replaced Brune in his command, induced me to remain there to await the events which were in preparation. He was, without doubt, the most intrepid, the most able, and the most estimable of all Bonaparte's lieutenants; since the peace of Campo Formio he had favoured the popular cause in Holland; he came into Italy resolved, notwithstanding the false policy of the Directory, to follow his own inclination, and to satisfy the wishes of the people, who anxiously desired liberty. I strongly urged him not to commit himself on my account, but to temporise. The commissary Rivaud, not daring to undertake anything while I remained at Milan, informed the committee-men of the Luxembourg of his situation, and the next courier was the bearer of some thundering dispatches.

The military authority was compelled to act, whether willingly or not. In the night of the 7th of December the guard of the directory and of the legislative body was disarmed and replaced by French troops. The people were not allowed to enter the place where the directory and the two councils assembled. A secret committee was held during the night, and on its breaking up the new functionaries were displaced to make way for the former ones. Seals were placed upon the doors of the constitutional circle, and the commissioner Rivaud ordered several arrests. I think that I myself should have been arrested, manacled, and passed from brigade to brigade up to Paris had not Joubert apprised me in time. I secreted myself in a country house near Monza, where I immediately received the proclamation addressed by citizen Rivaud to the Cisalpine Republic. In this disgraceful memento of political absurdity the irregularity and violence of the proceedings of the 20th of October were alleged and condemned on account of their having been promoted by the military power—a most ridiculous accusation, since it equally condemned the 18th Fructidor and the late and humiliating scene at Milan, performed by orders from Paris, without any investigation.

This parrot of a commissioner, in enigmatical terms, taxed both Brune and myself with being innovators and reformers, without character or mission; in short, he described the excess of our patriotism, which, said he, caused the popular government to be calumniated.

All this was truly pitiable, from its bad reasoning. Being informed that I had disappeared, and thinking that I was concealed in Milan, the Directory again dispatched an extraordinary courier, the bearer of a fresh order for my expulsion from Italy. "If you are aware," wrote immediately poor Rivaud to the Cisalpine directory, "that citizen Fouché is on your territory, I beg you will give me information accordingly." I smiled at his perplexity, and at the alarms of both directories; then, quitting my retreat, calmly took the road to the Alps, which I crossed. I arrived at Paris in the beginning of January, 1799. The credit and influence of Rewbel and Merlin were already considerably on the decline. Intrigues were being formed against them in both councils, and they began to lower their lofty tone. Therefore, instead of calling me to their bar and making me give an account of my conduct, they contented themselves with announcing in their official journal that I had returned from my mission to the Cisalpine Republic.

I now thought myself sufficiently strong to call them to an account for their vindictive proceedings towards me, and insisted upon indemnities for the loss of my employment, which I received, accompanied with an earnest entreaty not to give rise to any scandal.

These details, upon my first failure in an important political mission, appeared to me necessary to be known, for the better understanding of the state of the public mind at this period, and the ground upon which my first operations were to commence. I had, besides, already penned this *exposé* by desire of Bonaparte on the eve of his departure for Marengo ; and I own that, upon re-perusing it, recollections were brought to mind which gave me no small degree of satisfaction.

I found the Directorial authority shaken less by the public disasters than by the underhand machinations of discontented factions, who, without throwing off the mask, carried on their attacks in secret.

The public testified itself generally disgusted with the narrow and paltry spirit which actuated our "five routine kings " ; people were indignant that their authority was only made known by exactions, injustice, and incapacity. By rousing the dormant passions they provoked resistance. A few confidential conversations with men who either possessed influence or exercised their powers of observation, and my own reflections, enabled me to form a right judgment of the state of things.

Everything announced important events and an approaching crisis. The Russians advanced, and prepared to enter the lists. Note after note was dispatched to Austria to endeavour to stop their progress; at length, towards the end of February, the war signal was sounded, without our being in a state to enter the field. The Directory had provoked this second coalition, merely by depriving itself of its best generals. Not only was Bonaparte an exile in the sands of Africa ; not only had Hoche, escaped from the Irish expedition, ended his days by poison ; but

Pichegru[1] had been banished to Sinnamary, Moreau
was in disgrace, and Bernadotte, who had retired
from diplomacy after the failure of his embassy to
Vienna, had resigned his command of the army of
observation ; even the removal of Championnet was
decreed, for having wished to put a stop to the
rapacity of the agents of the Directory. In short,
Joubert himself, the brave and virtuous Joubert, had
received his dismissal on account of his desire of
establishing in Italy a wholesome liberty, which would
have drawn still closer together the ties that united
the two nations, whose destinies appeared to be the
same.

This second continental war, of which Switzerland,
Italy, and Egypt had only seen the prelude, commenced on the 1st of March ; and by the 20th
Jourdan had lost the battle of Stockach, which forced
him to repass the Rhine in the greatest precipitation.
This gloomy omen was soon followed by the breaking-
up of the congress of Rastadt, a political drama, the
last act of which was full of horrors. We were not
more fortunate in Italy than in Germany : Schérer,
Rewbel's favourite general, lost three battles on the
Adige ; these deprived us in a few days of the liberty
of Italy, together with the conquests which had cost
us three laborious campaigns. Till then we had
either invaded or resisted with firmness. The effect
produced by the intelligence that we were retreating
on all sides must be imagined ; it exceeds description !
Every revolutionary government, which can only make
malcontents, but cannot command victory, necessarily

[1] Succeeded in escaping. (See biographical notice.)

loses its power: upon the first reverses all the ambitious assume an hostile attitude.

I was present at several meetings of the discontented deputies and generals, and I concluded that, in reality, these parties had not all the same intentions, but that they reunited for the common purpose of overturning the Directory, that each might be enabled to further his own ambitious views. I set Barras right upon this subject, and persuaded him to effect, at any cost, the expulsion of Rewbel, being very sure that we should afterwards gain over Treilhard, Merlin, and Reveillère, on our own terms. These two last were particularly disliked, from having favoured the system of the electoral schisms, the object of which was to clear the legislative councils of the most ardent republicans. I was aware that Joseph and Lucien, Bonaparte's brothers, intrusted by him to watch over his interests during his warlike exile, were manœuvring with the same intentions. Lucien displayed an exalted patriotism; he was at the head of a party of disaffected with Boulay de la Meurthe. Joseph, on his side, lived at a great expense, and kept a magnificent establishment. His house was the rendezvous for the most powerful deputies of the councils, the highest functionaries, the most distinguished of the generals, and the women most fertile in expedients and intrigue.

The coalition being formed, Rewbel, disconcerted and abandoned by Merlin, to whom he was represented as the scapegoat, thought himself extremely fortunate in obtaining his expulsion, disguised by the chance of the dice, on the principal condition that his retreat in the council of ancients should be respected.

But who was to fill his place in the Directory? Merlin, and the other overgrown deputies, his creatures, determined upon appointing in his stead Duval, of the Seine Inférieure, a man of mediocre talents, and without influence, in other respects a worthy person; he at that time filled the office of minister of police, but was too short-sighted for his post. They were permitted to go on quietly, and all their measures being taken, every effort was made for Sieyès, the ambassador at Berlin, whose hidden abilities had been the theme of praise for the last ten years. I knew him to possess some strong and decided revolutionary opinions, but I also knew that his character was mistrustful and artificial; I also believed he cherished sentiments but little compatible with the basis of our liberties and institutions. I was not his partisan; but I associated myself with the faction so suddenly formed in his favour without my being able to conjecture from what motive. It was urged that it was necessary to have at the head of affairs, upon the commencement of a threatening coalition, a man who of all others knew how to keep Prussia in a neutrality so advantageous to her; it was even asserted that he had shown himself an experienced politician by giving the first hints of the coalition.

The election commenced: I still smile when I recollect the disappointment of the subtle Merlin and the worthy Duval his creature, who, whilst the council were proceeding in the election, having established a telegraphic line of agents from the Hôtel de Police to the Legislative Hall, whose duty it was to transmit intelligence to the happy candidate, learnt that a party of the *ventre* had deserted. Neither Merlin nor Duval could possibly comprehend how a *certain* majority could be suddenly transformed into a minority. But we, who knew the secret spring, often amused ourselves with the affair at excellent dinners, at which politics were discussed.

Merlin saw in Sieyès a dangerous competitor, and from that moment looked upon him with an evil eye. As to the worthy Duval, being soon replaced by Bourguignon, he became misanthropical. These two mediocre citizens were neither of them fitted to direct the police.[1] The work was as yet only in embryo. In order to bring it to perfection two legislative coalitions were formed. In one were Boulay de la Meurthe, Chénier, Français de Nantes, Chalmel, Texier-Olivier, Berlier, Baudin des Ardennes, Cabanis, Regnier, the two Bonapartes; in the other Bertrand du Calvados, Poulain-Grandpré, Destrem, Garrau, Arena, Salicetti, and several other vigorous *athletæ*. In both these, which had their auxiliaries without, I gained over several to Barras, while he on his side manoeuvred tolerably well. Underhand means were the only ones that could be employed at first; the time for throwing off the mask was not yet come.

In this respect our reverses served us admirably; they were inevitable. Could one hundred and sixty thousand men, exhausted and worn out by fatigue, dispirited by repeated defeats, and commanded by

[1] A little vanity of Fouché, who prepares everything in the style of a melodrama, in order to introduce himself upon the stage as alone capable of guiding the police helm, of turning to the best advantage his dark intrigues and fertile expedients.— *Note by the Editor.*

generals always liable to be disgraced, make head against more than three hundred thousand enemies seconded, in Italy and Germany, by the people, and brought, either by the ardour of victory or the desire of vengeance, upon the frontiers even of the Republic?

The dissatisfaction with the majority of the Directory soon became general. " It has only," as was observed, " displayed its authority in oppression, injustice, and incapacity; instead of signalising its dictatorship by some brilliant action, since the 18th Fructidor it has but abused its immense power; it has ruined our finances, and dug the abyss which now threatens to engulf the Republic."

It was now only in the councils that the Directory could still find defenders amongst the creatures in its interest, and its unskilful apologists. The exasperation was at its height when Bailleul wrote in a pamphlet that he feared more the Russians in the legislative body than the Russians approaching the frontiers.

A concerted message, addressed to the Directory, requiring information upon the exterior and interior situation of the Republic, became the signal for battle. It was at the moment when Sieyès, the new director, had just been installed. No answer arriving from the Luxembourg, the councils, on the 18th of June (28th Prairial), declared their sittings permanent. On its side, the Directory adopted the same resolution by way of reprisal; but it was already incapable of parrying the blows about to be aimed at its existence.

It was first deprived of the right of restraining the liberty of the press. The expression of opinion being no longer compromised, it was no longer possible for the lawyers to defend the field. Consequently, scarcely was the appointment of Treilhard contested and revoked than he retired without opening his lips.

Merlin and Reveillère, however, were obstinate, and endeavoured to maintain themselves in the Directorial chairs. Boulay de la Meurthe, and the deputies of his faction, proceeded to the Luxembourg to demand imperiously the dismissal of the two directors. At the same time Bertrand du Calvados, in the name of a commission of eleven, of which Lucien was one, ascended the tribune, and found means to alarm the directors by the preface of their act of accusation. " I will not speak to you," cried he, " of your Rapinats, your Ivauds, your Trouvés, and your Faypoults, who, not satisfied with exasperating our allies by injuries of every kind, have violated by your orders the rights of nations, have proscribed republicans, or have arbitrarily displaced them to make way for traitors ! " I was not ignorant of this sally, in which was implied an indirect approbation of my conduct, and a tacit condemnation of that pursued by the Directory with respect to me.

At length, on the 30th Prairial (18th of June), Merlin and Reveillère, upon a solemn assurance that they should not be impeached, sent in their resignation, and Sieyès became master of the field of battle. At that very instant the whole strength of the revolution rallied round Sieyès and Barras.

In perfect understanding with the head of the councils, they used every means to prevent the admission of any into the Luxembourg for their colleagues in place of the expelled directors, but such men as

Roger Ducos, Moulins, and Gohier, who were incapable of throwing them in the background by their abilities or the strength of their character. This arrangement tended greatly to make them masters of affairs, Roger Ducos being associated in vote and interest with Sieyès.

The first-fruit of the triumph of the councils over the Directory was the appointment of Joubert to the command of Paris, an appointment obtained from Sieyès by Barras, and to which I also was not a stranger. A few days afterwards I was appointed to the embassy of Holland : this was a species of reparation which the new Directory owed me. I went to take leave of Sieyès ; he told me that till then government had been directed by chance, without end and without fixed principles, and that it should not be so for the future. He expressed some uneasiness respecting the new flight of the anarchical spirit, with which, said he, it is impossible ever to govern. I answered that it was time this aimless and irregular democracy should give place to a republican aristocracy, or government of men of wisdom and experience, the only one which could establish and consolidate itself. "Yes, doubtless," replied he ; "and if that were possible, you should have it ; but how distant are we still from so desirable an object !" I then spoke to him of Joubert, as a pure and disinterested general whom I had an opportunity of being well acquainted with in Italy, and to whom might be safely intrusted, in case of need, a powerful influence ; nothing was to be feared either from his ambition or his sword, which he would never turn against the liberty of his country. Sieyès having,

attentively heard me to the conclusion, only replied by
a *C'est bien!* I could discover nothing else in his side
glance.

It is clear that I did not succeed in my intention
of sounding him and drawing out his confidence. I
knew, however, that a short time before he had had
a very significant conversation with one of M. Talleyrand's friends, who has since been made a senator;
that he owned to him that the Revolution wandered
without any object in performing a vicious circle; and
that no stability or safety could be found but by help
of another social organisation, which would present
us with a counterpart of the English revolution of
1688; adding, that in that country, for more than a
century, liberty and royalty were united together without satiety and without divorce. The objection was
started that there was no longer a William. " That is
true," he replied; " but there are in the north of
Germany wise princes, warriors, philosophers, who
govern their little principality as paternally as Leopold
governed Tuscany." Finding that he alluded to the
Duke of Brunswick, the manifesto of 1792 was mentioned. " He is not the author of that cursed
manifesto," replied he, with much warmth, " and it
would be easy to prove that he himself advised the
retreat from Champagne, refusing to deliver up France
to fire and bloodshed, and to fight for the emigrants."
" We must not, however," continued Sieyès, "think
of the son of the cowardly Egalité; not only has he
not headpiece sufficient, but it is certain that he has
become reconciled with the Pretender; he would not
dare to take a single step by himself. Among our

generals I do not see one who is capable of, or adequate to, placing himself at the head of a coalition of determined spirits to extricate us from the bog in which we are at present knee-deep, for it cannot be dissembled that our power and constitution are crumbling into ruin on all sides." This conversation required no commentary; I knew also that Sieyès had held, upon our interior situation, nearly the same language to Barras. These glimmerings were sufficient to let me into his views, and to form my opinion respecting his ultimate intentions.

There is no doubt he already indulged the project of favouring us with a social compact of his own fashion. The haughty priest had been for a long time preyed on by this ambition of raising himself to be the sole legislator. I set off with the firm persuasion that he had succeeded in making his views agreeable to some men of influence, such as Daunou, Cabanis, Chénier, Garat, and the greater part of the members of the council of the ancients, who, hurried on since that, went beyond the goal at which they were to stop. Such was the germ of the revolution which shortly began to be prepared, and without which France would inevitably have fallen prostrate in the convulsions of anarchy, or under the repeated blows of the European coalition.

I had scarcely time to go and present my credentials at the Hague, where I replaced Lombard de Langres—a kind of affected author, but in other respects a worthy man. I found this other young republic divided in its authorities into firm and weak men, into aristocrats and democrats, as everywhere else. I convinced myself that the Orange, or English, party would never have influence upon the destinies of the country so long as our armies were capable of protecting Holland. There I again met with Brune, who kept our troops firm in their obedience by shutting his eyes to the carrying on of a contraband trade, indispensable to prevent the ruin of the country. I let him do as he pleased; we could not fail of being on perfectly good terms; like me, he found himself sufficiently avenged by the overthrow of the ill-conducted governments which had injured and expatriated us so *mal à propos*.

Nothing, however, was as yet fixed at Paris. The greatest instability prevailed, and it was to be apprehended that the triumph of the councils over the executive power might end by enervating and disorganising the government. It was, above all, to be feared that the anarchists, by abusing the consequences of the late revolution, might wish to overturn everything in order to seize a power which they were incapable of directing. They relied upon Bernadotte, whom they had appointed to be minister of the war department, and whose ambition and character did not sympathise with the views of Sieyès and his party.

Fortunately, the faction of Bonaparte, directed by his two brothers, and having for council Rœderer, Boulay de la Meurthe, and Regnier, coincided in viewing the necessity of arresting the flight of the legislative movement. Lucien took upon him to speak from the tribune. By proposing some line of demarcation for the future, he drew round his own party the old directors and their followers, who were fearful

of being called to an account. The danger was press-
ing; the ultra party demanded the impeachment of
the co-directors, a measure which would bring to
light or unveil every malversation.

A strong opposition, therefore, immediately arose in
a portion of those deputies even who had concurred in
overthrowing the majority of the Directory, but merely
in order to change the system of the government, and
to get it into their own hands. They alleged in favour
of the accused that people were liable to make mistakes
in politics, to adopt false theories, and be unsuccessful ;
that they might even yield to the intoxication which is
attendant upon great power, and in that be more unfortunate than criminal. They above all invoked the
promise, or rather the moral promise given and received,
that no measure should be adopted against the ex-
directors if they made a voluntary resignation ; and,
finally, they recalled to remembrance that the councils
had more than once sanctioned by their plaudits the
expedition into Egypt and the declaration of war
against the Swiss ; the objects of so much declamation.
This impeachment, besides, would have revealed too
much, and this Barras wished to avoid ; it would also,
in other respects, have had consequences injurious to
power abstractedly considered, and this Sieyès considered as impolitic. These discussions were protracted
with the view of occupying the public attention till
other incidents and the march of events might operate
a diversion.[1] But how was it possible to stop at one

---

[1] All this is very clear, and we know no other production
which throws so much light upon the intrigues of this period.—
Note by the Editor.

and the same time the abuses of the press, which began to degenerate into licentiousness, and the contagion of the popular clubs, which had everywhere been reopened? Could Sieyès, at the head of his phalanx, composed of some forty philosophers, metaphysicians, and deputies, without any energy than that stimulated by worldly interest, flatter himself with being able to overthrow anarchy and erect a superstructure of social order without foundations? His coalition with Barras was precarious. In the Directory he could only calculate upon Roger Ducos. With regard to Moulins and Gohier, his only guarantee for them was their extreme sincerity and their limited political views. Men so insignificant might, at the critical moment, become the instruments of an enterprising faction. The ascendency which Sieyès exercised in the Directory might be diminished, or even turned against him by mistrust.

But when, indeed, he saw that it was in his power to strengthen himself by means of Joubert—invested with the command of Paris—and whose inclinations were about to be gained over by a marriage into which he allowed himself to be entrapped, Sieyès resolved to make him the pivot of his reforming coalition. In consequence, the chief command of the army of Italy was given him, in the hope that he would bring back victory to our standards, and thus acquire a quantum of glory sufficient for the elevation of the part allotted to him.

This arranged, Sieyès perceived that he wanted the instrumentality of a firm and active police. The police, as it was then constituted, naturally favoured the popular party, which had introduced into its body several of its creatures and of its leaders. The worthy Bourguignon, the then minister, owed his elevation to Gohier, but was entirely inadequate to such an office beset with so many difficulties. This was felt, and at the very moment when I had just drawn up for Barras a memoir upon the situation of the interior, in which I treated in its fullest extent the question of general police, Barras himself joined with Sieyès in order to dismiss Bourguignon, and afterwards with Gohier and Moulins, for the purpose of removing Alquier, Sieyès' candidate, and of calling me into office. I willingly exchanged my embassy for the direction of the police, although the ground on which I trod appeared slippery. I lost no time in taking possession of my post, and on the 1st of August I was installed.

The crown was lost in 1789 from the mere incapacity of the high police, the directors of it at that time not being able to penetrate the conspiracies and plots which threatened royalty. The first pledge for the safety of any government whatever is a vigilant police, under the direction of firm and enlightened ministers. The difficulties of the high police are immense, whether it has to operate in the combinations of a representative government, so incompatible with whatever is the least arbitrary, and that leaves to the factious legal arms with which to execute their projects; or whether it acts in behalf of a more concentrated form of government, aristocratical, directorial, or despotic. In the latter case the task is the more difficult, for nothing transpires from without: it is in obscurity and mystery that traces must be discovered which only present themselves to inquiring and penetrating glances. I found myself in the former case, with the double duty of discovering and dissolving the coalitions and legal oppositions against the established power, as well as the dark plots of royalists and foreign agents. The danger from these last was far less immediate.

I raised myself mentally above my functions, and felt not the least fear at their importance. In two hours I fully understood all my official powers. I did not, however, fatigue myself with considering the ministry intrusted to me in its minor details of arrangement. As things were situated, I felt that all the powers and abilities of a minister must be absorbed in the high police ; the rest might safely be left to the *chefs de bureau*. My only study was, therefore, to seize with a steady and sure hand all the springs of the secret police, and all the elements composing it. I first insisted that, for these essential reasons, the local police of Paris, called the *bureau central* (the prefecture did not then exist), should be placed entirely under my control. I found all the constituent elements in the most deplorable state of confusion and decay. The treasury was empty; and without money, no police. I soon had money at my command, by making the vice inherent in this great city contribute to the safety of the state. My first act was to put a stop to a tendency to insubordination, in which some of the *chefs de bureau* belonging to active factions indulged themselves; but I judged it necessary not to introduce hasty reforms or ameliorations in the details. I restricted myself simply to concentrating the high police within my own cabinet, with the

assistance of an intimate and faithful secretary. I felt
that I alone should be judge of the political state of
the interior, and that spies and secret agents should
only be considered as indications and instruments
often doubtful: in a word, I felt that the high police
was not administered by memorials and long reports;
that there were means far more efficacious; for
example, that the minister should place himself in
contact with the men of greatest influence, over all
opinions and doctrines, and over the superior classes
of society. This system never failed me, and I was
better acquainted with France, veiled in mystery by
means of oral and confidential communications, and
by widely-grasping conversations, than by the heaps
of written rubbish which continually passed under
my eyes. Thus, nothing essential to the safety of
the state ever escaped me, as will be proved in the
sequel.

These preliminaries being settled, I informed myself of the political state of the interior—a kind of
examination which I had already prepared in my
mind. I had scrutinised every vice, and probed every
wound of the social compact of the year III., by
which we were governed; and, to speak sincerely, I
considered that compact incapable of being executed
constitutionally. The two shocks it had sustained on
the 18th Fructidor, and the 30th Prairial, in a contrary
sense, changed the assertion into a positive fact. From
a government purely constitutional, the nation had
passed under the dictatorship of five men; this did
not succeed. Now that the executive power was
mutilated and weakened in its very essence, every-

thing indicated that the despotism of a few would be changed into a popular delirium, unless a strong barrier could be opportunely raised. I knew also that the man who had obtained the greatest influence, Sieyès, had from the commencement regarded this political establishment as absurd, and that he had even refused to direct the helm. If he had now surmounted his repugnance, it was because the opportunity of substituting a more reasonable organisation appeared to have arrived; he could not demolish the bastions without approaching the fortress itself. I explained myself to Barras, who, as much as I, mistrusted the sinuous policy of Sieyès. But he had certain engagements with him, and, moreover, dreaded on his own account the exaggerations and encroachments of the popular party. This party had the upper hand of him, but only from political considerations, and with the hopes of opposing Sieyès, who was beginning to throw off the mask. In the eyes of the republicans, Barras was considered as an old worn-out director, with whom the preservation of the public weal was incompatible. On one side he found himself pressed by the club of the Manège, which, assuming the tone and attitude of the Jacobins, declaimed against dilapidators and public robbers; and on the other, by Sieyès, who, taking advantage of some degree of influence, had some ulterior views which he did not care to intrust in confidence to Barras.

Sieyes had no doubt already prepared a constitution to his own taste, which should restrain and counterpoise power, according as events should develop themselves; his coalition was complete, and he

thought himself certain of the co-operation of Joubert.
A letter from this general showed me his real intentions : he cherished the noble hope of returning,
strengthened by the ascendency of victory, to conciliate all parties. Sieyès had been heard to say,
" Nothing can be accomplished with fools and drivellers ; we only want two things, a headpiece and a
sword." I was in great hopes that the sword upon
which he so much relied would not place itself entirely at his discretion.

Although his position was critical—temporising with
Barras, and not being able to rely either upon Gohier
or Moulins, who were both attached to the established
order of things — he could, however, still rely upon
his colleagues in their acquiescence to measures necessary to oppose the new legislative encroachments and
the attempts of the anarchists. Sieyès had, in the
council of ancients, an organised band. It became
necessary to assure himself of a numerical majority
in the council of five hundred, in which the ardent
and ultra party fixed their headquarters. The union
of the directorials and politicals sufficed to keep it in
check. Sure of the majority, the Directory determined
to make trial of their strength. As minister of police
in this state of affairs, I had only to manœuvre with
dexterity and promptitude upon the line of operations.
The first step was to render any dangerous coalition
against the executive government totally impossible.
I took upon myself to arrest the licentiousness of the
public journals, and the bold march of the political
societies which arose from their ashes. Such was the
first proposition which I made to the Directory, in

full sitting, after an explanatory report which Barras
had concerted with Sieyès. A *carte-blanche* was granted
me, and I resolved to suppress the clubs first.

I began by a kind of proclamation, or circular,
in which I declared that I had just taken upon myself
the duty of watching for all, and over all, in order
to re-establish the tranquillity of the interior, and to
put an end to the *massacres*. This last assurance, and
the word which ended it, displeased the demagogues,
who had flattered themselves with finding me accom-
modating. It was still worse when, on the 18th Thermidor (5th of August), four days after my entrance
into office, the Directory transmitted to the council
of ancients, who sent it to the council of five hundred,
my report upon the political societies. This was my
avowed production. In this report, which was guarded
in its expressions, for fear of irritating republican sus-
ceptibility, I began by establishing the necessity of
protecting the interior discussions of the clubs, by
coercing them exteriorly with all the power of the
Republic; then adding that the first steps of these
societies had been attempts against the constitution,
I concluded by praying for measures which should
compel them to re-enter the constitutional boundaries.

The sensation which the communication of this
report produced in the chamber was very strong.
Two deputies (who, I believe, were Delbrel and
Clémanceau) considered this mode of transmission,
on the part of the council of ancients, as an incipient
blow to the constitution. The deputy Grandmaison,
after having applied the terms *false and calumnious* to
my report, said it was the signal of a new reaction

against the most ardent supporters of the Republic.
A very warm discussion then took place, whether the
report should be printed—a discussion which produced
some animated observations from Briot and Garrau,
who demanded it might be put to the vote; this did
not take place, and the printing of *the report was
not ordered.

Thus, to speak the truth, in this first skirmish the
battle was a drawn one; but I experienced a disadvantage : not one voice was raised in my favour, which
led me to observe how little reason there is, in a
revolution, for relying upon cold and calculating spirits,
whatever may have been the bait with which they were
allured.   They afterwards give you good reasons for
justifying their silence ; but the only true one is the
fear of committing themselves.   The same day I was
attacked with still greater violence in the society of
the Manège.

I was neither disconcerted nor alarmed by this
discouraging *début*. To have flinched would have been
to work my own destruction, and abandon fortune in
the road she opened to me. I resolved to manœuvre
skilfully in the midst of kindling passions and of
interests which clashed without the least disguise.
Sieyès, finding that the Directory was not firm, and
that Barras did not keep pace with his wishes, ordered
the commissioner of inspectors of the council of ancients,
who were sitting at the Tuileries, to close the hall of
the Manège.   This stroke of authority caused a sensation.   I thought Sieyès certain of his object, and
still more so when, at the commemoration of the 10th
of August, which was held with much pomp in the

Champ de Mars, he made in his state speech, as
president, the most violent attack upon the Jacobins,
declaring that the Directory knew all the enemies
which were conspiring against the Republic, and that
it would oppose them with equal vigour and perseverance, not by counterpoising one against the other,
but by suppressing them all alike.

As if at that very instant it was wished to punish
him for having fulminated forth these menacing words,
at the moment when the salvos of artillery and musketry terminated the ceremony, two or three balls were
heard, or were said to have been heard, whistling round
Sieyès and Barras, followed by some shouts.   Upon
returning to the Directory, whither I closely followed
them, I found them both exasperated and enraged to
the utmost degree.   I said that if indeed there had
been a plot, it could only have been planned by some
military instigators ; and fearing that I should myself
become suspected by Sieyès, who would not have failed
demanding my sacrifice, I insinuated to him, in a
pencilled note, that he should remove General Marbot,
commandant of Paris.   It was notorious that this
general showed himself completely devoted to the party
of the high republicans, who were opposed to Sieyès'
politics.   Upon the proposition of Sieyès, that very
night, without the advice of Bernadotte, at that time
the war minister, and without his knowledge, an order
was made out directing that Marbot should be employed on active service.   The command of Paris was
conferred upon General Lefèvre, an illustrious sergeant,
whose ambition was limited to being the instrument
of the majority of the Directory.   The diâtribe of

Sieyès at the Champ de Mars, and the *Houra* against
the Jacobins, were considered by one half of the
council of five hundred as an appeal to the counter-
revolution. The passions fermented still more and
more, and the Directory itself became divided and
irritated. Barras was in doubt whether he should
attach himself to Gohier and Moulins, which would
have isolated Sieyès. His incertitude could not escape
me; I was convinced that it was not yet time to determine: I told him so candidly. Three days after
the harangue of Sieyès, I took upon myself to recom-
mend the closing of the hall of the Jacobins of the
Rue du Bac. I had my reasons.[1] A message from
the Directory announced that the violation of the constitutional forms by this reunited society had determined it to order the closing of it. This bold step
completed the irritation of a violent faction, which
now experienced nothing but checks either from the
government or the councils.

It became also necessary to show that measures as
decisive could be adopted against the royalists, who
began to stir in the west, and who had just made a
futile effort in La Haute Garonne. Upon my report,
the Directory required and obtained, by a message,
the authority of making, for the space of one month,
domiciliary visits to discover the emigrants, *embaucheurs*,
assassins, and robbers. A few military measures in

---

[1] What, then, were Fouché's views in thus manœuvring against
those centres of the popular government, or rather against the
sovereignty of the people—a favourite dogma of our author's?
He has himself told us, he aspired to become one of the first
heads of the revolutionary *aristocracy.—Note by the Editor.*

La Haute Garonne were sufficient to stifle this ill-conceived and ill-directed insurrection.[1] As to the excesses perpetrated afresh by the Chouans in Brittany and La Vendée, as it was an inveterate evil proceeding from a vast cause, the remedy was not so easy in its application. The law of hostages, which prescribed measures against the relations of emigrants and nobles, instead of appeasing the troubles in their birth, did but increase them. This law, which but too much recalled to memory the Reign of Terror, appeared to me very odious, and well calculated to raise us up still more enemies. I contented myself with neutralising its execution as much as depended upon myself, taking care at the same time that my repugnance did not irritate in too great a degree the Directory and the departmental authorities. I perceived that these troubles were connected with one wound of the state, which the cabinet of London did its utmost to enlarge. I dispatched into the western departments intelligent emissaries, to give me exact information of the state of things. I then gained over a certain number of royalist agents, who, having fallen into our power in the different disturbed departments, had to fear either death, exile, or perpetual imprisonment. The greater part of these had offered their services to the government. I contrived means for their escape without their being liable to be suspected by their own party, whose ranks they again went to fill. They almost all rendered valuable services, and I can even say that

[1] He was here no longer the Fouché of the revolutionary aristocracy, but the Fouché of the Convention; his police was like Janus, it had two faces.—*Note by the Editor.*

through them and the information they furnished I succeeded at a later period in putting an end to the civil war.[1]

The greatest obstacles proceeded from amongst ourselves; they were raised by the schism of the revolutionists, who divided themselves into the possessors of power and the aspirants after office. The latter, impatient and irritated, became more and more exacting and hostile. How could it be hoped to govern and reform the state while the licentiousness of the press was permitted? It was at its height. "The Directory, now nearly royalty," said the *Journal des Hommes Libres*, "has ostensibly sanctioned the massacre of republicans by the speech of its president on the 10th of August, and by its message on the shutting up of political societies." Upon arriving at the Luxembourg I found, as I expected, Sieyès and his colleagues exasperated against the journals. I immediately suggested a message, requiring from the councils measures calculated to curb the counter-revolutionary journalists and the libellers. The message was being drawn up when the first intelligence arrived of the loss of the battle of Novi and the death of Joubert. The Directory was thunderstruck and discouraged. Although overcome with grief myself, I was nevertheless mindful that the reins should not be let fall; nothing, however, could be decided on that day. In the circumstances in which we were placed the loss of the battle was a disaster, the death of Joubert a calamity. He had set off with special instructions to come to an engage-

[1] Here Fouché appears as the precursor and promoter of the imperial *régime.—Note by the Editor.*

ment with the Russians. Unfortunately, the delay of a month, occasioned by his marriage with Mademoiselle de Montholon, had given the enemy time to reinforce itself.

The death of Joubert, who was struck down at the first discharge of musketry, and which has justly been deemed suspicious, has never been clearly explained. I have questioned ocular witnesses respecting the event, who seemed persuaded that the murderous ball was fired from a small country-house, by some hired ruffian, the musketry of the enemy not being within reach of the group of staff officers, in the middle of which was Joubert, when he came up to encourage the advance guard, which was giving way. It has even been said that the shot was fired by a Corsican chasseur of our light troops.

But let us not endeavour to unravel a dreadful mystery by conjectures or facts not sufficiently substantiated. "I leave you Joubert!" said Bonaparte, on setting off for Egypt. I will add, that his valour was heightened by his simplicity of manners and his disinterestedness, and that in him a correct *coup d'œil* was found united with rapidity of execution—a cool head with a warm heart. And this warrior was just snatched from us, perhaps by the hand of a murderer, at the moment when he might have raised and saved the country!

The progress of the policy of the government was suspended for nearly fifteen days; we could not, however, see ourselves perish. I urged Barras; and well assured that Sieyès was meditating an important blow, which it was essential to parry, these two directors

reunited to Roger Ducos, resolved, upon my suggestions, to resume their counteracting plans. Resolved
to restrain the licentiousness of the press, I determined
upon a decisive blow; I at one stroke of my pen suppressed eleven of the most popular journals among the
Jacobins and the royalists. I caused their presses to
be seized ; and even arrested the authors, whom I
accused of sowing dissension among the citizens, of
establishing it by persisting to suppose its existence,
of blasting private character, misrepresenting motives,
reanimating factions, and rekindling animosities.[1] By
its message the Directory restricted itself to inform the
councils that the licentiousness of several journalists
had determined it to cite them before the tribunals,
and to put seals upon their printing presses. Upon
my report being read, murmurs were heard, and much
agitation pervaded the hall. The deputy Briot declared
that some *coup d'état* was in preparation ; and, after a
personal attack upon me, demanded the suppression
of the ministry of the police. The next day the Directory caused a eulogium upon my administration to be
inserted in the *Redacteur* and *Moniteur.*

We had resumed our plans; we had secured Moreau
to our party, a republican in his heart, but detesting
anarchy. He was indeed but a poor politician, and
we did not find a great occasion of security in his
co-operation. Indifferent, and easily alarmed, he was

[1] Always the same when a government equally free from
contradictors and contradictions is the object in view; Fouché
does but follow, in this place, the errors of the Convention, of
the Committee of Public Safety, and of the Directory on the
18th Fructidor; he will do the same under Bonaparte, and he
will *prove* to us he is right.—*Note by the Editor.*

constantly in need of a stimulus. But we had no longer a power of choice; for, among the generals then in credit, there was not a single one upon whom we could safely rely.

The political horizon daily became more gloomy. We had just lost Italy, and were menaced with the loss of Holland and Belgium; an Anglo-Russian expedition had landed, on the 27th of August, in the north of Holland. From these reverses the ultra party derived fresh vigour. Their meetings became more frequent and active; they nominated for their leaders Jourdan and Augereau, who had seats in the five hundred and in the council, and Bernadotte, who was minister of war. Nearly two hundred deputies had recruited their party; it was, indeed, a minority, but an alarming one. As its roots in the Directory, it had also the directors Moulins and Gohier, at the moment when Barras, affecting to preserve a kind of equilibrium, believed himself by this manœuvre the arbiter of affairs. If he did not detach himself from Sieyès, it was solely from the fear that too violent a movement might deprive him of the power. I carefully preserved him in this disposition, much less to preserve my own stability than from love for my country:[1] too violent a convulsion in favour of the popular party would have been our destruction at this crisis.

The motion for declaring the country in danger, proposed by Jourdan, was the signal of a grand effort on the part of our adversaries. I had been informed

[1] What candour, what disinterestedness, in Fouché!—*Note oy the Editor.*

of it the night before. So that all our majority, assembled not without difficulty, after a meeting at the house of the deputy Frégeville, marched to their post, determined to stand firm. The picture of the dangers which surrounded us on every side was first drawn: "Italy under the yoke, the barbarians of the north at the very barriers of France, Holland invaded, the fleets treacherously given up, Helvetia ravaged, bands of royalists indulging in every excess in many of the departments, the republicans proscribed under the name of *Terrorists* and *Jacobins*." Such were the principal traits of the gloomy picture which Jourdan drew of our political situation. "One more reverse upon our frontiers," cried he, "and the alarm-bell of royalty will ring over the whole surface of the soil of France, as that of liberty did on the 14th of July."

After having conjured the Directory, from the legislative tribune, to discard the lukewarm friends of the Republic, in a crisis in which energy alone could be the salvation of France, he concluded by a motion, the object of which was to declare the country in danger. The adoption of this proposition would have hastened the movement which we were anxious to prevent, or at least to regulate. It produced the most violent discussion. The intention of the party had been to carry it with a high hand; but whether from shame or irresolution, they consented to adjourn the debate till the next day: this gave us breathing time.

I was informed that the most ardent among the patriots had earnestly solicited Bernadotte to mount his horse and declare for them, aided by a tumult at once civil and military. Already, in spite of the efforts and opposition of the police, an appeal had been made to the old and new Jacobins, to the old and new Terrorists. Upon Barras and myself devolved the task of dissuading Bernadotte from an enterprise which would have made him the Marius of France, a part compatible neither with his character nor habits. Ambition was doubtless his ruling passion; but it was a useful and generous ambition, and liberty was the object of his sincere devotion. We both touched these sensitive chords, and succeeded in overcoming him. He was, however, aware of the projects founded under the ægis of Joubert, together with the proposals made to Moreau, to change the form of government. We assured him that these were mere undigested ideas, mere chance projects, proposed by those theorists with which governments are continually annoyed in critical times; that nothing in this respect had been determined upon; that the constitution would be respected as long as our enemies did not wish to destroy it themselves. Barras hinted to him that it was advisable he should express his wish to be appointed commander-in-chief of an army, as while he held the war portfolio, he was the rallying point for an active party opposed to government. He avoided explaining himself respecting the hint thrown out, and left us.

Sieyès and Roger Ducos were extremely fearful of any failure; the more so as I had certain intelligence that vast crowds would be assembled round the Legislative Hall, and that the party flattered themselves they should carry their object by a *coup de main*, with the assistance of three generals devoted to their interests. Sieyès, in his quality of president, having sent for

Bernadotte, talked him over, and with much ability
got him to say that he would consider the chief command of an army as an honourable reward for his
labours as minister. Upon which Sieyès proposed immediate action. General Lefèvre had already received
orders to concert with me the necessary military
measures for dispersing any popular assembling by
force, after being well assured of the good disposition
of the soldiery. I found him full of confidence, and I
believed I could rely upon his soldierlike inflexibility.
My secret informations coinciding with other confidential communications, Sieyès and Barras, united with
Roger Ducos, dismissed Bernadotte without any communication whatever to Moulins or Gohier. As a
douceur, we were compelled to assure them that they
should be consulted upon the choice of the new
minister—a choice which Gohier, seconded by Barras,
directed a few days after upon Dubois de Crancé.

The debate was opened in rather an imposing
manner, upon the motion of Jourdan. Two opinions
were expressed. One party was desirous that the
government should preserve its ministerial and secret
character, the other that it should develop one more
national and public. These were so many masks to
conceal the real views of both parties. Jourdan's
motion was opposed with much talent and ingenuity
by Chénier and Lucien Bonaparte, and with less
ability by Boulay de la Meurthe. Lucien declared
that the only way to surmount the crisis was by
intrusting a great extent of power to the executive
authority. He, however, thought it his duty to combat
the idea of a dictatorship. " Is there one among us,"

cried he—this is very remarkable—"who would not
arm himself with the poniard of Brutus and chastise
the base and ambitious enemy of his country?" This
was anticipating the affair of the 18th Brumaire—a
day the triumph of which Lucien himself insured two
months afterwards. It is clear that he at this time
thought less of avoiding an inconsistency than at
keeping at a distance all kind of dictatorship, for this
would have dashed down the hopes which his brother
cherished in Egypt, to whom he had dispatched
courier after courier to hasten his return. Lucien's
grand object was that he should find the field clear,
being well assured that neither hesitation nor irresolution would be found in him—superior in this respect
to our timorous generals, who, fearful of the responsibility of a precarious power, saw no other mode of
reform but that of a new organisation, consented to
by men who were averse to any.

The debate in the council of five hundred was very
stormy. The report of Bernadotte's dismission had
irritated it considerably. Jourdan perceived in this the
certain prognostics of a *coup d'état*, and demanded the
permanence of the councils. His motions were nega-
tived by two hundred and forty-five votes against one
hundred and seventy-one. One hundred and two of
the warmest among the deputies entered their protests.
The mobs and crowds assembled around the hall were
dreadful, and their shouts and vociferations threatening.
The mass of the population of Paris testified their
alarm. But, whether from imbecility or sluggishness,
or from the efficacy of the measures of the military,
and the manœuvres of my agents, all the elements of

trouble and discord were dissipated, and tranquillity began to reappear.

The victory gained by the executive was complete; the council of ancients rejected the resolution which was to have deprived the Directory of the power of introducing troops within the constitutional radius.

These were, however, but evasive means. The country was really in danger; angry factions lacerated the state. The removal of Bernadotte, disguised under the appearance of a dismissal, solicited on his part, was doubtless a decided act, but one which might be interpreted to the disadvantage of the Directory. In a letter which was made public, Bernadotte replied in these terms to the official notification of his retirement, " I did not give in the resignation *which was accepted*, and I make known this fact for the honour of truth, which equally belongs to contemporaries and to history." Then, declaring his want of repose, he solicited his retiring pension (*traitement de reform*), " which I think to have deserved," added he, " by twenty years of uninterrupted services."

Thus were we again plunged into chaos by the effect of this grand division of opinion which pervaded both the legislative body and the Directory. " The vessel of the state," said I often to myself, " will float without any direction till a pilot presents himself capable of bringing it safe into port." [1]

Two sudden events brought about our safety. First, the battle of Zurich, gained on the 25th of September by Masséna, who, by again defeating the Russians,

[1] Fouché ably prepares us for the 18th Brumaire.—*Note by the Editor.*

and by preserving our frontier, permitted us to linger on without any interior crisis till the 16th of October, the day on which Bonaparte, who had landed on the 9th at Fréjus, made his entry into Paris, after having violated the laws of quarantine, so essential to the preservation of the public health.

Here let me pause an instant. The course of human events is, doubtless, subjected to an impulse which is derived from certain causes, the effects of which are inevitable. Imperceptible to the vulgar, these causes strike either more or less the statesman. He discovers them either in certain signs or in fortuitous incidents whose inspirations enlighten and direct him. This was precisely what happened to me five or six weeks before Bonaparte's landing. I was informed that two persons, employed in the *bureau de police*, discussing the state of affairs, had said that Bonaparte would be soon seen again in France. I traced this remark to its source, and found it to have no other origin than one of those gleams of the mind which may be considered as a species of involuntary foresight. This idea made its impression upon me.

I soon discovered by the temporising of Lucien and Joseph what were their real thoughts. They were persuaded that if their letters and packets arrived in Egypt, in spite of the British cruisers, Bonaparte would do his utmost to return; but the chances appeared to them so uncertain and hazardous that they dared not trust to them. Réal, one of Bonaparte's secret correspondents, went still further; he owned to me his hopes. I imparted them to Barras, but found him without any decided opinion upon the matter. As to myself, concealing previous discoveries, I made several advances, both to the two brothers and to Josephine, with the view of making both families favourable; they were divided. I found Josephine much more accessible It is well known by what ill-judged profusion she perpetuated the disorder and the embarrassments of her family: she was always without a sou. The income of forty thousand francs, secured to her by Bonaparte before his departure, was insufficient for her, independent of two extraordinary remittances, amounting together to the same sum, which had been sent her from Egypt in less than one year. Besides this, Barras having recommended her to me, I had included her in the number of those who received secret pecuniary assistance from the funds arising from gambling licenses. I gave her, with my own hands, one thousand louis—a ministerial gallantry which completed her favourable opinion of me.[1] Through her means I obtained much information, for she saw all Paris; with Barras, however, she was reserved, being more intimate with Gohier, at that time president of the Directory, and receiving his lady at the house; complaining at the same time very heavily of her brothers-in-law, Joseph and Lucien, with whom she was on very bad terms. My information from different quarters at length convinced me that Bonaparte would suddenly burst upon us; I was therefore, as it were, prepared for this event, at a time when everyone else was struck with surprise at it.

[1] This is truly being *l'homme habile*, and it is pretty well known what the signification of the adjective *habile* is with revolutionists. —*Note by the Editor.*

There would have been no great merit in coming to take possession of an immense power, which was offered to the most enterprising, and of gathering the fruits of an enterprise in which, to succeed, the display of audacity was alone requisite; but to abandon a victorious army, to pass through hostile fleets, arrive in the very nick of time, hold all parties in suspense, and decide for the safest—to weigh, balance, and master everything in the midst of so many contrary interests and opposing passions, and all this in twenty-five days, supposes wonderful ability, a firm character, and prompt decision. To enter into the details of the short interval between the arrival of Bonaparte and the 18th Brumaire would fill a volume, or rather, it would require the pen of a Tacitus.

Bonaparte, with much ability, had caused his own arrival to be preceded by that of the bulletin announcing the victory of Aboukir. It did not escape my notice that in certain coteries it was made much of, and that much inflation and hyperbole was put in requisition. Since the last dispatches from Egypt, much more movement and cheerfulness were perceptible at Josephine's and also at Joseph's and Lucien's. "Ah! if he should arrive for us!" said Josephine to me; "it is not impossible: should he have received the news of our disasters in time, nothing would prevent his flying hither to repair and save all!" A fortnight had scarcely elapsed after hearing these words, and Bonaparte suddenly landed. The most lively enthusiasm was excited on his passing through Aix, Avignon, Valence, Vienne, and especially Lyons. It might have been supposed that the universal feeling was that a chief was wanting, and that this chief had arrived under auspices the most fortunate. Upon being announced at Paris, in the theatres, the intelligence produced an extraordinary sensation, a universal delirium of joy.

Perhaps there might have been something prepared in all this, some concealed impelling power; but the general opinion cannot be commanded, and certainly it was very flattering to this unexpected return of a great man. From this moment he appeared to regard himself as a sovereign who had been received as such in his dominions. The Directory at first conceived a hidden disgust for him, and the republicans, from instinct, many fears. A deserter from the army of the East, and a breaker of the quarantine laws, Bonaparte would have been arrested by a firm government. But the Directory, a witness of the general delirium, dared not be severe : it was besides divided. How can it agree upon so important an affair without a unanimity of views and intentions ?

The very next day Bonaparte repaired to the Luxembourg to render an account, in a private sitting, of the situation in which he had left Egypt. There, compelled to account for his sudden return by the intention of sharing and averting the dangers of the country, he swore to the Directory, grasping at the same time the pommel of his sword, that it should never be drawn but in defence of the Republic and its government. The Directory appeared convinced, so disposed was it to deceive itself. Finding himself thus welcomed and courted by the governors themselves, Bonaparte, firmly resolved upon seizing upon the chief authority, considered himself certain of his object. All depended upon the dexterity of his manœuvres. He first considered the state of parties. The popular one, or that of the Manège, of which Jourdan was one of the chiefs, floundered, as we have seen, in the void of an interminable revolution. Next succeeded the party of the speculators upon revolution, whom Bonaparte called the *pourris*, at the head of which was Barras; then the moderates or *politiques*, conducted by Sieyès, who endeavoured to fix the destinies of the Revolution, that they might be the directors or arbiters of it. Could Bonaparte ally himself with the Jacobins, even had they been inclined to confer the dictatorship upon him? But after having been victorious with them, he would have been under the necessity of being victor independent of them. What had Barras really to offer him but a rotten seat (*planche pourrie*), Bonaparte's own expression? The party of Sieyès remained, which he was compelled to deceive, the illustrious deserter being unwilling to employ, otherwise than as an instrument, him who affected to remain at the head of affairs. Thus, in fact, Bonaparte could calculate upon no party in his favour, having for its object the foundation of his fortune in an open usurpation; and yet he succeeded —by deceiving everyone, by deceiving the directors Barras and Sieyès, and especially Moulins and Gohier, who alone possessed sincerity and good faith.

Bonaparte first formed a kind of privy council, composed of his brothers, of Berthier, Regnault de St. Jean d'Angely, Rœderer, Réal, Bruix, and another person, who soon eclipsed the others by his acuteness and ability—I mean M. de Talleyrand, who, harassed by the party of the Manège, and forced to abandon the ministry, made himself of consequence in the new intrigues. He at first feared that he should not be well received by Bonaparte on account of the expedition to Egypt, or rather for having advised it. He, however, adroitly sounded his way, presented himself, and employed all the resources of his insinuating and supple spirit to captivate the man, who, with a single *coup d'œil*, perceived all the advantage to be derived from him. It was he who disclosed to him the weaknesses of the government, and made him acquainted with the state of parties and the bearings of each character. From him he learnt that Sieyès, followed by Roger Ducos, meditated a *coup d'état;* that he was exclusively occupied with the project of substituting for that which existed a government after his own fashion; that if on the one hand he had against him the most determined of the republicans, who repented having elected him, on the other hand he had a party already formed, the centre of which was in the council of ancients, an advantage possessed by no other director, not even Barras, who fluctuated between Sieyès on the one part and Moulins and Gohier on the other; that the two last, blindly attached to the existing order of things, were somewhat inclined towards the most ardent republicans, and even to the Jacobins, and that with more talent and decision of character they might dispose as they thought fit of the council of the five hundred, and even of a considerable part of the other council.

Bonaparte found all Talleyrand's information con-

firmed by the opinions of his other advisers. As to
himself, nothing of his real intentions was yet to be
known. He apparently manifested much coolness
towards Sieyès, but little confidence in Barras, much
openness and intimacy with Moulins and Gohier; he
even went so far as to propose to them to get rid of
Sieyès, upon condition of himself being elected in his
place. But not being yet qualified by age to enter
the Directory, and the two directors fearing perhaps
his ambition, the objection was firmly maintained to
be insuperable. It was then doubtless that his agents
brought him upon more friendly terms with Sieyès.
In this affair Talleyrand had employed Chénier and
Daunou. In a first conference between him, Daunou,
Sieyès, and Chénier, he gave them the assurance of
leaving the direction of the government to them, pro-
mising to be satisfied with being the first officer of the
executive authority. This I have from Chénier himself.

It was immediately after this conference that the
first meetings of the deputies were held, sometimes
at Lemercier's, and sometimes at Frégeville's. Who
would credit it? Bonaparte had at first his own
brother Lucien against him. "You know him not,"
said he to them who wished to intrust him with the
entire direction of the movement which was in preparation; "you know him not; once there, he would
think himself in his camp: he would command all,
would aspire to be all."

But eight days after this utterance Lucien's co-
operation was warm and powerful. As with so many
others, the republican mistrust was not able to resist
the tempting bait of riches and honour.

It has been asserted that I took no part whatever in these wholesale plottings; that I had temporised, but that I had gathered the fruits of them with the greatest dexterity. Certainly, the moment in which I am now writing is not very favourable for laying claim to the honour of having contributed to Bonaparte's elevation; but I have promised the truth, and I feel a satisfaction in telling it, superior to all the calculations of self-love, and all the disappointments of disappointed hope.

The revolution of St. Cloud would have failed had I opposed it. It was in my power to mislead Sieyès, put Barras on his guard, and enlighten Gohier and Moulins; I had only to back Dubois de Crancé, the only opposing minister, and the whole would have fallen to the ground. But it would have been stupidity in me not to have preferred some future prospects to an unpromising blank. My ideas were fixed. I considered Bonaparte as alone capable of effecting the political reforms imperiously called for by our manners, vices, and excesses, by our disasters and fatal divisions.

Bonaparte, indeed, was too cunning to let me into the secret of his means of execution, and to place himself at the mercy of a single man. But he said enough to me to induce my confidence, and to persuade me, of what I was already convinced, that the destinies of France were in his hands.

In two conferences at Réal's house, I did not conceal the obstacles he had to surmount. What chiefly engaged his attention I knew to be the having to combat the republican spirit, to which he could only oppose the moderates or the bayonet. He at this time appeared to me, politically speaking, inferior to Cromwell; he had also to dread the fate of Cæsar, without possessing either his fame or genius.

But, on the other hand, what a difference between him, Lafayette, and Dumouriez! All the advantages of the revolutionary sword, which those men wanted, he was in possession of, to command or seize upon supreme power. All parties already seemed motionless and in expectation before him. His return, his presence, his renown, the crowds of his adherents, his immense credit in public opinion, caused much inquietude among the sombre lovers of liberty and of the Republic. The two directors, Gohier and Moulins, now become their hope, endeavoured to gain him by dint of attentions and proofs of confidence. They proposed to their colleagues to confer upon him the command of the army of Italy. Sieyès opposed it; Barras said that he had already executed his mission there so well that there was no necessity for his return. This proposal, of which he was informed, caused him to come to the Directory to provoke an explanation. There his firm and elevated tone showed that he was above all fear. Gohier, president of the Directory, leaving him the choice of an army, he replied very coolly to his observations. I saw clearly he was hesitating whether he should effect his revolution in conjunction with Barras or Sieyès.

It was now that I pointed out to him the necessity of prompt action, by persuading him to distrust Sieyès and draw closer to Barras, so anxious was I that he should associate him in his views. "Have Barras on your side," said I to him, "manage the military party,

paralyse Bernadotte, Jourdan, and Augereau, and lead
Sieyès." I thought for a moment that my own sugges-
tions and those of Réal would overcome his dislike to
Barras; he even went so far as to promise us either
to make him overtures or to receive his. We informed
Barras of this, who sent him an invitation to dine
with him the next day; this was the 8th Brumaire.
In the evening Réal and I waited upon Bonaparte at
his residence to know the result of his conference with
Barras. We there found Talleyrand and Rœderer. His
coach was soon heard approaching: he appeared.
" Well," said he to us, " do you know what this
Barras of yours requires? He freely owns that it is
impossible to proceed in the present state of things:
he is very desirous of having a president of the Republic; but it is himself whom he proposes. What
ridiculous pretensions! And this hypocritical wish of
his he masks by proposing to invest with the supreme
magistracy—whom do you suppose? Hédouville, a
very blockhead! Does not this sufficiently prove to
you that it is upon himself he wishes to fix the public
attention? What madness! It is impossible to have
anything to do with such a man."

I owned that in this there was certainly nothing
practicable, but I said that, notwithstanding, I did not
despair of convincing Barras that some arrangement
might be made for saving the public affairs; and that
Réal and I would go to him and reproach him with
his dissimulation and want of confidence; that to all
appearance we should make him consent to more
reasonable arrangements, by proving to him that in
this case deceit was out of season, and that he could

do nothing better than unite his own destinies with those of a great man. " We will do our utmost," added we, " to bring him over to us." " Well, dc so," said he. We immediately proceeded to Barras. He told us at first that it was very natural he should require guarantees which Bonaparte continually eluded. We alarmed him by giving a picture of the real state of things, and of the ascendency which the General exercised over the whole of the government. He at last agreed with us, and promised to go early the next day and place himself at his disposal. He kept his word; and, upon his return, appeared persuaded that nothing could be done without him.

Bonaparte had, however, decided for Sieyès. He had entered into engagements with him; besides, by his manœuvres in every direction, he had enabled himself to choose the intrigue most useful to his politics and ambition. On the one hand, he circumvented Gohier and Moulins; on the other, he held Barras in suspense, and Sieyès and Roger Ducos fettered. As for me, I was only informed of his operations through Réal, who served, so to speak, as mutual guarantee between Bonaparte and me.

Reckoning from the 9th Brumaire, the conspiracy developed itself rapidly. Each made his recruits. Talleyrand gave us Sémonville, and among the principal generals, Beurnonville and Macdonald. Among the bankers, we had Collot; he lent two millions. This set the enterprise in full sail. They commenced secretly tampering with the garrison of Paris, amongst others, two regiments of cavalry which had served in Italy under Bonaparte. Lannes, Murat, and Leclerc were employed in gaining over the commanders of corps, and in seducing the principal officers. Independently of these three generals, and of Berthier and Marmont, we could soon rely upon Serrurier and Lefèvre. Moreau and Moncey were already certain. Moreau, with a self-denial of which he had afterwards to repent, owned that Bonaparte was the man necessary to reform the state. He thus spontaneously pointed him out to play the lofty part which had been destined for himself, but for which he had neither disposition nor political energy.

On his side the most active and able of the faction, Lucien, seconded by Boulay de la Meurthe and by Regnier, concerted measures with the most influential members devoted to Sieyès. In these meetings figured Chazal, Frégeville, Daunou, Lemercier, Cabanis, Lebrun, Courtois, Cornet, Fargues, Baraillon, Villetard, Goupil-Préfeln, Vimar, Bouteville, Cornudet, Herwyn, Delcloy, Rousseau, and Le Jarry. The plotters of the two councils were deliberating upon the best and surest means of execution when Dubois de Crancé went to denounce the conspiracy to directors Gohier and Moulins, requiring them to arrest Bonaparte instantly, and offering himself to see the order of the Directory to this effect executed. The two directors, however, felt themselves so certain of Bonaparte that they refused to give any credit to the information of the minister of war. They required proofs from him before they opened the matter to Barras or took any other measure. They required proofs at a time when a conspiracy was being openly carried on, as is the custom in France. Conspiracy was afoot at Sieyès', at

Bonaparte's, at Murat's, at Lannes', and at Berthier's; conspiracy was being carried on in the saloons of the inspectors of the council of ancients and of the principal members of the commissions. Failing to persuade either Gohier or Moulins, Dubois de Crancé dispatched to them at the Luxembourg a police-agent who was well acquainted with the plot, and who revealed the whole of it to them. Gohier and Moulins, after having heard him, caused him to be confined while they deliberated upon his revelations. This man, uneasy at a proceeding the motive of which he could not understand, alarmed and terrified, escaped out of a window, and came to inform me of what had passed. His evasion and my own counter-mines soon effaced from the minds of the two directors the impression which the proceeding of Dubois de Crancé had made. I informed Bonaparte of all.

The impulse was immediately given. Lucien assembled Boulay, Chazal, Cabanis, and Emile Gaudin; each had his part assigned to him. It was in the house of Madame Récamier, near Bagatelle, that Lucien arranged the legislative measures which were to coincide with the military explosion. The presidency of the council of five hundred, with which he was invested, was one of the principal supports on which the conspiracy rested. Two powerful passions at this time agitated Lucien — ambition and love. Deeply enamoured of Madame Récamier, a woman full of sweetness and charms, he considered himself the more unfortunate, because, having interested her heart, he could not suspect the cause of her cruel severities. In this tumult of his senses, however, he lost none of his

activity and political energy. She who possessed his
heart could read all there, and was discreet. It had
been agreed that the more effectually to disguise the
plot, a splendid banquet should be given by subscription to Bonaparte, to which should be invited the
chief of the high authorities and of the deputies of
both parties. The banquet was given, but was utterly
destitute of cheerfulness and enthusiasm; a mournful
silence and an air of restraint pervaded it; the parties
were watching each other. Bonaparte, embarrassed
with the part he had to act, retired at an early hour,
leaving the guests a prey to their reflections.

With Lucien's consent, Bonaparte had, on the 15th
of Brumaire, a secret interview with Sieyès, in which
were discussed the arrangements for the 18th. The
object was to remove the Directory and to disperse
the legislative body, but without violence, and by
means to all appearance legal, but prepared with all
the resources of artifice and audacity. It was determined to open the drama by a decree of the counci
of ancients, ordering the removal of the legislative corps
to St. Cloud. The choice of St. Cloud for the assembling of the two councils was to prevent all possibility
of a popular movement, and, at the same time, to
afford a facility for employing the troops with greater
security, away from the contact of Paris.

In consequence of what was agreed upon between
Sieyès and Bonaparte, the secret council of the principal conspirators, held at the Hôtel de Breteuil, gave,
on the 16th, its last instructions to Lemercier, the
president of the council of ancients. These were to
order an extraordinary convocation in the hall of the

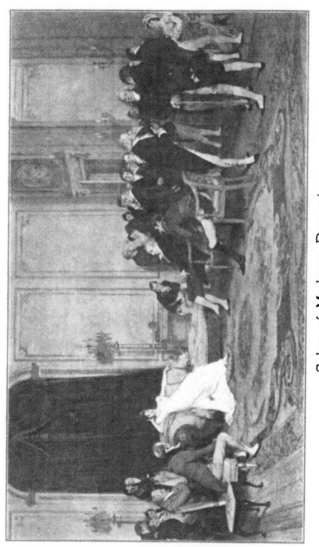

Salon of Madame Recamier

ancients at the Tuileries, on the 18th, at ten o'clock
in the morning. The signal was immediately given to
the commission of the inspectors of the same council,
over which the deputy Cornet presided.

The third article of the constitution invested the
council of ancients with the power of removing the
two councils out of Paris. This was the *coup d'état*
which had been proposed to Sieyès by Baudin des
Ardennes even before the arrival of Bonaparte. Baudin
was at that time president of the commission of the
inspectors of the ancients and an influential member
of the council. In 1795 he had a great part in drawing up the constitution ; but, disgusted with his work,
he entered into the views of Sieyès. It had always
been his opinion that an arm for action was required ;
that is to say, a general capable of directing the
military part of an event which might assume a
serious character. The execution of it had been put
off. On the news of Bonaparte's landing, Baudin,
struck with the idea that Providence had sent the
man for whom he and his party had so long searched
in vain, died the very same night from excess of joy.
He was succeeded by Cornet in the presidency of the
commission of inspectors of the ancients, now become
the principal centre of the conspiracy. He possessed
neither the talent nor the influence of Baudin des
Ardennes, but he substituted in their stead great zeal
and much activity.

It was of great importance to neutralise Gohier,
president of the Directory. With the view, therefore,
of the better deceiving him, Bonaparte engaged him
to dine with him on the 18th, with his wife and

brothers. He also caused to be invited to breakfast for the same day, at eight o'clock in the morning, the generals and chiefs of corps; announcing also that he would receive the visits and respects of the officers of the garrison, and of the adjutants of the national guard, who had in vain solicited admission to his presence. One only obstacle caused uneasiness; this was the integrity of the president Gohier, who, being undeceived in sufficient time, might rally round him all the popular party, and the generals opposed to the conspiracy. Indeed, I was awake to this. However, for better security, it was proposed to draw the president of the Directory into a snare. At midnight Madame Bonaparte sent him, by her son, Eugène Beauharnais, a friendly invitation for himself and his lady to breakfast with her at eight o'clock in the morning. "I have," wrote she, "some very important things to communicate to you." But the hour appeared suspicious to Gohier, and, after Eugène's departure, he decided that his wife should go alone.

Already Cornet, the president of the commission of the ancients, had secretly assembled in his bureau at five o'clock in the morning (the hour of the meeting), such members as were in the secret, or upon whom he could rely. The two commissions of both councils were in permanence. The ostensible meeting of the deputies of the ancients was fixed for ten in the morning, and the assembling of the deputies of the five hundred at twelve. This last council was about to find itself obliged to close the sitting, after the mere reading of the decree of removal, which was secured in the ancients. I had arranged everything, in order to be informed in time of what took place, either at the commissions, at Bonaparte's, or at the Directory.

At eight o'clock in the morning I learnt that the president of the commission of the ancients, after having formed, by his extraordinary convocation, a fictitious majority, had, upon concluding a long and turgid harangue, in which he represented the Republic in the greatest danger, moved to transfer the legislative corps to St. Cloud, and to invest Bonaparte with the chief command of the troops. It was at the same time announced to me that the decree would pass. I instantly got into my coach, and going first to the Tuileries, learnt that the decree had been made; and about nine o'clock I arrived at the hotel of General Bonaparte, the courtyard of which was full of military. Every avenue was filled with officers and generals, and the hotel was not spacious enough to contain the crowds of his friends and adherents. All the corps of the garrison of Paris and of the military division had sent officers to take his orders. I entered the oval cabinet in which Bonaparte was; he was impatiently awaiting, with Berthier and Lefèvre, the resolution of the council of ancients. I announced to him that the decree of removal, which conferred upon him the chief command, had just passed, and that it would be instantly laid before him. I reiterated to him my protestations of devotion and zeal, informing him that I had just closed all the barriers, and had stopped the departure of couriers and mails. "All that is useless," said he to me, in presence of several generals who entered; "the numbers of citizens and

brave men around me must sufficiently convince all
that I act with and for the nation. I shall take care
to cause the decree of the council to be respected, and
to maintain the public tranquillity." At that instant
Josephine came up to him, and told him, with much
dissatisfaction, that the president Gohier had sent his
wife, but would not come himself. "Write to him,
by Madame Gohier, to come as quick as possible,"
cried Bonaparte. A few minutes after the deputy Cornet
arrived, quite proud at having executed for the General
the functions of state messenger. He brought him the
decree which placed in his hands the destiny of the
Republic.

Bonaparte, leaving his cabinet immediately, made
known to his adherents the decree which invested him
with the chief command; then placing himself at the
head of the generals, of the superior officers, and of
1,600 cavalry, forming part of the garrison of Paris,
which had just been brought him by Murat, he began
his march towards the Champs Elysées, after desiring
me to ascertain what resolution the Directory had
adopted upon learning the decree of removal.

I first repaired to my hotel, where I gave orders
for placarding a proclamation, signed by myself, in the
spirit of the revolution which had just commenced;
I then directed my steps towards the Luxembourg.

It was a little after nine o'clock, and I found
Moulins and Gohier, who with Barras formed the
majority of the Directory, completely ignorant of what
was passing in Paris. Madame Tallien, in defiance of
the countersign, had entered the apartments of Barras,
whom she surprised in the bath; she was the first to

Fouché

From the E. Lami portrait

inform him that Bonaparte had acted without him.
"What do you mean?" cried the indolent epicure.
"That man" (designating Bonaparte by a coarse epithet) "has included all of us in the affair." However,
in the hope of negotiating, he sent to him his confidential secretary, Botot, modestly to inquire what he
might expect from him. Botot found Bonaparte at the
head of the troops, and, delivering his message, received
this harsh reply : "Tell that man that I will never see
him more!" He had just detached Talleyrand and
Bruix from his interests for the purpose of forcing him
to resign.

Having entered the apartments of the Luxembourg,
I announced to the president the decree which trans-
ferred the sittings of the legislative corps to the château
of St. Cloud. "I am much astonished," said Gohier
peevishly to me, "that a minister of the Directory
should thus transform himself into a messenger of the
council of ancients."

"I considered it," replied I, "a part of my duty
to give you intelligence of so important a resolution,
and at the same time I thought it expedient to come
and attend the orders of the Directory." "It was far
more your duty," rejoined Gohier, in an altered tone,
"not to have let us remain in ignorance of the
criminal intrigues which have produced such a decree;
this is no doubt but the prelude to all that has been
plotted against the government in the meetings which,
in your quality of minister of the police, you ought
to have discovered and made known to us." "But,"
returned I, "the Directory was not without this information. I myself, finding I did not possess its

confidence, employed indirect means to give it the
necessary information ; but the Directory would never
give credit to my agents ; besides, is it not by its own
members that this blow has been struck ?   The directors
Sieyès and Roger Ducos are already in coalition with
the commission of the inspectors of the ancients."
"The majority is at the Luxembourg," replied Gohier
vehemently ; "and if the Directory have any orders
to give, it will intrust the execution of them to men
worthy of its confidence."

Upon this I withdrew, and Gohier lost no time in
summoning his two colleagues, Barras and Moulins.
I had scarcely got into my carriage when I saw the
messenger of the ancients arrive, bringing to the president the communication of the decree of removal to
St. Cloud.   Gohier immediately repaired to Barras,
and made him promise to meet him and Moulins in
the Hall of Deliberations to determine what steps
were to be taken in the present conjuncture.

Such, however, was the perplexity of Barras that
he was incapable of adopting any vigorous resolution.
In fact, he did not hesitate a moment to forget his
promise to Gohier when he saw two agents from
Bonaparte enter his apartment, Bruix and Talleyrand,
who were commissioned to negotiate his retreat from
the Directory.   They at first declared to him that
Bonaparte was determined to employ against him all
the means of force in his power should he attempt
to make the least opposition to his plans.   After
having thus acted upon his fears, the two adroit
negotiators made him the most magnificent promises
if he would consent to send in his resignation.   Barras

exclaimed against this treatment for some time, but
at length yielded to the arguments of two artful men.
They repeated to him the assurance that he should
want for nothing that could contribute to a luxurious
and tranquil life, free from the anxieties of a power
he was no longer able to retain. Talleyrand had a
letter already drawn up, which Barras was advised to
address to the legislature to notify his determination
of retiring into private life. Thus placed between hope
and fear, he ended by signing all that was required
of him; and having thus placed himself at Bonaparte's
mercy, he quitted the Luxembourg and set off for his
estate at Grosbois, escorted and watched by a detachment of dragoons.

Thus, by nine o'clock in the morning, no majority
in the Directory existed. About this time arrived
Dubois de Crancé, who, persisting in his opposition,
solicited from Gohier and Moulins an order for the
arrest of Bonaparte, Talleyrand, Barras, and the principal conspirators, taking upon himself as minister of
war to arrest Bonaparte and Murat on the road even
to St. Cloud. Perhaps Moulins and Gohier, at length
undeceived, would have yielded to the urgent remonstrances of Dubois de Crancé had not Lagarde, chief
secretary to the Directory, and who had been gained
over, declared that he would not countersign any
decree which should not have the sanction of the
majority of the Directory. " At the worst," said
Gohier, rather damped by this observation, " how can
there be any revolution at St. Cloud? I have here,
in my quality of president, the seals of the Republic."
Moulins added that Bonaparte was to dine with him

at Gohier's and that he would soon discover his real intentions.

I had for some time formed an opinion of the abilities of these men so little calculated to govern the state. Nothing could equal their blindness and incapacity; it may justly be affirmed that they betrayed themselves.

Events already began to develop themselves. Bonaparte on horseback, followed by a numerous staff, first took the road to the Champs Elysées, where several corps were drawn up in order of battle. After being acknowledged by them as their general, he proceeded to the Tuileries. The weather was extremely fine, and favoured the utmost display of military pomp in the Champs Elysées, on the quays, and in the national garden, which was in a moment transformed into a park of artillery, and where the crowd became excessive. Bonaparte was greeted at the Tuileries by the shouts of the citizens and the soldiery. Having presented himself with a military suite at the bar of the council of ancients, he eluded taking the constitutional oath; then descending from the château, he came to harangue the troops already disposed to obey him. There he learnt that the Directory was disorganised; that Sieyès and Roger Ducos had sent in their resignations to the commission of the inspectors of the ancients; and that Barras was on the point of subscribing to the conditions offered him.

Passing on to the commissions of the assembled inspectors, the General there found Sieyès, Roger Ducos, and several deputies of their party. Gohier, president of the Directory, together with his colleague,

Moulins, now arrived, both of whom refused their adhesion to what had taken place. An explanation took place between Gohier and Bonaparte. " My plans," said the latter, "are not hostile; the Republic is in danger—it must be saved. *I will it !* " At this very moment intelligence arrived that the Faubourg St. Antoine was rising at the instigation of Santerre, who was a relation of Moulins. Bonaparte, turning to him and questioning him upon the subject, told him that he would send a detachment of cavalry to shoot Santerre if he dared to make the least stir. Moulins removed Bonaparte's apprehensions, and declared that Santerre could not assemble four men round him. He was, in fact, no longer the instigator of the insurrection of 1792. I myself repeated the assurance that there would not be the least shadow of popular tumult, and said that I would answer for the tranquillity of Paris.

Gohier and Moulins, finding that the impulse was given, that the movement was irresistible, re-entered the Luxembourg to witness the defection of their guards. Both were there soon besieged by Moreau, for Bonaparte had already made certain military arrangements which placed in his power all the public authorities and establishments. Moreau was sent with a detachment to invest the Luxembourg; General Lannes was intrusted with a corps to guard the legislative body; Murat was dispatched in all haste to occupy St. Cloud; while Serrurier was in reserve at the Point-du-Jour. All proceeded without any obstacle —or, at least, no opposition manifested itself in the capital, where, on the contrary, the revolution appeared to meet with general approbation.

In the evening a council was held at the commission of the inspectors', either for the purpose of preparing the public mind for the events which the next
day was to produce, or to determine upon what was
to be done at St. Cloud. I was present, and saw
there, for the first time, undisguised, and in presence
of each other, the two parties now united for the
same object, but of which the one appeared already to
be alarmed at the ascendency of the military faction.

At first much discussion took place without anything being well understood, and without coming to
any determination. All that Bonaparte himself proposed, or that his brothers proposed for him, smacked
of the dictatorship of the sabre. The legislative party
who had embraced his cause took me aside and made
me the remark. "But," said I to them, "it is done;
the military power is in the hands of General Bonaparte; you yourselves invested him with it, and you
cannot proceed a step without his sanction."

I soon perceived that the majority would willingly
have receded, but they had no longer the power of so
doing. The most timorous separated themselves, and
when we had got rid of the fearful and those we could
not depend upon, the establishment of three provisional consuls was agreed upon; namely, Bonaparte,
Sieyès, and Roger Ducos. Sieyès then proposed to
arrest about forty of the leaders who were hostile, or
imagined to be so. I advised Bonaparte, through
Saint-Réal, not to consent to it; and, in his first steps
on the road to supreme power, not to render himself
the instrument of the fury of a vindictive priest. He
understood me, and alleged that the idea was prema-

ture; that there would be neither opposition nor resistance. "You will see that to-morrow, at St. Cloud,"
said Sieyès, rather hurt.

I confess that I was not myself very confident
respecting the issue of the next day. All that I had
just heard, and all the information I could gather,
agreed in one point, that the authors of this movement could not rely upon the majority among the
members of the two councils, almost all conceiving
the idea that the object was to destroy the constitution in order to establish the military power on its
ruin. Even a great party of the initiated repelled the
idea of a dictatorship, and flattered themselves with
being able to avert it. But Bonaparte already exercised
an immense influence both within and without the
sphere of these tottering authorities. Versailles, Paris,
St. Cloud, and St. Germain were favourable to his
revolution; and his name among the soldiers operated
as a talisman.

His privy council appointed as leaders to the
deputies of the ancients, Regnier, Cornudet, Lemercier,
and Fargues; and for guides to the deputies of the
councils of the hundred devoted to the party, Lucien
Bonaparte, Boulay de la Meurthe, Emile Gaudin,
Chazal, and Cabanis. On their side the opposing
members of the two councils, united to the leaders of
the Manège, passed the night in secret deliberations.

The next day, at an early hour, the road from
Paris to St. Cloud was covered with troops, officers
on horseback, spectators, coaches full of deputies,
functionaries, and journalists. The hall for the two
councils had just been hastily prepared. It was soon

perceived that the military party in the two councils
was reduced to a small number of deputies, more or
less ardent for the new order of things.

I remained at Paris seated in my cabinet, with all
my police in hand, observing all that passed, receiving
and examining myself every report which arrived. I
had detached to St. Cloud a certain number of able
and intelligent emissaries for the purpose of placing
themselves in contact with the persons who were
pointed out to them; and other agents, who, returning thence every half-hour, came to inform me of the
position of affairs. I was thus made acquainted with
the least incident, the most trifling circumstance, that
could affect the expected *dénouement*. I was decidedly
of opinion that the sword alone could cut the knot.

The sitting opened at the five hundred, over which
Lucien Bonaparte presided, with an artful speech by
Emile Gaudin; the object of which was the appointment of a commission charged to present an immediate report upon the situation of the Republic.
Emile Gaudin, in his prearranged motion, also required that no measures whatever should be determined upon till the report of the proposed commission
had been heard. Boulay de la Meurthe held the
report in his hand, already prepared.

Scarcely, however, had Emile Gaudin concluded
his motion than a most dreadful tumult agitated the
whole assembly. The cries of " Long live the Constitution ! " " No Dictatorship ! " " Down with the
Dictator ! " were heard on all sides. Upon the motion
of Delbrel, seconded and supported by Grandmaison,
the assembly, rising in a body at the cry of " Long

The 18th Brumaire

Engraved by Burdet after picture by **Raffet**

live the Republic!" resolved that they would renew individually the oath of fidelity to the constitution. Those even who had come for the professed object of destroying it took the oath.

The hall of the ancients was almost equally agitated; but there the party of Sieyès and Bonaparte, who were anxious to accelerate the establishment of a provisional government, had asserted as a fact, upon a false declaration of the Sieur Lagarde, chief secretary of the Directory, that all the directors had sent in their resignation. The oppositionists immediately demanded that substitutes should be provided according to the prescribed forms. Bonaparte, informed of this double storm, thought it was time to appear upon the stage. Crossing the Salon de Mars, he entered the council of the ancients. There, in a verbose and disjointed speech, he declared that there was no longer any government, and that the constitution could no longer save the Republic. Conjuring the council to hasten to adopt a new order of things, he protested that, with respect to the magistracy they should appoint, his only wish was to be the arm commissioned to maintain and execute the orders of the council.

This speech, of which I only give the substance, was delivered in a broken and incoherent manner, which fully testified the agitation the General suffered, who sometimes addressed himself to the deputies, and then turned towards the soldiery, who remained at the end of the hall. Cries of "Long live Bonaparte!" and the acquiescence of the majority of the ancients having given him fresh courage, he withdrew, hoping to make a like impression upon the other council. He was not without some apprehensions, knowing what had passed there, and with what enthusiasm they had sworn fidelity to the republican constitution. A message to the Directory had just been decreed there. A motion was being made to require from the ancients an explanation of the motives of its removal to St. Cloud, when they received the resignation of the director Barras, transmitted to them by the other council. This resignation, of which till then they had been ignorant, caused a great astonishment throughout the assembly. It was considered as the result of some deep-laid intrigue. At the very moment the question was being discussed, whether the resignation was legal and according to the forms, Bonaparte arrived, followed by a platoon of grenadiers. Scarcely, however, had he entered the hall when the assembly were thrown into the utmost disorder. All the members, standing up, expressed in loud cries the effect produced upon them by the appearance of the bayonets and of the general who thus advanced armed into the temple of the legislature. "You are violating the sanctuary of the laws; withdraw instantly!" exclaimed several deputies. "What are you doing, rash man?" cried Bigonnet to him. "Is it then for this you have been a conqueror?" said Destrem. In vain Bonaparte, who had ascended the tribune, endeavoured to stammer out a few sentences. On all sides he heard the cries repeated of "Long live the Constitution!" "Long live the Republic!" On all sides he was saluted by cries of "Down with the Cromwell!" "Down with the Dictator!" "Down with the Tyrant!" "Away

with the Dictator!" Some of the more furious
deputies rushed upon him and pushed him back.
"You will make war then upon your country!" cried
Arena to him, showing him the point of his stiletto.
The grenadiers, seeing their General grow pale and
tremble, crossed the room to form a rampart around
him. Bonaparte threw himself amongst them, and they
escorted him away. Thus rescued, and almost frantic,
he remounted his horse, set off at a gallop, and riding
towards the bridge of St. Cloud, cried aloud to his
soldiers, "They have attempted my life! They have
wished to put me out of the protection of the laws!
They do not know, then, that I am invulnerable, for
I am the god of thunder."

Murat having joined him on the bridge, "It is not
fitting," said he to him, "that he who has triumphed
over such powerful enemies should fear drivellers. . .
Come, General, courage, and the victory is our own!"
Bonaparte then turned his horse's head and again
presented himself before the soldiers, endeavouring to
excite the generals to bring matters to a conclusion
by a *coup de main*. But Lannes, Serrurier, and Murat
himself seemed but little disposed to direct the bayonets
against the legislature.

In the meantime the most horrible tumult reigned
in the hall. Firm in the president's chair, Lucien
made vain efforts to re-establish tranquillity, earnestly
entreating his colleagues to allow his brother to be
recalled and heard, and obtaining no other answer
than, "Outlawry! Let the outlawry of General Bonaparte be put to the vote!" They even went so far as
to call upon him to put to the vote the motion of

outlawry against his brother.   Lucien, indignant, quitted
the chair, abdicated the presidency, and laid aside its
ensigns.   He had scarcely descended from the tribune,
when some grenadiers arrived, and carried him out
with them.   Lucien, astonished, learnt that it was by
order of his brother, who was anxious for his advice,
being determined upon employing force to dissolve the
legislature.   Such was the advice of Sieyès; seated in
a chaise drawn by six post horses, he awaited the issue
of the event at the gates of St. Cloud.   There was no
longer time for hesitation; pale and trembling, the
most zealous partisans of Bonaparte were petrified,
whilst the most timid among them already declared
against his enterprise.   Jourdan and Augereau were
observed standing aloof, watching the favourable moment
for drawing the grenadiers into the popular party.   But
Sieyès, Bonaparte, and Talleyrand, who had come to
St. Cloud with Rœderer, were of opinion, as well as
myself, that the party would want both *an arm and
a head*.   Lucien, inspiring Bonaparte with all his energy,
mounted a horse, and, in his quality of president, requested the assistance of force to dissolve the assembly.
The grenadiers in close columns, with Murat at their
head, followed him into the hall of the five hundred,
whilst Colonel Moulins caused the charge to be beaten.
The hall is invaded amidst the noise of drums and
the shouts of the soldiers, the deputies escape out of
the windows, throw away their togas, and disperse
themselves.   Such was the result of the day of St.
Cloud (19th Brumaire, 10th of November).   Bonaparte
was particularly indebted for it to the energy of his
brother Lucien, to the decision of Murat, and perhaps

to the weakness of the generals, who, being opposed to him, dared not openly show their hostility.

But it became necessary to render national an anti-popular event, in which force had triumphed over a representative rabble, alike incapable of showing either a real orator or chief. It was requisite to sanction what history will call the triumph of military usurpation.

Sieyès, Talleyrand, Bonaparte, Rœderer, Lucien, and Boulay de la Meurthe, who were the soul of the enterprise, decided that the deputies of their parties who were wandering through the apartments and galleries of St. Cloud should be instantly assembled. Boulay and Lucien went in search of them, assembled between twenty or thirty, and constituted them the council of five hundred. From this meeting a decree was issued, the burden of which was that General Bonaparte, the general officers, and the troops which seconded him, had deserved well of their country. The leaders then determined upon asserting in the next day's newspaper that several deputies had endeavoured to assassinate Bonaparte, and that the majority of the council had been ruled by a minority of assassins.

Then came the promulgation of the Act of the 19th Brumaire, likewise concerted among the chiefs, to serve as a legal foundation for the new revolution. This Act abolished the Directory, instituted a consular executive commission, composed of Sieyès, Roger Ducos, and Bonaparte, adjourned the two councils, and excluded from them sixty-two members of the popular party, among whom figured General Jourdan; it likewise established a legislative commission of fifty members, chosen equally from both councils, whose

duty it was to prepare a new draft of the constitution of the state. Upon being brought from the
assembly of the five hundred to the council of the
ancients, to be transformed into a law, this Act was
only voted for by the minority, the majority maintaining a mournful silence. Thus the intermediary
establishment of the new order of things was converted into a law by some sixty of the members of
the legislature, who declared themselves to be duly
qualified for the employment of ministers, diplomatic
agents, and delegates of the consular commission.

Bonaparte, with his two colleagues, came into the
council of the ancients to take the oaths, and on the
11th of November, about five o'clock in the morning,
the new government, quitting St. Cloud, came to
instal itself in the palace of the Luxembourg. I had
foreseen that all the authority of this executive triumvirate would fall into the hands of him who had
already been invested with the military power. Of
this there was no longer any doubt after the first
sitting which the three consuls held together that
very night. There Bonaparte, with the authority of
a superior, took possession of the president's arm-
chair, which neither Sieyès nor Roger Ducos dared
to dispute with him. Roger, already gained over,
declared that Bonaparte alone could save the country,
and that he would henceforth follow his opinion in
everything. Sieyès sat silent, biting his lips. Bonaparte, knowing him to be avaricious, abandoned to
him the private treasury of the Directory; it contained
800,000 francs, which Sieyès immediately seized, and
adopting the lion's mode of division, left only 100,000

francs to his colleague Roger Ducos. This trifling *douceur* calmed his ambition a little, for he waited till Bonaparte should engage in military affairs, and resign the civil affairs into his hands. But hearing Bonaparte at their first sitting treat upon the finances, the administration, the laws, the army, politics in general, and discuss these various subjects with much ability, he said, upon entering his house, in presence of Talleyrand, Boulay, Cabanis, Rœderer, and Chazal, "Gentlemen, you have found a master."

It was easy to perceive that a mistrustful and avaricious priest, surfeited with gold, would not dare to contend a long time with a general, young, active, possessed of immense renown, and who had by force already made himself supreme. Besides, Sieyès possessed none of those qualities which could have insured him a great influence with a proud and warlike nation. His title of priest alone had made him unpopular with the army: here artifice could do nothing against force. By wishing to make a trial of it with respect to me Sieyès fell.

In the second sitting held by the consuls, the change of the ministry was discussed. The chief secretary of the executive commission was first named, and the choice fell upon Maret. Berthier was the first called to be minister of war; he replaced Dubois de Crancé, whom Bonaparte never pardoned for his opposition to him. Robert Lindet yielded the finance to Gaudin, formerly a chief clerk devoted to Bonaparte; Cambacérès was left at the head of justice. In the ministry of marine, Bourdon was replaced by Forfait; the geometrician Laplace succeeded Quinette in the interior ; the ministry of foreign affairs was reserved *in petto* for Talleyrand, and in the interim the Westphalian Reinhard served him as a cloak. When they came to the police, Sieyès, alleging some insidious reasons, proposed that I should be replaced by Alquier, who was his creature. Bonaparte objected that I had conducted myself very well on the 18th Brumaire, and that I had given sufficient proofs of it. In fact, not only had I favoured the development of his preliminary dispositions, but had also, at the critical moment, succeeded in paralysing the efforts of several of the deputies and generals who might have injured the success of the day. Scarcely had the intelligence reached me, than I caused to be placarded that very night all over Paris, a proclamation full of attachment and obedience to the saviour of the country. I was retained in an office, without doubt, the most important of all, in spite of Sieyès, and in defiance of the intrigues which had been played off against me.

Bonaparte judged better of the state of things; he felt that he had many obstacles yet to overcome, that it was not sufficient to vanquish, but that he must subdue : that it was not too much to have at his command a minister experienced against the anarchists. He was equally convinced that his interest rendered it imperative upon him to lean for support upon a man whom he believed most capable of keeping him on his guard against a cheat who had become his colleague. The confidential report which I placed in his hands the very evening of his installation, at the Luxembourg, had convinced him that the police was as clear as it was quick-sighted.

Sieyès, in the meantime, who was anxious for proscriptions, was continually exclaiming against such as
he called opposers and anarchists. He told Bonaparte
that public opinion, empoisoned by the Jacobins, had
become detestable; that the police bulletins supported
it, and that severe examples were necessary. "See,"
said he, "in what colours they have painted the
glorious day of St. Cloud! To believe them, its only
springs, its only lever, were artifice, falsehood, and
audacity. The consular commission is nothing but a
triumvirate invested with a terrific dictatorship, which
corrupts in order the better to enslave; the Act of the
19th Brumaire is the work of a few deserters, abandoned by their colleagues, and who, deprived of a
majority, are not less eager to sanction the usurpation. You should hear what they say of you, of me!
We must not suffer ourselves to be thus dragged
through the mire, for if once debased we are lost. In
the Faubourg St. Germain, some say that it is the
military faction which has just snatched the reins of
government out of the hands of the lawyers; others
assert that General Bonaparte is about to perform the
part of Monk. Thus by some we are classed with the
Bourbons, and by others among the most furious of
Robespierre's creatures. Severity is necessary to prevent public opinion from being left to the mercy of
the royalists and anarchists. These must be struck
first. It is always in its *début* that a new power
should show its force."

Upon concluding this artful speech, Sieyès suggested that the head of the police should be required
to put in execution a measure highly essential to the

public weal and the general security; and he persuaded
Bonaparte. It had been declared on the 19th Brumaire that there should be no more oppressive acts,
no more lists of proscription, and yet on the 26th I
was required to furnish names in order to form a list
of the proscribed. That same day a decree was
issued, condemning to banishment, without previous
trial, fifty-nine of the principal opposers—thirty-seven
to French Guiana and twenty-two to the island of
Oleron. On these lists were seen names blasted and
odious, followed by those of amiable and esteemed
citizens. What I had prognosticated to the consuls
came to pass: the voice of the public loudly disapproved of this impolitic and useless proscription.

They were compelled to yield, and commenced
by naming exceptions. I solicited and obtained the
liberty of several proscribed deputies, and represented
how much France and the army would be shocked at
seeing people persecuted on account of their opinions
—Jourdan, for example, who had gained the battle of
Fleurus, and whose probity was unassailable. The
proscriber, Sieyès, finding Bonaparte alarmed, did not
dare to follow up any more the execution of an odious
measure, which he carefully imputed to me, it was
reported; and they contented themselves, upon my
proposition, with placing their opponents under the
surveillance of the high police. The three consuls
then felt how necessary it was for them to consult
and gain public opinion. Many of their acts were
calculated to deserve the confidence of the people.
They lost no time in revoking the law respecting
hostages and loans, which was so unpopular.

A few days sufficed to make it certain that the
transactions of the 18th Brumaire had obtained the
consent of the nation.   This has now become an historical truth; it was at that time a fact which decided
between the government of the many and that of a
single person.

The strict republicans, the desponding friends of
liberty, alone saw with regret Bonaparte's accession
to the supreme power.   They at first drew from it
the most gloomy consequences and anticipations. They
were right in the end; we shall see why, and shall
assign the reasons of it.

I had declared myself against the proscriptions,
and against all other general measures. Certain henceforth of my credit, and finding myself firmly established
in the ministry, I endeavoured to impart to the general
police a character of dignity, justice, and moderation,
which, to render more lasting, has not depended upon
myself.   Under the Directory the women of the town
were employed in the vile trade of espionage.   I forbade
the use of such disgraceful instruments, wishing to give
to the scrutinising eye of the police the direction of
observation only, not of accusation.

I also caused misfortune to be respected by obtaining an alleviation of the fate of emigrants shipwrecked upon the northern coasts of France, among
whom were persons belonging to the flower of the
ancient nobility.   I was not satisfied with this first
attempt towards a return to national humanity: I made
a report to the consuls, in which I solicited the liberty
of all emigrants whom the tempest had cast upon the
shores of their country.   I forced from them this act

of clemency, which from that time gained me the confidence of the royalists disposed to submit to government.

My two instructions to the bishops and prefects, which were published at this time, produced likewise a great sensation upon the public. They were the more remarked as I spoke a language in them which had fallen into disuse; that of reason and toleration, which I have always considered to be very compatible with the policy of a government strong enough to be just. These two instructions were, however, differently interpreted. In the opinion of some they bore the stamp of that foresight and of that profound art of influencing the human heart, so essential to a states-man; according to others, they tended to substitute morality for religion, and the police for justice. But the supporters of this last opinion did not reflect upon the circumstances and times in which we were placed. My two circulars are still extant; they are in print; let them be read once again, and it will be seen that some courage, and some fixed principles, were neces-sary to render the doctrines and sentiments therein expressed palatable.

Thus salutary modifications and a more certain tranquillity were the first pledges offered by the new government to the expectations of the French. They applauded the sudden elevation of the illustrious General, who, in the administration of the state, manifested equal vigour and prudence. With the exception of the demagogues, each party persuaded itself that this new revolution would turn to its advantage. Such especially was the dream of the royalists; they saw in Bonaparte the Monk of the expiring Revolution, a dream which was particularly favourable to the views of the First Consul. Fatigued and disgusted with the Revolution, the moderate party itself, confounding its views with those of the counter-revolutionists, openly desired the modification of the republican *régime*, and its amalgamation with a mixed monarchy. But the time had not yet arrived for transforming the democracy into a republican monarchy; for this could only be obtained by the fusion of all parties, which was still very far off. The new administration, on the contrary, favoured a kind of moral reaction against the Revolution and the severity of its laws. The writings most in vogue tended to royalism. To judge from the clamours of the republicans, we were rapidly approaching it. These clamours were accredited by imprudent royalists, and by works which recalled the recollection and the distresses of the Bourbons—" Irma," for example, which at that time was the rage in Paris, because it was supposed to contain the recital of the affecting misfortunes of Madame Royale.[1]

[1] The history of " Irma " appeared under the form of an allegory. The scenes were laid in Asia, and all the names were changed; but the key to them was easily found by anagrams. This able manner of publishing the history of the misfortunes of the house of Bourbon excited curiosity in a high degree, and warmly interested the public. The work was devoured; by following the events and arriving at the catastrophes, the names were easily guessed at. Under a false appearance of liberty, the First Consul permitted everything to be published respecting the Revolution that could disparage it; then successively appeared the Memoirs of the Marquis de Bouillé, of Bertrand de Moleville, of the Princess Lamballe those of the

At any other time the police would have caused a similar work to be seized ; but I was obliged to sacrifice public opinion to reasons of state, and these reasons required that the royalists should be deceived. The maxims and interests of the Revolution had, however, still too much life to be injured with impunity. I thought it my duty to cool the hopes of the counter-revolutionists, and to raise the courage of the republicans. I observed to the Consul that he still acted a part of great delicacy ; that, having manœuvred with men sincerely attached to the republican forms and to the liberties of the public, and the army itself having imbibed the same sentiments, he could not separate himself without danger, either from his own party or the army ; besides that, it was necessary for him to quit a provisional and create for himself a permanent establishment.

The attention of the government had just been engaged at this period in the preparatory labours of two intermediary legislative commissions. That of the five hundred was conducted by Lucien, Boulay, Jacqueminot, and Daunou; that of the ancients by Lemercier, Lebrun, and Regnier. The man of most ability was unquestionably Lebrun. Bonaparte desired his advice, and received it with deference. The object was to discuss in grand conference the new project of social organisation which Sieyès was anxious to present, in place of the constitution of the year III., whose

Mesdames of France, the " History of Madame Elizabeth," the "Cimetière de la Madeleine," &c. But this toleration ceased as soon as the First Consul found himself securely seated, as will be seen in the sequel of these Memoirs.—*Note by the Editor.*

obsequies he was eager to superintend. Sieyès, with whose real thoughts Bonaparte was acquainted, affected great mystery. He said he had nothing ready; that he had not time to arrange his papers. He played off silence. In this he resembled those fashionable authors who, eaten up with the desire manifested by the public of reading their works, insist upon being first entreated by coquetry and fashion before yielding to the prayers of a curious and oftentimes satirical public. I was commissioned to penetrate his mystery, and I employed Réal, who, using much address, with an appearance of great good-nature, discovered the bases of Sieyès' project by getting Chénier, one of his confidants, to chatter upon rising from a dinner at which wine and other intoxicating liquors had not been spared.

Upon this information a secret council was held, to which I was called. Bonaparte, Cambacérès, Lebrun, Lucien, Joseph, Berthier, Réal, Regnault, and Rœderer were present. There we discussed the counter-projects and the conduct to be pursued by Bonaparte in the general conferences which were impatiently awaited by all of us.

At length, towards the middle of December, the three consuls and the two legislative commissions assembled in Bonaparte's apartment. The conferences commenced at nine o'clock in the evening, and were prolonged far into the night. Daunou was charged with the drawing up of them. Sieyès, at the first sitt.ng, did not utter a word. At length, pressed on all sides, he yielded, and then gave several detached parts of his theories, inclosed in separate papers. With the tone of an oracle, he successively explained to us the bases of his favourite constitution. It created tribunals composed of one hundred members, who were to discuss the laws; a legislative body more numerous, whose province was to receive or reject them by vote in an oral discussion; and lastly, a senate composed of members elected for life, and charged with the important office of watching over the laws and the constitution of the state. All these principles, against which Bonaparte made no serious objections, were successively adopted. As to the government, he gave it the drawing up of laws, and for this purpose created a council of state, charged with perfecting and improving the projects and regulations of the public administration. It was known that the government of Sieyès was to terminate in a pinnacle, in a species of monarchical shaft, erected upon republican foundations; an idea to which he had been for a long time attached; an attention and even impatient curiosity was manifested, till at last he discovered the capital of his constitutional edifice. What was Sieyès' proposal? *A grand elector*, chosen for life by the conservative senate, sitting at Versailles, representing the majority of the nation, with a revenue of six millions, a guard of three thousand men, and having no other functions than to nominate two consuls, one for *peace* and another for *war*, both independent of each other in the exercise of their functions. And this *grand elector*, in case of a bad choice, could be *absorbed* by the senate, which was invested with the right of drawing back into its own body, without explaining its reasons, every depositary of public authority, the two consuls and the grand elector not excepted; the latter having become a member of the senate, would no longer have any direct share in the operations of government.

Here Bonaparte could no longer contain himself; rising up and bursting into a loud laugh, he took the paper from the hands of Sieyès, and, with one dash of his pen, *sabred* what he called metaphysical nonsense. Sieyès, who generally yielded to, instead of resisting, objections, defended, nevertheless, his grand elector; and said that after all a king ought to be nothing else. Bonaparte replied, with much warmth, that he mistook the shadow for the substance, the abuse for the principle; that there could not be in the government any active power without an independence founded upon, and defined by, prerogative. He also made several other preconcerted objections, to which Sieyès replied very lamely; and becoming gradually more warm, he finished by addressing his colleague thus : " How could you have supposed, citizen Sieyès, that a man of honour, of talent, and of some capacity in affairs, would ever consent to be nothing but a hog fattened up by a few millions in the royal château of Versailles ? " Amused by this sally, the members of the conference began to laugh; and Sieyès, who had already testified indecision, remained confounded, and saw his *grand elector* sink never to rise again.

It is certain that Sieyès concealed some deep projects in this ridiculous form of government, and that had it been adopted, he would soon have remained sole master. It was he, doubtless, whom the senate was to have nominated *grand elector*, and he would have appointed Bonaparte consul for war, sure of *absorbing* him at a convenient opportunity. By this means everything would remain in his own hands, and it would have been easy for him, by causing himself to be absorbed, to have called a similar personage to the head of the government, and to have transformed, by a transition artfully prepared, an elective executive power into an hereditary royalty, in favour of any dynasty it was necessary for him to establish for the interests of a revolution of which he was the supreme pontiff.

But his circuitous and suspicious proceedings brought against him the determined resistance of the consul, which he ought to have expected; and thence the overthrow of all his projects. He had not, however, neglected to secure, as will shortly be seen, a retirement proof against all the shafts of adverse fortune.

It was not sufficient to do away with the project of Sieyès; it was necessary, besides, that the adherents and intimate advisers of the General Consul should be brought into the government, in order to make themselves master of the supreme power. All was ready. But notwithstanding the personal retreat of Sieyès, the party who were attached to his opinions returned to the charge, and, in despair at their cause, proposed the adoption of forms purely republican. To this was opposed the creation of a president, similar to the plan of the United States, for ten years, free in the choice of ministers, of his council of state, and all the members of the administration. Others, also, who were gained over, advised to disguise the sole magistrateship of the president; for which purpose they offered to conciliate conflicting opinions by forming a government of three consuls, of which two should only be advisers as occasion required (*conseillers néces-saires*). But when they were called upon to decide that there should be a First Consul, invested with supreme power, having the right of nominating to, and dismissing from all appointments, and that the two consuls should only have consulting voices, then objections arose. Chazal, Daunou, Courtois, Chénier, and many others besides, insisted upon constitutional limits. They represented that if General Bonaparte should take upon himself the supreme magistracy, with-out a previous election, it would denote the ambition of a usurper, and would justify the opinion of those who had asserted that the events of the 18th Brumaire were solely intended for his own aggrandisement. Making a last effort to prevent it, they offered him the dignity of generalissimo, with the power of making peace and war, and of treating with foreign powers. " I will remain at Paris," replied Bonaparte with vivacity, and biting his nails; I will remain at Paris; I am Consul." Then Chénier, breaking silence, spoke of liberty, of the Republic, of the necessity of putting some restrictions upon power; insisting, with much force and courage, upon the adoption of the measure of *absorption* into the senate. " That shall not be ! " cried Bonaparte, in a rage, and stamping with his feet; " we will rather wade to our knees in blood ! " At these words, which changed into a scene a delibera-tion hitherto kept within the bounds of moderation, everyone remained speechless; and the majority rising placed the power not into the hands of three consuls, the second and third having consulting voices, but to a single one nominated for three years, re-eligible, promulgating laws, appointing and dismissing at his will all the members of the executive power, making peace and war, and, in fact, nominating himself. And so Bonaparte, by avoiding to make a previous institution of the senate, would not even condescend to be First Consul by the act of the senators.

Whether from spite or pride, Sieyès refused to be one of the accessory consuls. This was expected, and the choice which was already made by Bonaparte *in petto* fell upon Cambacérès and Lebrun, who differed but very little in politics. The one, a member of the Convention, having voted for the death of the king, had embraced the Revolution in its principles as well as its consequences; but, like a cold egotist, the other, brought up in the maxims of ministerial despotism, under the Chancellor Maupeou, whose intimate secretary he was, caring little about theories, attached himself solely to the action of power; the one, a powerless defender of the principles of the Revolution and of its interests, was inclined for the return of distinctions, honours, and abuses; the other was a warmer and a juster advocate of social order, of morals, and of public faith. Both were enlightened and men of probity, although avaricious.

As to Sieyès, nominated a senator, he concurred with Cambacérès and Lebrun in organising the senate, of which he was first president. As a reward for his docility in resigning the helm of affairs into the hands of the General Consul, he was voted the estate of Crosne, a magnificent present of a million of francs, independent of twenty-five thousand francs a year as senator, and exclusive of his *pot de vin* as director, which amounted to six hundred thousand francs, and which he called his *poire pour la soif*. From that time, fallen from all consideration and sunk in secret sensuality, he was politically dead.

A decree of the 20th of November ordained that the two preceding legislative councils should assemble of their own right in February, 1800. In order to elude with more effect this decree, the execution of which would have compromised the consular dignity, a new constitution was submitted to the acceptance of the French people. There was no longer any question of collecting them in primary assemblies by consecrating again the democratic principle, but of opening registers in all the government departments and public offices—registers in which the citizens were to inscribe their votes. These votes amounted to three millions and more, and I can affirm that there was no deception in the computation, so favourably received was the *Révolution de Brumaire* by the great majority of Frenchmen.

Nine times in less than seven years, since the fall of the royal authority, the nation had seen the helm pass from hand to hand, and the vessel of state dashed upon new shoals. But this time the pilot inspired more universal confidence. He was considered to be steady and skilful, and his government, in other respects, assumed the forms of durability.

The day on which Bonaparte declared himself First Consul, and was recognised in that character, he judged that his reign was substantially to date from that period, and he did not disguise that opinion in the internal action of his government. Republicanism was observed to lose every day some portion of its gloomy austerity, and conversions in favour of unity of power were seen to multiply.

The Consul induced us to believe, and we willingly persuaded ourselves, that this necessary unity in the government would cause no encroachment on the republican structure; and, in fact, up to the period of the battle of Marengo, the forms of the Republic still subsisted; no person dared to stray from the language and the spirit of that government. Bonaparte, when First Consul, constrained himself to appear in no other light than as magistrate of the people and chief of the army. He assumed the reins of government on the 25th of December, and his name was from that time inscribed at the head of all public Acts, an innovation unknown since the birth of the Republic. Till then the chief magistrates of the state had inhabited the palace of the Luxembourg; none of them had yet dared to invade the abode of the kings. Bonaparte, with more assurance, quitted the Luxembourg and went in state, accompanied by great military display, to occupy the Tuileries, which became from that time the residence of the First Consul. The senate held its sittings at the Luxembourg, and the tribunal at the Palais Royal.

This magnificence pleased the nation, which approved of being represented in a manner more suited to her dignity. Splendour and etiquette resumed a portion of their empire. Paris beheld its circles, its balls, and sumptuous entertainments revived. Observant of forms, punctilious even in matters of public decency, Bonaparte, breaking through the ancient connections of

Josephine, and even his own, excluded from the palace all females of decried or suspected morals who had figured in the most brilliant circles, as well as in the intrigues carried on at the Luxembourg under the reign of the Directory.

The commencement of a new reign is almost always auspicious. It was the same with the consulship, which was distinguished by the reform of a great number of abuses, by acts of wisdom and humanity, and by the system of justice and moderation which the consuls adopted. The recall of a portion of the deputies, against whom were levelled the decrees of the 19th Fructidor, was an act of wisdom, decision, and equity. The same may be said of the measure for closing the list of emigrants. The consuls permitted the erasure of a great number of the distinguished members of the Constituent Assembly. I enjoyed the satisfaction of re-calling and erasing from the fatal list the celebrated Cazalès, as well as his old colleague Malouet, a man of real talent and strict integrity. As well as myself, the ex-elector Malouet had formerly taken his degree at the Oratoire, and I entertained for him an extreme regard. It will be seen that he repaid my friendship by a per-severing and sincere return.

The reorganisation of the judicial system, and the establishment of prefectures, equally distinguished that auspicious opening of the consulship, of which the com-position of the new authorities felt the beneficial results. But, to confess the truth, this flattering picture was soon overshadowed. " It is not my intention to govern in the character of a beau magistrate," said Bonaparte to me one evening ; " the pacification of the west does

not proceed; there is too much license and boasting
in the journals." The awaking moment was terrible.
The execution of young Toustain, that of the Count de
Frotté and his companions in arms, the suppression of
a portion of the journals, the threatening style of the
last proclamations, while they filled both republicans
and royalists with dismay, dissipated through nearly
the whole of France the fond hopes which had been
cherished of an equitable and humane government. I
caused the First Consul to feel the necessity of dispersing these clouds. He relaxed a little; gained over
the emigrants by favours and employments; restored
the churches to the Catholic worship; kept the republicans either in a state of minority or dispersion,
but without persecuting them: he proclaimed himself
at the same time the scourge of contractors.

All the sources of credit were either dried up or
destroyed at the accession of the Consul by the effect
of the disorders, the dilapidations, and the profusion
which had crept into all the branches of the public
administration and revenue. It was rèquisite to create
new resources in order to meet the war and all the
departments of service. Twelve millions were borrowed
of the commercial interest of Paris; twenty-four millions
were expected from the sale of the domains of the
house of Orange; and at length one hundred and fifty
millions of *bons de rescription de rachat de rentes*, were
put into circulation. In decreeing these measures, the
First Consul perceived how difficult it would be for
him to depart from the ruinous control of the contractors. He had a perfect horror of them. The
following note, of which he subsequently remitted me

a copy, prejudiced and singularly exasperated him against our principal bankers and brokers. This is the note:

"The individuals whose names are subscribed are masters of the public fortune; they give an impulse to the course of public stock, and each of them possesses about a hundred millions of private capital; they, moreover, dispose of twenty-four millions of credit; namely, Armand Séguin, Vanderberg, Launoy, Collot, Hinguerlot, Ouvrard, the brothers Michel, Bastide, Marion, and Récamier. The partisans of Haller the Swiss have triumphed, because that Swiss, whose measures of finance the First Consul did not choose to adopt, predicted the fall which has at this moment taken place."

Bonaparte could not support the idea of fortunes so suddenly made and so gigantic; it seemed as if he feared to be subjected to them. He regarded them generally as the disgraceful results of public dilapidation and usury. He had only been able to triumph on the 18th of Brumaire with the money which Collot had lent him; and he was humiliated by the reflection. Joseph Bonaparte himself only obtained possession of Morfontaine with the two millions lent him by Collot. "Yes," said he to his brother, "you wished to play the great man with other people's money; but the whole weight of the usury will fall upon me."

I had much trouble, as well as the Count Lebrun, to mitigate his indignation against bankers and brokers, and to divert him from the violent measures which from that time he purposed instituting against them. He comprehended little of the theory of public credit; and it was obvious that he had a secret inclination to conduct the finance department amongst us, on the system of the averages adopted in Egypt, Turkey, and throughout the East.   He was, however, compelled to recur to Vanderberg in order to open the campaign ; to him he committed the charge of the necessary loan.   His prejudices extended to all the secret parts of the government.   I was always the person to whom he assigned the duty of verifying or controlling the secret notes which intriguers and place-hunters never failed transmitting to him.   Some idea of the delicacy of my functions may be formed from that circum- stance.   I was the only one capable of correcting his prejudices or of triumphing over them, by placing daily under his eye, by means of my police bulletins, the expression of all kinds of opinions and ideas, and the summary of such secret circumstances, a knowledge of which interested the safety and tranquillity of the state.   In order not to exasperate him, I took care to make a separate summary of all which might have mortified him in his conferences and communications with the two other consuls.   My communications with him were too frequent not to be of a ticklish character. But I maintained a tone of truth and frankness tem- pered with zeal, and that zeal was sincere.   I found in that unique personage precisely all that was wanted in order to regulate and maintain that unity of power in the executive authority, without which everything would have fallen back into disorder and chaos.   But I found also that he possessed violent passions and a natural tendency to despotism, derived from his character and martial habits.   I flattered myself with being able successfully to restrain it by the exercise of prudence and reason, and I pretty often succeeded beyond my hopes.

At this period Bonaparte had no further cause to fear any material opposition in the interior of France, except that of some royalist bands which still retained their arms in the departments of the east, and chiefly in Morbihan. In Europe his power was neither so well consolidated nor so undisputed. He was perfectly aware beforehand that he could strike its roots deeply only by new victories. Of these he was therefore greedy.

But France was then emerging from a crisis; her finances were exhausted; if anarchy had been quelled, it was not so with royalism; and the republican spirit was fermenting secretly beyond the sphere of power. As to the French armies, notwithstanding their recent successes in Holland and Switzerland, they were still in no condition to resume the offensive. The whole of Italy was lost; even the Apennines were not able to prescribe bounds to the soldiers of Austria.

What, then, did Bonaparte do? By the excellent advice of his minister for foreign affairs, he sagaciously availed himself of the passions of the Emperor Paul I., in order to detach him entirely from the coalition. He next made appearance on the ostensible stage of European diplomacy by publishing his famous letter to the King of England. It contained overtures offered in an uncustomary form. In that circumstance the First Consul foresaw the double advantage of obtaining credit for his pacific intentions, and of persuading France, in the event of the refusal which he expected, that in order to conquer that peace which was the

object of all his desires, it was necessary to supply
him with gold, steel, and men.

When one day, on issuing from his private cabinet
council, he told me, with an air of inspiration, that he
felt assured of reconquering Italy in three months, I
was, in the first instance, struck with the seeming
audacity of the proposal, and nevertheless was induced
to give it credit. Carnot, who a short time previously
had become minister of war, perceived as well as I
that there was one thing which Bonaparte understood
above all others, and that was the practical science of
war. But when Bonaparte positively told me that he
understood, before his departure for the army, that all
the departments of the west were tranquil, and pointed
out to me measures connected with the subject, coinciding with my own views, I not only recognised in
him the character of a warrior, but also of an able
politician; and I seconded his exertions with a good
fortune, for which he manifested his obligations.

We were, however, not able to break up the royalist
league, except by means of the great *primum mobile*,
subornation. In this respect Bernia, the curate, and
two viscountesses, desirably assisted in favouring the
opinion that Bonaparte was exerting himself to replace
the Bourbons on the throne. The bait took so well
that the King himself, then at Mittau, deceived by his
correspondents in Paris, conceived that the favourable
moment was come for him to claim his crown, and
transmitted to the consul Lebrun, by means of the
Abbé de Montesquiou, his secret agent, a letter addressed to Bonaparte, wherein, in the most mincing
terms, he endeavoured to convince him of the honour

he would acquire by replacing him on the throne of his ancestors. "I can do nothing for France without you," said that prince, "and you cannot contribute to the welfare of France without me. Hasten, then, to undertake the task."

At the same time the Count d'Artois sent the Duchess de Guiche, a lady of great attraction and talent, from London, in order, on his side, to open a negotiation of a parallel description by means of Josephine, who was considered the tutelary angel of the royalists and emigrants. She obtained some interviews, and I was informed of them by Josephine herself, who, in conformity with our mutual treaty, cemented by a thousand francs per day, informed me of all that took place within the interior of the château.

I confess that I was mortified in not receiving from Bonaparte any instruction respecting circumstances so essential. I therefore went to work. I employed extraordinary means; and I learnt in a positive manner the proceedings of the Abbé de Montesquiou with the consul Lebrun. I made it the subject of a memorial, which I addressed to the First Consul, in which I referred equally to that mission and the proceedings of the Duchess de Guiche. I represented to him that, in sanctioning such negotiations, he gave occasion to suspect that he sought to secure to himself, in case of a reverse of fortune, a brilliant means both of fortune and security; but that he miscalculated greatly, if, indeed, it were possible for a spirit so magnanimous as his to stoop to so erroneous a policy; that he was, essentially, the man of the Revolution, and could be

no other; and that the Bourbons could by no chance
re-ascend the throne, except by reaching it over his
dead body.

This memorial, which I took the pains to compile
and write myself, proved to him that nothing which
concerned the secrets and safety of the state could
escape my notice. It produced the result which I expected; that is to say, it made a vivid impression on
the mind of Bonaparte. The Duchess de Guiche was
dismissed with an order to repair without delay to
London; and the consul Lebrun was taunted with the
fact of having received a letter from the king through
an underhanded channel. My credit from that time
assumed the solidity which befitted the eminence and
importance of my functions.

Other scenes were about to commence; but they
were scenes of blood and carnage on different fields of
contention. Moreau, who had passed the Rhine on the
25th of April, had already defeated the Austrians in three
encounters before the 10th of May, when Bonaparte,
between the 16th and 20th, in an enterprise worthy
of Hannibal, passed the great St. Bernard, at the
head of the entire army of reserve. Surprising the
enemy which, either through negligence or delusion,
persisted, on the Var and toward Genoa, in invading
the frontier of France, he directed his march upon
Milan, through the valley of Aoste and Piedmont, and
arrived in time to cut off the communication of the
Austrian army, commanded by Melas. The Austrian,
disconcerted, concentrated himself between the cannon
of Alessandria, at the confluence of the Tanaro and the
Bormida, and, after some partial defeats, courageously

The Passage of Mount St. Bernard

Engraved by Outhwaite after picture by Karl Girardet

advanced to confront the First Consul, who, on his side, was marching in the same direction.

The decisive crisis was approaching, and kept the public mind in suspense. Feelings and opinions were in a state of ferment in Paris, especially among the two extreme parties, popular and royalist. The moderate republicans were not less moved. They felt a kind of misgiving in seeing at the head of the government a general more disposed to employ the cannon and the sabre than the cap of liberty or the scales of justice. The malcontents cherished the hope that the individual whom they already called the Cromwell of France, would be arrested in his course, and that, owing his elevation to war, he would owe to war his destruction.

Things were in this state when, on the evening of the 20th June, two commercial expresses arrived with news from the army, announcing that on the 14th instant, at five o'clock in the evening, the battle fought near Alessandria had turned to the disadvantage of the consular army, which was retreating; but that the contest was still continued. This intelligence, diffused with the rapidity of lightning throughout all such classes as were interested, produced upon the public mind the same effect as the electric shock does upon the human body. Meetings were held, assemblies called; visits were made to Chénier, to Courtois, to the coterie of Staël; some hurried to the house of Sieyès, others to that of Carnot. The common pretence was that it was necessary to withdraw the endangered Republic from the grip of the Corsican; that it was necessary to remodel it on a wiser and freer system; that it was requisite to have a chief magistrate, but not an arrogant dictator, nor a mere emperor of the soldiers. Every eye and every thought were bent on the minister of war, Carnot.

I was at once informed of the news and of the public ferment which it occasioned. I hastened instantly to the two consuls, and I found them in a state of consternation. I immediately applied myself to the task of raising their fainting resolution. But I confess that, on returning to my own house, my brain stood in need of all its energy. My *salon* was full of company. I took care not to show myself; at length I was besieged even in my closet. In vain I gave orders to be denied to all but my intimate friends; the heads of the file penetrated into my fastness. I fatigued myself to death in telling everybody that the news was exaggerated; that probably it was a result of stock-jobbing; that, moreover, Bonaparte had always performed miracles on the field of battle. "Above all things," I added, "wait; let us have no caprice, no imprudence, no bitter reflections, and no overt and hostile acts."

The next day an express arrived from the First Consul, loaded with the laurels of victory; the disenchantment of one party was incapable of suppressing the universal intoxication. The battle of Marengo, like that of Actium, enabled our young triumvir to triumph, and raised him to the pinnacle of power: a triumvir, equally fortunate, but not so discreet as the Octavius of Rome. He departed in the character of the first magistrate of a nation, still free, and he was about to reappear in the character of a conqueror. It seemed,

in fact, as if he were less the conqueror of Italy at
Marengo than of France. From this period is to be
dated the first essay of that disgusting and servile
flattery with which all the magistrates and public
authorities conspired to turn his head during the fifteen
years of his predominance. One of his councillors of
state, named Rœderer, was observed to apotheosise his
new master, and apply to him, in a public journal, the
well-known line of Virgil :

Deus nobis hæc otia fecit.

I foresaw all the fatal consequences that this adulatory
tendency (perfectly unworthy of a great people) would
produce on France and on her chief. But the intoxication was at its height, and the triumph was complete.
At length, in the night between the 2nd and 3rd of
July, the conqueror arrived.

I observed, from the first moment, an appearance
of moroseness and constraint on his countenance. That
very evening, at the hour devoted to business, he darted
a gloomy look at me on entering his closet, and broke
out in ejaculations : " What ? so ! I was thought to
be lost, and an experiment was about to be again
made on a Committee of Public Safety. I know everything — and these were the men whom I saved and
spared. Do they take me for Louis XVI. ? Let them
try, and find the difference. There must be no more
deception ; a battle lost in my case is a battle gained.
I fear nothing ; I will crush all those ungrateful men
and traitors into dust. I am able to save France in
spite of factions and disturbers." I represented to him
that there had only been an access of the republican
fever excited by an inauspicious report, a report that I

had contradicted, and the ill effects of which I had restrained; that my memorial to the two consuls, a copy of which I had transmitted to him, would enable him to appreciate at its true value that diminutive movement of fermentation and misgiving; and that, in fine, the *dénouement* was so magnificent, and the public satisfaction so general, that a few clouds, which only rendered the brilliancy of the picture more dazzling by contrast, might easily admit of toleration. " But you do not tell me all," replied he; " was there not a design to place Carnot at the head of the government? Carnot, who suffered himself to be mystified on the 18th Fructidor, who is incapable of maintaining his authority for two months, and who would inevitably be sent to perish at Sinnamary." I affirmed that the conduct of Carnot had been unimpeachable; and I remarked that it would be very hard to render him responsible for the extravagant projects engendered by sickly brains, and of which he (Carnot) had not the least idea.

He was silent; but the impression had struck deep. He did not forgive Carnot, who some time after found himself under the necessity of resigning the portfolio of war. It is probable that I should have shared his anticipated disgrace had not Cambacérès and Lebrun been witnesses of the circumspection of my conduct and the sincerity of my zeal.

Becoming more jealous as he became more powerful, the First Consul armed himself with precautionary measures, and surrounded himself with a military equipage. His prejudices and distrusts were more especially directed against those whom he called the

perverse, whether they wished to preserve their attachment to the popular party or dissipated their strength
in lamentations at the sight of dying liberty. I proposed mild measures in order to bring back the malcontents within the circle of government. I demanded
means of gaining the chiefs of the party by pensions,
gifts, and places. I received *carte blanche* with respect
to the employment of pecuniary means; but my credit
did not extend to the distribution of public employments and rewards. I saw clearly that the First
Consul persisted in the system of only admitting the
republicans into his counsels and high employments in
the form of a minority, and that he wished to maintain in full force the partisans of monarchy and absolute power. I had scarcely sufficient credit to nominate
some half-dozen prefects. Bonaparte did not like the
Tribunat, because it contained a nucleus of staunch
republicans. It was well known that he more especially
dreaded the zealots and enthusiasts known by the
name of anarchists, a set of men always ready to be
employed as instruments of plots and revolutions. His
distrusts and his alarms were inflamed by the persons
who surrounded him, and who urged him towards
monarchy — such as Portalis, Lebrun, Cambacérès,
Clarke, Champagny, Fleurieu, Duchâtel, Jollivet, Bene-
zech, Emmery, Rœderer, Cretet, Regnier, Chaptal,
Dufresne, and many others. To this effect must be
added the secret reports and clandestine correspondence of men employed by him, which were couched
in the same spirit, and swam with the torrent of
the prevailing opinion. In these I was not spared.
I was exposed to the most malevolent insinuations :

my system of police was therein often run down and denounced. I had Lucien against me, who was then minister of the interior, and who had also his private police. Sometimes obliged to bear the reproaches of the First Consul about facts which he believed concealed in obscurity, he suspected me of keeping spies upon him in order to depreciate him in my reports. I had a former order to keep nothing concealed, whether popular reports or the gossip of the *salons*. The result was that Lucien, making abusive use of his credit and his position, playing the part of a debauchee, seducing wives from their husbands, and trafficing in licenses for the exportation of corn, was often an object of rumours and innuendoes. In the character of head of the police, it was not proper for me to disguise how important it was that the members of the First Consul's family should be irreproachable and pure in the eyes of the public.

The nature of the conflict in which I was thus engaged may be conceived. Luckily, I had Josephine in my interest; Duroc was not against me; and the private secretary was devoted to my views. This personage, who was replete with ability and talent, but whose greediness of gain very shortly caused his disgrace, always exhibited so much cupidity that there is no occasion to name him in order to point him out. Having the control over the papers and secrets of his master, he discovered that I spent 100,000 francs monthly, for the purpose of incessantly watching over the existence of the First Consul. The idea came into his head to make me pay for such intelligence as he might supply me, in order to furnish means of accomplishing the aim I had in view. He sought me, and offered to inform me exactly of all the proceedings of Bonaparte for 25,000 francs per month; and he made me this offer as a means of saving 900,000 francs per annum.

I took care not to let this opportunity slip, of having the private secretary of the chief of the state in my pay; that chief whom it was so requisite for me to follow step by step, in order to know what he had done, and what he was about to do. The proposal of the secretary was accepted, and he every month very punctually received a blank order for 25,000 francs, the promised sum, which he was to draw out of the treasury. On my side, I had full reason to congratulate myself on his dexterity and accuracy. But I took care not to starve the funds which I employed, in order to protect the person of Bonaparte from any unforeseen attack. The palace alone dried up more than half the resource of my 100,000 francs, which were monthly available. In fact, I was by that means very accurately apprised of all that was important for me to know; and I was enabled, reciprocally, to control the information of the secretary by that of Josephine, and that of the latter by the secretary. I was stronger than all my enemies put together.

But what were the next measures resorted to in order to destroy me? I was formally accused to the First Consul of protecting republicans and demagogues; and the accusers went so far as to point out General Parain, who was personally attached to me, of being the intermediate agent whom I employed for the purpose of supplying information to the anarchists, and of distributing money among them. The real fact is that I employed all my ministerial influence in order to counteract the designs of zealots, to appease passions, to divert them from the means of combining any plot against the chief magistrate; and that many individuals were greatly indebted to me for salutary assistance and admonition. In doing this I only availed myself of the latitude allowed me by my functions in the superior police. I thought, and I still think, that it is better to prevent criminal attempts than subsequently to exert the power of punishing them. But the means of rendering me suspected finally succeeded in exciting the distrust of the First Consul. In a short time he found pleas to limit my functions, by especially charging the prefect of police with the duty of superintending the malcontents. That prefect was Dubois; an old lawyer, avaricious and blindly devoted to power; a magistrate before the Revolution, who, after having adroitly insinuated himself into the *bureau central*, got himself appointed prefect of police, after the 19th Brumaire. In order to obtain a little private administration for himself, he threw difficulties in my way in the matter of the secret fund; and I was obliged to give him a large bonus out of the *curée des jeux*, under pretext that money was the sinew of all political police. But afterwards I succeeded in detecting him in the employment of the funds of his budget, which were derived from the base and disgraceful vices which dishonour the metropolis.

The Machiavellian maxim, *Divide et impera*, having prevailed, there were shortly no less than four distinct systems of police: the military police of the palace, conducted by the aides-de-camp and by Duroc; the police of the inspectors of gendarmerie; the police of the prefecture, managed by Dubois; and my own. As to the police of the home department, I lost no time in abolishing it, as will shortly be seen. Accordingly, the Consul daily received four bulletins of separate police establishments, derived from different quarters, and which he was enabled to compare together, without mentioning the reports of his privately accredited correspondents. This was what he called feeling the pulse of the Republic; the latter was considered as in a very bad state of health under his hands. All that it was possible for me to have done, in order to keep up her strength, would have turned to her disadvantage.

My adversaries laboured to reduce my functions to that of a simply administrative and theoretical police. But I was not a man to be so put down. The First Consul himself—it is fair to do him justice—was capable of firmly withstanding all manœuvres of this description. He said that in thus wishing to deprive him of my services, he was exposed to the hazard of remaining defenceless in presence of the counter-revolutionists; that no one understood better than I how to manage the police departments of the English and Chouan agents, and that my system suited him. I nevertheless was aware that I was only a counterpoise in the machine of government. Besides, its march was more or less subordinate to the course of public events and the chances of politics.

Everything at that time seemed to intimate an approaching peace. The battle of Marengo had, by the results of a military convention more wonderful than the victory itself, thrown into the power of the First Consul Piedmont, Lombardy, Genoa, and the strongest places in Upper Italy. It was only after having re-established the Cisalpine republic that he departed from Milan.

On his side, Moreau approaching Vienna, after having made himself master of Munich, the Austrians also were induced to solicit an armistice; that of Italy not extending to the German territory. To this Moreau consented; and on the 15th of July the preliminaries of peace were signed at Paris between Austria and France.

Successes so decisive, far from disarming the republican malcontents, exasperated them more and more. Bonaparte created bitter enemies by his absolute and military habits. There were, even at that time, counted in the ranks of the army a great number of oppositionists whom a republican spirit induced to form secret associations. General officers and colonels moved their secret strings. They flattered themselves with having in their party Bernadotte, Augereau, Jourdan, Brune, and even Moreau himself, who already began to repent of having assisted the elevation of the individual who had now erected himself into a master. In fact, no visible sign, no positive datum, furnished the government with a hint of these intrigues; but some broken indications and disclosures prompted it to the frequent removal from one place to another of the regiments and officers who had rendered themselves objects of suspicion.

In Paris affairs were in a more gloomy condition,

and the operation of the malcontents was more obvious. The more violent were withheld from employments, and watched. I was informed that, since the institution of the consular government, they held secret assemblies and fabricated plots. It was in order to render those plots abortive that I exerted all my energies ; by that means hoping to mitigate the natural inclination of the government to react upon the individuals of the Revolution. I had even succeeded in obtaining from the First Consul some exterior demonstrations favourable to republican ideas. For example, on the anniversary of the 14th of July, which had just been celebrated under the auspices of concord, the First Consul had given at a solemn banquet the following remarkable toast: "The French people ; our sovereign."

I had supplied much assistance to indigent and unfortunate patriots ; on the other hand, by the vigilance of my agents, and by means of timely information, I retained in obscurity and inactivity the most violent of those demagogues who, before the departure of Bonaparte for Italy, had assembled and devised the project of perpetrating his murder on the road, in the vicinity of the capital. After his return, and his triumphs, resentments became blind and implacable. There were secret divans held, and one of the more intemperate conspirators, muffled up in the garb of a gendarme, took an oath to assassinate Bonaparte at the Comédie Française. My measures, combined with those of General Lannes, chief of the counter-police, caused the frustration of this plot. But one baffled conspiracy was quickly followed by another. How,

indeed, could the possibility be expected of restraining
for any length of time men of a turbulent character
and of an unconquerable fanaticism, exposed, moreover,
to a condition of private distress so well calculated to
inflame them ?   It is with such instruments that conspiracies are formed and fomented.   I soon received
information that Juvenot, an old aide - de - camp of
Henriot, with some twenty zealots, were plotting the
attack and murder of the First Consul at Malmaison.
I put a stop to this, and caused Juvenot to be
arrested.   But it was impossible to extract any confession ; we were unable to penetrate the secret of
these intrigues and to reach their real authors.   Fion,
Dufour, and Rossignol passed for the principal agents
of the conspiracy ; Talot and Laignelot for the in-
visible directors.   They had their own pamphleteer ;
this was Metge, a resolute, active, and untraceable
individual.

Towards the middle of September intimation was
given me of a plot to assassinate the First Consul at
the opera. I caused Rossignol and some other obscure
persons who were suspected to be arrested and conveyed to prison in the Temple.   The interrogatory
elicited no light ; and I ordered them to be set at
liberty, with directions to follow them.   Five days
after, the same conspiracy was resumed ; at least, an
individual named Harel, one of the accomplices, in
the hope of large remuneration, made some disclosures,
in concert with the commissary Lefebvre, to Bourienne,
secretary of the First Consul.   Harel himself being
brought forward, corroborated its first information, and
designated the conspirators.   According to him they

were Roman emigrants named Ceracchi and Diana ; Arena, brother of the Corsican deputy who had de- clared against the First Consul ; the painter Topino- Lebrun, a fanatical patriot ; and Demerville, an old clerk to the Committee of Public Safety, intimately connected with Barère. This affair procured for me at the palace a tolerably vehement *sortie,* made up of reproaches and bitterness. Luckily I was not thrown off my guard. "General Consul," I calmly replied, "if the indiscreet zeal of the accuser had been less interested, he would have come to me, who direct, and ought to direct, all the secret strings of the superior police, and who secure the safety of the chief magistrate against all organised conspiracy—organised, I say—for there is no answering for the solitary madness of a fanatical scoundrel. In this case, beyond a doubt, there is a plot, or, at least, a real design to commit violence. I had myself full knowledge of it, and caused the incoherent projectors, who seem to have deluded themselves with reference to the possibility of its execution, to be observed. I can produce proofs of what I advance by the immediate production of the person from whom I derived my information!" It was Barère, who was then charged with the political department of journals written under ministerial in- fluence. "Very well," replied Bonaparte in an ani- mated tone; "let him be produced and make his declaration to General Lannes, who is already ac- quainted with the affair, and with whom you will concert the proper measures."

I soon perceived that the policy of the First Consul led him to impart substance to a shadow, and that it was his wish to have it believed that he had incurred great danger. It was decided—and to this I was a stranger—that the conspirators should be entrapped into a snare which Harel was ordered to devise ; in procuring them, as he had promised, four armed men, who should be employed to assassinate the First Consul on the evening of the 10th of October while present at the performance of the opera of the *Horatii*.

This being decided, the Consul, in a privy council, to which the minister of war was summoned, spoke of the dangers by which he was surrounded, the plots of the anarchists and demagogues, and of the perverse direction which men of irritable and ferocious republicanism imparted to the public mind. He instanced Carnot, and reproached him with his connection with men of the Revolution, and with his morose disposition. Lucien spoke in the same strain, but in a more artificial manner ; and he referred (the whole scene being got up for the occasion) to the prudence and wisdom of the consuls Cambacérès and Lebrun, who, pleading reasons of state, had alleged that the portfolio of the war department must be withdrawn from Carnot. The fact is that Carnot had frequently allowed himself to defend public liberty and remonstrate with the First Consul against the favours granted to royalists, against the royal magnificence of the court, and against the inclination which Josephine manifested of performing the part of Queen, and surrounding herself with females whose name and rank flattered her self-love. The next day Carnot, in conformity with the notice which I was instructed to give him, sent in his resignation.

On the day following, at the performance of the *Horatii*, the mock attempt on the life of the First Consul occurred. On that occasion persons were stationed in readiness by counter-police, with respect to whom the conspirators had been deluded, and those persons arrested Diana, Ceracchi, and their accomplices.

This affair made a great stir, and it was what was wanted. All the superior authorities hurried to congratulate the First Consul on the danger he had escaped. In his reply from the tribune he said that he had in reality run no danger; that, independently of the assistance supplied by all good citizens who were present at the performance which he attended, he had with him a picket of his brave guard. "The wretches," exclaimed he, "were incapable of braving the looks of those gallant men."

I immediately proposed measures of superintendence and precaution for the future, and, amongst others, to disarm all the villages from Paris to Malmaison, and to institute a search into all the detached houses on the same road. Special instructions were drawn up in order to impart redoubled vigilance to the agents of police. The counter-police of the palace also ordained extraordinary measures. Less facility of access to the chief magistrate was permitted; all the avenues by which he reached the boxes of the theatres were secured from all risk of individual violence.

Every government of recent origin generally profits by the occasion of a danger which it has provoked, either to corroborate or to extend its power; to have escaped a conspiracy is sufficient ground for acquiring

more energy and vigour. The **First Consul** was in-
stinctively induced to follow a policy adopted by all
his predecessors. In this latter case he was more particularly prompted thereto by his brother Lucien, who
was equally ambitious as himself, although his ambition exhibited a different shape and character. It had
not escaped his notice that he curbed and eclipsed his
brother, either by boasting with too much arrogance
and self-complacency of the 18th of Brumaire, or by
desiring to exercise too great a predominance in the
operations of government. He had at first entertained
a secret design of urging Bonaparte to establish a
species of consular duumvirate, by means of which he
meant to have retained in his own hands all the civil
power, and to have thus effected a participation of
power with a brother who never contemplated the
idea of any participation whatsoever.

This project having failed, he sought every means
of re-establishing his credit, which had declined in
consequence of his wants, and of that iron barrier
which he found in his way, and to the construction
of which he had himself so much contributed.

Availing himself of the impression produced by the
species of a republican conspiracy just suppressed, and
exaggerating to the eye of his brother the inconvenience attending on the instability of his power and the
dangers stirred up against him by the republican spirit,
he hoped from that time to induce him to establish
a constitutional monarchy, of which he meant himself
to be the directing minister and support. I was
openly opposed to this project, which was at that
time impracticable ; and I was well aware that the

First Consul himself, however devoured by the desire of rendering his power immovable, founded the anticipated success of his encroachments upon other combinations.

Lucien, however, persisted in his projects; and wishing to complete the work, which according to him was only yet a sketch, at least (conceiving himself to be secure of the tacit assent of his brother), he caused a pamphlet to be secretly composed and written, entitled, "Parallel of Cromwell, Monk, and Bonaparte," where the cause and principles of monarchy were overtly advocated and cried up. Great numbers of this pamphlet having been struck off, Lucien in his private office inclosed as many packets of them under cover as there were prefectures, and each packet contained copies equal in number to the functionaries of the departments. No official notice, it is true, accompanied this mission, which was sent to each prefect by coach; but the character of the envoi, the superscription bearing the marks of a ministerial mission, and other indications, gave sufficient intimation of the source and political object of the publication. I on the same day received a copy, unknown to Lucien; and hastening to Malmaison, I laid it under the eye of the First Consul, with a report, in which I exhibited the serious inconveniences likely to result from so ill-disguised an initiative. I designated it as unseasonable and imprudent, and I supported my arguments effectually by referring to the state of secret irritation in which the mind of the army at that time was, especially among the generals and superior officers, who personally were little attached to Bonaparte, and

who being indebted for their military fortunes to the
Revolution, were attached more than it was imagined
to republican forms and principles. I said that a
monarchical establishment could not without danger
be abruptly made to succeed them, and that it would
be obnoxious to all those who beforehand raised the
cry of usurpation. I concluded, in short, by making
the premature character of such tests obvious, and I
subsequently obtained an order publicly to prevent the
further propagation of the pamphlet.

I afterwards ordered the circulation to be stopped,
and in order with more effect to obviate the suspicion
that it emanated from government, I designated it in
my circular as the work of " some contemptible and
culpable intriguer." Lucien, in a rage at this, and concluding that I should not have employed such expressions
without being authorised, hurried in his turn to Malmaison, in order to extort an explanation, which was
of a stormy character. From this epoch the opposition
between the two brothers assumed a complexion of
hostility, which concluded by degenerating into violent
scenes. It is certain that Lucien, at the conclusion
of one intemperate altercation, passionately threw on
his brother's desk his portfolio of minister, exclaiming
that he divested himself the more readily of a public
character as he had suffered nothing but torment from
subjection to such a despot; and that, on the other
hand, his brother, equally exasperated, called his aides-
de-camp on duty to turn out of his closet the *citizen*
who forgot the respect due to the First Consul.

Both decorum and state reasons required the separation of the two brothers without more scandal and

violence. M. de Talleyrand and myself laboured at this task; all was politically made up. Lucien in a short time departed for Madrid, with the title of ambassador, and with an express mission to change the inclinations of the King of Spain, and urge him to a war against Portugal; a kingdom which the First Consul beheld with chagrin subjected to dependence upon England.

The causes and the circumstances of the departure of Lucien could scarcely remain secret. On this occasion the opportunity was not lost in private correspondence and in the Parisian saloons to exhibit me upon the stage; to represent me as having triumphed in a contest for favour against the brother of the First Consul himself. It was pretended that by such means I had enabled the party of Josephine and the Beauharnais to preponderate over the party of the brothers of Napoleon. It is true that, looking to the advantage of the maturity and unity of authority, I was fully persuaded that the mild and benignant influence of the Beauharnais was preferable to the excessive and imperious encroachments of Lucien, who alone wished to domineer over the state, and to leave his brother nothing but the management of the army.

New plots, engendered by extreme parties, succeeded these domestic quarrels of the palace. Ever since the latter end of October the fanatics had renewed their sinister designs; I perceived that they were organised with a secrecy and ability which disconcerted all the vigilance of the police. At this period two parallel and almost identical plots were formed against the life of the First Consul by demagogues and royalists. As the latter, which was more dangerous because entirely devised in darkness, appeared to me to be connected with the political situation which the chief magistrate then held, I will give a summary of that situation in a few words.

The Emperor of Austria had received news of the preliminaries of peace being signed in his name at Paris by the Count St. Julien, at the very moment when that monarch had signed a subsidiary treaty with England. The cabinet of Vienna, thus embarrassed between peace and English gold, courageously resolved on a new recourse to the risks of war. M. de St. Julien was thrown into prison for having exceeded his powers; and, the armistice being about to expire in a short time, preparations for renewing hostilities were made on both sides. The armistice, however, was prolonged till November. In this manner both sides balanced between peace and war. The First Consul and his government were at that time inclined to peace, which then solely depended on the operations of Moreau in Germany; of that Moreau whose troublesome reputation Bonaparte even at that time envied.

He was the only man whose renown could bear competition with his in point of strategic skill. This kind of military rivalry, and the position of Moreau in regard to public opinion, subjected Bonaparte, in some sort, to the mercy ot his success, while in the interior of France he was exposed to the plots of demagogues and hostile royalists. In their eyes he was the common enemy. The vigilance of the police, far from discouraging the anarchists, appeared to imbue them

with more audacity and vigour. Their leaders sometimes assembled at the house of Chrétien, the *limon-
adier ;* sometimes at Versailles ; sometimes in the
garden of the .Capucines, organising insurrection, and
already devising a provisional government. Determin-
ing to bring the matter to a conclusion, they proceeded to desperate resolutions. One of them, named
Chevalier, a man of delirious republicanism and atrocious spirit, who was employed in the great artillery
magazine at Meudon, under the Committee of Public
Safety, conceived the first idea of destroying Bonaparte
by means of an infernal machine stationed on his
road. Stimulated by the approbation of his accomplices, and still more by his native disposition, Chevalier, seconded by a man named Veycer, constructed
a kind of barrel, hooped with iron, furnished with nails,
and loaded wlth gunpowder and case-shot, to which
he affixed a firmly adapted and loaded battery, which
was calculated to be discharged at any given moment
by the aid of a match held by an engineer, who must
himself, of course, be sheltered from the effects of the
explosion.

The work proceeded rapidly ; all the conspirators
exhibited an impatience to blow up, by means of the
infernal machine, the " Little Corporal," a name which
they gave to Bonaparte. This was not all ; the most
daring among them, with Chevalier at their head, had
the audacity to make an experiment of the infernal
machine among themselves. The night between the
17th and 18th of October was chosen. The chiefs of
the plot proceeded to the back part of the Hospital
de la Salpêtrière, believing themselves in that place

secure from detection. The explosion was so great there that the fanatics themselves, seized with terror, dispersed. As soon as they recovered from their first alarm, they deliberated on the effects of the horrible invention ; some considered it well adapted to effect their purpose ; others (and Chevalier was of this opinion) thought that as it was not the object of their plot to destroy many persons, but to secure the destruction of one, the effect of the infernal machine depended on too many hazardous chances. After some deep reflection, Chevalier decided on the idea of constructing a kind of incendiary bomb, which being hurled against the First Consul's carriage, either at his arrival or departure from the play, would blow it up by a sudden and inevitable explosion. Accordingly, he again set himself to work.

But the nocturnal explosion had already attracted my attention ; and the boast of the conspirators transpiring from one to the other, very shortly drew the whole police after their heels. The greater part of the secret intelligence referred to an infernal machine which was intended to blow up the " Little Corporal." I consulted my notes, and I felt assured that Chevalier must be the principal artificer of this perfidious machination. He was found concealed on the 8th of November, and arrested, as well as Veycer, in the Rue des Blancs Manteaux ; all those suspected of being their accomplices being taken at the same time. Powder and ball were found, the relics of the first machine, and a rough model of the incendiary bomb ; in short, all the materials of the crime. But no confession was to be obtained either by menaces or bribes.

It will naturally be believed after this discovery that the life of Bonaparte would be secure against means so atrocious and attempts so perverted. But the other hostile party, following the same object by the same intrigues, already conceived the scheme of robbing the demagogues of the invention of the infernal machine. Nothing is more extraordinary, and nevertheless more true, than this sudden change of actors on the same stage, in order to perform the same tragedy. It would appear incredible did I not myself retrace its secret causes, as they successively appear to classify themselves in my own mind.

At the opening of the campaign, Georges Cadoudal, the most decided and inveterate of all the unsubjected chiefs of Lower Britanny, disembarked at Morbihan, on a mission from London, to get up a new revolt. He was invested with the command-in-chief of all Brittany, the military details of which command he deputed to his principal lieutenants, Mercier la Vendée, De Bar, Sol de Grisolles, and Guillemot. These intrigues were connected with others in Paris among correspondents and fellow-conspirators, as well as in the departments of the west. In this particular I had more than indications: I had full knowledge of a projected insurrection, which, at that epoch, namely, the passage of St. Bernard by the First Consul, furnished great cause of alarm to the two other consuls, Cambacérès and Lebrun. I immediately adopted vigorous measures. My agents and the whole of the gendarmerie took the field; I caused several of the old suspected chiefs to be closely watched and arrested, and among others, some very dangerous heads of parishes. But the

operations of the police were more or less subordinate
to the chances of external war.

In a report transmitted to the First Consul at Milan,
I did not disguise from him the symptoms of a crisis
which displayed themselves in the interior of France;
and I told him that he must absolutely return victorious, and that instantly, in order to disperse the newly-
collected elements of troubles and storms.

In fact, as it has been shown, fortune on the plain
of Marengo loaded him with all kinds of favours at the
very moment when his enemies considered him lost for
ever. This sudden triumph disconcerted all the designs of England, and destroyed all the hopes of
Georges Cadoudal, without however quelling his iron
resolution. He persevered in remaining in Morbihan,
which he considered as his domain, and the royalist
organisation of which was supported by his exertions.
Informed by his correspondents at Paris of the irritation and the reviving plots of the popular party, he
sent thither, toward the end of October, his most decided confidential officers, such as Limolan, Saint-
Regent, Joyaux, and Haie-Saint-Hilaire. It is even
probable that he had already conceived, or adopted,
the idea of borrowing the infernal machine from the
Jacobins, of which machine his agents had furnished
him information. In the disposition of the public
mind, and of the government also, this crime, originated by royalists, did not fail of being ascribed to
Jacobins; besides, the royalists were, at all events, in a
condition to gather the harvest of the crime. A com-
bination so audacious appeared more especially political.
Such was the origin of the attempt made on the 24th

of December (3rd Nivôse) by the agents, or rather the delegates, of Georges. This double plot remained for a short time concealed by a thick veil, so exclusively did the suspicions and attention of all parties direct themselves toward the anarchists.

One circumstance appeared favourable to confer a great probability of success on this new design. The oratorio of the *Creation*, by Haydn, was announced for the 24th of December, at the opera; all Paris was aware that the First Consul would be present with his retinue. So profound was the perversity of the conspiracy that the agents of Georges deliberated whether it would not be more certain to station the infernal machine beneath the foundations of the opera pit in such a manner as to blow up at the same time Bonaparte and the entire *élite* of his government. Whether it was the idea of so horrible a catastrophe, or the uncertainty of destroying the individual against whom such an outrage was designed, which caused the crime to be put off, I am incapable, indeed I tremble, to pronounce. Nevertheless, an old officer of the marines, named Saint-Régent, assisted by Carbon, called "Little Francis," a subaltern, was directed to station the fatal machine in the Rue Saint-Nicaise, which it was necessary for Bonaparte to pass, and to apply the match in time to blow up his carriage. The burning of the match, the effect of the powder and explosion, was all computed by the time which the coachman of the First Consul ordinarily employed in coming from the Tuileries to that upper portion of the Rue Saint-Nicaise where the infernal machine was to be placed.

The prefect of police and myself were apprised the

evening before that there was much whispering in certain clubs of a great blow that was to be struck on the following day. This information was very vague; besides, notices equally alarming were brought to us every day. The First Consul, however, was instantly apprised of it by our diurnal reports. He at first appeared to exhibit some hesitation; but, on the report of the counter-police of the palace that the opera-house had been inspected, and all kinds of precautionary measures taken, he called for his carriage and departed, accompanied by his aides-de-camp. On this occasion, as on so many others, it was Cæsar, accompanied by his fortune. It is well known that the hope of the conspirators was only baffled by a slight accident.[1] The First Consul's coachman, being half intoxicated

[1] The infernal machine did not accomplish its design, which was that of destroying the First Consul; but it caused the death of some twenty persons, and wounded fifty-six others, more or less severely. Medical assistance was given to the unfortunate wounded, according to the greater or less severity of their wounds. The maximum of that medical assistance was 4,500 francs, and the minimum twenty-five francs. The orphans and widows received pensions, as well as the children of those who perished; but only till they arrived at their majority; and then they were to receive 2,000 francs for their fitting out. The following are the names of the persons who received assistance by order of the First Consul, with the amount of the sum allowed them:—

	FRANCS
Banny, Jean Frédéric, garçon traiteur, Rue des Grands Augustins	1000
Barbier, Marie Geneviève Viel, veuve, Rue Saint-Honoré .	1000
Bataille, Madame, épicière, Rue Saint-Nicaise . . .	100
Beirlé, Alexandre, marchand gantier peaussier, Rue Saint-Nicaise	800
Boiteux, Jean-Marie-Joseph, ci-devant frère de la charité .	50
Bonnet, Madame, Rue Saint-Nicaise	150

on that day, having driven his horses with more than usual celerity, the explosion, which was computed with rigorous precision, was retarded about two seconds, and that scarcely perceptible fraction of time, deducted

	FRANCS
Boulard (veuve), musicienne, Rue J. J. Rousseau	4000
A second supply was granted her on account of her wounds: it was	3000
Bourdin, Françoise Louvrier, femme, portière, Rue Saint-Nicaise	50
Boyeldieu, Marie Louise Chevalier, veuve, Rue Saint-Placide	1000
Buchener, Louis, tailleur, Rue Saint-Nicaise	25
Chapuy, Gilbert, officier civil de la marine, Rue du Bac	800
Charles, Jean Etienne, imprimeur, Rue Saint-Nicaise	400
Clément, garçon maréchal, Rue de Petit Carrousel	50
Cléreaux, Marie Joséphine Lehodey, épicière, Rue Neuve de l'Egalité	3800
Collinet, Marie Jeanne Cécile, revendeuse à la halle	200
Corbet, Nicolas Alexandre, employé à l'état-major de la 17ᵉ division, Rue Saint-Honoré	240
Couteux, vermicellier, Rue des Prouvaires	150
Duverne, Louis, ouvrier serrurier, Rue du Harlay	1000
Fleury, Cathérine Lenoir, veuve, Rue de Malte	50
Fostier, Louis Philippe, remplaçant au poste de la Rue Saint-Nicaise	25
Fridzery, Alexandre Marie Antoine, musicien aveugle, Rue Saint-Nicaise	750
Gauther, Marie Poncette, fille, Rue de Chaillot	100
Harel, Antoine, garçon limonadier, Rue de Malte	3000
Hiblot, Marie Anne, fille, Rue de Malte	240
Honoré, Marie Thérèse Larue, veuve, Rue Marceau	100
Honoré, Thérèse, fille, ouvrière	50
Huguet, Louis, cuisinier aux Champs Elysées	50
Jardy, Julien, remplaçant au poste Saint-Nicaise	100
Kalbert, Jean Antoine, apprenti menuisier	100
Lambert, Marie Jacqueline Gillot, femme, Rue Fromenteau	100
Leclerc, élève en peinture, mort à l'hospice	200
Lefèvre, Simon François, garçon tapissier, Rue de la Verrerie	200
Leger, Madame, limonadière, Rue Saint-Nicaise	1500

from the preconcerted time, sufficed to save the life of the First Consul and consolidate his power.

Without expressing any astonishment at the event, Bonaparte exclaimed on hearing the report of the frightful explosion, "That is the infernal machine"; and, without desiring to retrograde or fly, he made his appearance at the opera. But with what a wrathful countenance and terrible aspect ! What

	FRANCS
Lemierre, Nicolas, Rue de Malte, tenant maison garnie .	200
Lepape, Elisabeth Satabin, femme, portière, Rue Saint-Nicaise	100
Lion, Pierre Nicolas, domestique, Allée d'Antin . . .	600
Masse, Jean François, garçon marchand de vin, Rue des Saints-Pères	150
Mercier, Jean Baptiste, rentier, Rue Saint-Honoré . .	4500
Mitaine, Jeanne Prevost, veuve, Rue de Malte . . .	450
Orilliard, Stéphanie Madeleine, fille, couturière, Rue de Lille	900
Orphelins—Lister, Agnès, Adélaide	1200
Palluel, portier, Rue Saint-Nicaise.	50
Platel, Jeanne Smith, veuve	1000
Préville, Claude Barthélemi, tapissier, Rue des Saints-Pères	4500
Proverbi, Antoine, homme de confiance, Rue des Filles Saint-Thomas	750
Regnault, femme, ouvrière, Rue de Grenelle Saint-Honoré.	200
Saint-Gilles, Louis, femme, ouvrière en linge, Galérie des Innocens	400
Selleque, veuve, Rue Saint-Denis	200
Thirion, Jean, cordonnier en vieux, Rue Saint-Nicaise .	25
Trepsat, architecte, Rue de Bourgogne.	4500
Varlet, Rue Saint-Louis, remplaçant au poste Saint-Nicaise	25
Vitriée, Elizabeth, femme, cuisinière, Rue Saint-Nicaise .	100
Vitry, perruquier, Rue Saint-Nicaise	50
Warmé, N., marchand de vin, Rue Saint-Nicaise . .	100
Wolff, Arnoult, tailleur, Rue de Malte	150
Zambrini, Félix, garçon limonadier chez Corazza . .	600

The sum total was 77,601 francs ; the overplus was paid into the fund at the Mont de Piété, in order to pay the pensions.— *Note by the Editor.*

gloomy thoughts must have rushed on his suspicious
mind!   The news of the attempt soon circulated
from box to box; the public indignation was vivid,
and the sensation profound among the ministers, the
courtiers, and the relations of the First Consul; in
short, among all individuals attached to the car of
his fortune.   Anticipating the opera, all followed his
carriage; and, on his return to the Tuileries, there
opened a scene, or, rather, an orgie of blind and
furious passions.   On my arrival thither—for I hurried
there without delay—I calculated, from the mental
irritation which I perceived from the frozen glance
which his adherents and councillors darted at me,
that a storm was about to burst upon my head, and
that the most unjust suspicions were directed against
the police.   For this result I was prepared, and determined not to suffer myself to be put down by the
clamours of the courtiers nor the apostrophes of the
First Consul.   " Eh bien ! " exclaimed he, advancing
towards me with a countenance inflamed with rage;
" Eh bien! you will not now pretend to say that
these were royalists ? "   " Yes," I replied, as if inspired, and with perfect presence of mind, " beyond
a doubt I will say so; and, what is more, I will
prove it."

My reply at first caused a universal astonishment;
but the First Consul repeating with more and more
bitterness, and with obstinate incredulity, that the
horrible attempt just directed against his life was the
work of a party too much protected and not sufficiently restrained by the police—in short, of the
Jacobins—" No," I replied; " it is the work of the

royalists, of the Chouans; and I only require eight
hours to furnish the demonstration." Having thus
obtained some attention, I gave a summary of recent
notices and facts, and justified the entire police; ad-
verting at the same time to its subdivision into different
centres, in order to exonerate myself from all personal
responsibility. I even went further. I recriminated
against that tendency of the public mind which, within
the atmosphere of the government, was urged to impute
everything that was culpable to the Jacobins and the
men of the Revolution. I attributed to this false bias
the circumstance of the whole vigilance of the counter-
police being directed against individuals who were
doubtless dangerous, but who were now paralysed and
disarmed; while the emigrants, the Chouans, the agents
of England, would not have been able, if my timely
warning had been attended to, to strike the metropolis
with terror, and fill the public mind with indignation.
General Lannes, Réal, Regnault, and Josephine were
of my opinion; and corroborated by a respite of eight
days, I felt no doubt that proof sufficient would instantly be supplied in support of my conjectures. I
had soon, in fact, possession (by means of the single
bait of 2,000 louis) of all the designs of the agents of
Georges, and I was furnished with the secret of their
hearts. I was apprised that, on the day of the explosion
and the day following, four-and-twenty chiefs of the
Chouans had clandestinely arrived at Paris, from different quarters and through by-ways; that if all of
these were not in the secret of the meditated crime,
they at least were all in expectation of some great
event, and were all supplied with a pass-word. At

length the true author and instrument of the attempt were revealed to me, and the proofs accumulating in a few days, I concluded by triumphing over every incredulity and prejudice.

I had not failed to perceive that this last attempt made on the life of the First Consul had irritated his gloomy and haughty spirit, and that in the resolution to suppress his enemies he looked to such an increase of power as would render him the master. His inclination was but too well seconded through all the hierarchies of government.

His first essay as a military dictator was to pass an Act of deportation beyond the seas against those individuals among the demagogues and anarchists in worst repute at Paris, of whom I was desired to provide a list. The senate, impelled by the public feeling, and conceding all that was required, made no hesitation in conferring its sanction on this extra-judicial Act. I succeeded, but not without difficulty, in saving some forty of the proscribed, whom I caused to be struck out of the list before the publication of the Senatus Consultum authorising deportation into Africa. Through my means that cruel decree of deportation pronounced against Charles de Hesse, Felix Lepelletier, Choudieu, Talot, Destrem, and other persons suspected of being the ringleaders of plots which gave inquietude to Bonaparte, was changed to a simple measure of exile and surveillance beyond the limits of Paris. Measures were not limited to a banishment of the most violent Jacobins. The First Consul found the forms of the constitutional tribunals too dilatory; he demanded an active and inexorable justice; he wished to abstract the accused from the sphere of their natural judges. It was deliberated in the council of state, whether the establishment of special tribunals, without jury, appeal, or revision, should not be solicited as a law of exception from the legislative body.

It was my task to make it felt how necessary it at least was to abstract from the jurisdiction of the tribunals none but persons accused of conspiracies, or individuals who had attacked and robbed the diligences on the high roads. I represented that the roads were infested by brigands; accordingly, a decree was published by the consuls on the 7th of January, ordaining that no diligence should depart from Paris without having four soldiers commanded by a sergeant or corporal on the imperial, and without having a night escort. The diligences were still attacked; such was the system of petty warfare carried on by the Chouans. At the same epoch, some scoundrels, known under the name of *chauffeurs*, desolated the provinces. Strong measures were necessary; for the government felt more alarm than it permitted itself to testify. Persons accused of conspiracy were punished without mercy.

Two military commissions were erected: one sentenced Chevalier and Veycer, the persons accused of having fabricated the infernal machine, and caused them to be executed; the other pronounced the same penalty against Metge, Humbert, and Chapelle, charged with having conspired against the government. They were executed, like Chevalier and Veycer, on the plain de Grenelle. At the same time, Arena, Ceracchi, Demerville, and Topino-Lebrun, appeared before the criminal tribunal, where they were allowed the benefit of a trial by jury; but the period was inauspicious, and the public prejudice decisive. They were condemned to die, and their four accomplices acquitted. No tribunal before, on the attempt of the life of the First Consul, would have dared to condemn them on the single testimony of Harel, a hireling accuser.

The trial relative to the explosion of the 3rd Nivôse came on later. In order to complete its details, I had possessed myself, as I had promised, of the necessary proofs. There was no longer any doubt of the quarter from whence the crime originated. It was in evidence that Carbon had bought the horse and waggon in which the infernal machine had been placed; it was equally proved that he and Saint-Régent had taken back the same waggon; had provided the casks; brought the baskets and boxes filled with small shot; and, in short, that Saint-Régent, having fired off the machine, had been wounded by the effect of the explosion.

The analogy remarked between these different attempts caused a presumption that some understanding had existed between their authors, although of different parties. The only analogy, in reality, was the common hatred which induced both to conspire against the same obstacle; nor were there any other relations between them than those of a secret agency, which rendered the royalists acquainted with the terrible instrument projected by the Jacobins for the destruction of Bonaparte.

Blood enough was doubtless shed in order to strike terror into the hearts of his enemies; and from that moment his power might be considered as established.

He had in his favour all those who surrounded him. Fortune, moreover, which seemed ever watchful for his advantage, loaded him with the consummation of her favours in the great game of war. His German armies, commanded by Moreau, had resumed the offensive at the expiration of the armistice, and Moreau, following up his successes, had just gained the battle of Hohen-linden: on that occasion, and on the theatre of his glory, he exclaimed, in addressing his generals: "My friends, we have conquered peace." In fact, in less than twenty days he had rendered himself master of eighty leagues of vigorously disputed territory; had forced the formidable lines of the Inn, the Salza, the Traun, and the Ens; had pushed on his advanced posts to within twenty leagues of Vienna; had dispersed the only troops which covered his approaches; and not till he was stopped in his career by policy, or envy, concluded a fresh armistice at Steyer.

Convinced of the emergency of circumstances, the cabinet of London consented to Austria's desisting from the conditions of the alliance, and opening negotiations for a separate peace; which gave occasion for the remark that Bonaparte had triumphed for his own interest, Moreau for the peace of his country. Such were the first seeds of that rivalry which were sown between the two great captains. Difference of character, and the relics of the republican spirit, naturally produced between them at a later period an open rupture.

This spirit exhibited itself in the capital, and created there a sort of fermentation about a *projet de loi*, having reference to the establishment of a special criminal tribunal, wherever such an institution might be deemed necessary. To speak plainly, the question concerned an unlimited commission, to be composed of one-half judges, and the other military men. This project, when introduced to the tribunal, embittered the minds of all the tribunes who cherished a regard for liberty. To their view it was a re-establishment of the *justice prévôtale* of the old *régime*.

The government orators alleged that the social fabric was attacked at its foundation by an organisation of crime more powerful and more extensive than the laws. "The laws," said they, "have no longer any relation with that scum of society which rejects all justice, and which contends to the utmost extreme against the entire social system." The discussion was skilful and animated. It occupied seven sittings. Isnard, Benjamin Constant, Daunou, Chénier, Ginguené, and Bailleul advanced as the rear-guard of the public, and disputed with vigour, but with limitation and decency, the proposal of the government. It only passed by a small majority, and by means of the influence of the cabinet. The *projet* concluded with the grant of a power to the consuls of banishing from the city, where the primary authorities held their sittings, and even from every other town, all persons whose presence attracted suspicion. This grant constituted a dictatorship of the police, and it did not fail to be said that I was about to become the new Sejanus of a new Tiberius. All that the First Consul required was thus conceded.

Invested with legal dictatorship, armed with power to punish his enemies with death or banishment, the

First Consul soon gave reason to understand that his
government had no other *primum mobile* but force.
But he gave peace to the world—and peace was a
talisman which, while offering a tranquil haven after
so many storms, dissipated a multitude of clouds.

The congress of Lunéville, at the end of forty days,
produced a definitive treaty of peace, which was signed
on the 9th of February, 1801, between France and
Austria.

The possession of the entire left bank of the Rhine,
from the point where it quits the Helvetic territory to
that where it enters the Batavian, was confirmed to
France. Austria reserved in Italy her ancient Venetian
jurisdiction; the river Adige was its boundary. The
independence of the Batavian, Helvetian, Cisalpine, and
Ligurian republics was mutually guaranteed.

The First Consul had taken so much umbrage at
the opposition manifested by the tribunal against the
march of his government that, in order to signify his
displeasure, he made no reply on the occasion of the
peace of Lunéville to the orator of that body.

Other points required regulation in Italy, whence
Masséna had been recalled on suspicion of republicanism. Since the preceding month of August he
had been superseded by Brune; himself originally
suspected at the *camp du dépôt* at Dijon, and whom I
had succeeded in getting restored to favour by softening
down certain secret disclosures; for there were spies
upon every staff officer.

But, however that may be, Brune had made himself
master of Tuscany, and confiscated Livourne, and every
kind of English property.

At the solicitation of the Emperor Paul, and in deference to his mediation, Bonaparte, who from that time had designed the conquest of the two Sicilies, stopped the march of Murat upon Naples, and negotiated with the Holy See.

The treaty of peace with Naples soon followed; by virtue of which, until the establishment of a definitive peace between France and Great Britain and the Ottoman Porte, four thousand French soldiers occupied the northern Abruzzo, and twelve thousand the peninsula of Otranto. It was I who first suggested the idea of this in a privy council. The stipulations were to remain secret. By this occupation of Abruzzo, Tarentum, and the fortresses, France supported, at the expense of the kingdom of Naples, a military corps which, as occasion required, might either pass into Egypt, Dalmatia, or Greece.

The treaty of Lunéville had stipulated for Austria and the Germanic Empire; it was ratified by the Diet; and in this manner peace was established on the European continent. Throughout this affair the First Consul appeared charmed with the dexterity of his minister of state for foreign affairs, Talleyrand-Périgord. But at bottom he began to be tired of what the gazetteers of London constantly represented, his being under the diplomatic tutelage of M. de Talleyrand, and, in point of fact, of being subjected to mine, as he could not move a single step without us, whose ability was purposely exaggerated in order to render us obnoxious and suspected. I wearied him myself by constant remarks that, when governments are not just, their prosperity is only transitory; that, in the elevated sphere where fortune had placed him, he ought to quench the hateful passions engendered by a long revolution in the torrents of his renown, and thus recall the nation to generous and benevolent habits, which are the only real source of public prosperity and happiness.

But how, on emerging from a long-protracted hurricane, could anyone expect to find at the head of an immense Republic transformed into a military dictatorship, a chief at once just, energetic, and discreet? The heart of Bonaparte was not alien from vengeance and hatred, nor was his mind shut against prejudice; and it was easy to perceive through the veil in which he shrouded himself a decided inclination to tyranny. It was precisely that inclination that I exerted myself to mitigate and combat; but for that purpose I never employed any other weapons than the ascendency of truth and reason. I was sincerely attached to that personage, fully persuaded as I was that there was no one in the career of arms and in the civil order who possessed a character so firm, so persevering; such a character, in short, as was requisite to direct the government and suppress faction. I even persuaded myself at that time that it was possible to mitigate that great character, in all that it comprised of too much violence and intractability. Others calculated on a passion for women; for Bonaparte was by no means insensible to their charms; at all events, it was obvious that the fair sex would never obtain an influence over him prejudicial to public affairs. The first in this direction was not successful. Having been struck on his last passage through Milan with the theatrical beauty of the singer G——, and still more by the sublime accents of her voice, he made her some rich presents, and wished to attach her to him. He charged Berthier with the task of concluding a treaty with her on liberal terms, and conducting her to Paris; she even performed the journey in Berthier's carriage. Having a tolerably rich establishment of fifteen thousand francs a month, she exhibited her brilliancy at the theatre and the concerts at the Tuileries, where her voice performed wonders. But at that time the chief magistrate made a point of avoiding scandal; and not wishing to give Josephine, who was excessively jealous, any subject of complaint, his visits to the beautiful vocalist were abrupt and clandestine. Amours without attention and without charms were not likely to satisfy a proud and impassioned woman, who had something masculine in her character. G—— had recourse to the usual infallible antidote; she fell violently in love with the celebrated violin player, Rode. Equally smitten himself, he was incapable of preserving any terms in his attachment; equally defying the vigilance of Junot and Berthier.

While these intrigues were going on, Bonaparte one day told me that he was astonished, with my acknowledged ability, that I did not conduct the police better, and that there were circumstances of which I was ignorant. " Yes," I replied, " there are things of which I was ignorant, but of which I am so no longer; for instance, a little man, muffled up in a grey great-coat, often issues, on dark nights, from a back door of the Tuileries, accompanied by a single attendant, mounts a shabby vehicle, and proceeds to ferret out a certain Signora G——; that little man is yourself; and the misjudging vocalist sacrifices her fidelity to you in favour of Rode, the violin-player." At these words the Consul, turning his back upon me and remaining silent, rang the bell, and I withdrew. An aide-de-camp was commissioned to perform the part of a black eunuch to the unfaithful fair one, who indignantly refused to submit to the regulations of the seraglio. She was first deprived of her establishment and pension, in the hope of reducing her to terms by famine; but, deeply in love with Rode, she remained inflexible, and rejected the most brilliant offers of the Pylades, Berthier. She was then compelled to quit Paris. She first retired into the country with her lover; but afterwards both made their escape, and went to Russia to recruit their fortune.

As it was commonly pretended that war was the only element of the First Consul, I urged him to show the world that he could, when it was necessary, govern an empire in a state of calm and in the midst of pacific enjoyments. But the pacification of the continent was not enough for him; his desire was to disarm England. Hereditary rival of France, she had become our inveterate enemy, from the moment that the impulse of the Revolution had invested us with a colossal power. Considering the state of Europe, the power and prosperity of the two countries connected by the bonds of peace appeared incompatible. The policy of the First Consul and his privy council soon desired the solution of this grave question — must England be forced to make peace before the establishment of an internal and external pacific system? The affirmative was decided

by necessity and reason. Without a general peace every other description of peace could only be considered in the light of a suspension of arms.

As after Campo Formio the result was to threaten Great Britain with an invasion, in favour of which there was a strong prejudice in the more versatile and capricious portion of public opinion, camps were formed and occupied by numerous select troops on the shores facing England. A combined fleet was assembled at Brest, under the French and Spanish flag; an effort was made to re-establish our marine; and the port of Boulogne became the principal rendez-vous of the flotilla designed to effect the descent. Such was the chimera we then indulged.

On her side, England made great preparations, watching all our movements, blockading our ports and naval roads, and bristling all her coasts with warlike apparatus. She had at that time subject for alarm. I refer to the Northern League established against her naval preponderance, and of which the Emperor Paul had declared himself the chief. Its direct object, loftily promulgated, was to annul the naval system maintained by England, and in virtue of which that power arrogated to herself the empire of the seas.

It is well understood how pleased the First Consul must have been in imbuing his diplomacy with all his activity and address, in order to impart life to that maritime league of which Paul I. was the soul. All the mobiliary force of the cabinet was exerted either to captivate Paul, to win Prussia, to exasperate Denmark, or drag Sweden upon the field of battle.

Prussia, having received her impulse, closed the mouths of the Elbe, the Weser, and the Ems, and took possession of the Hanoverian territory. England now perceived that the object of the quarrel could only be decided by arms. Admirals Hyde Parker and Nelson suddenly sailed to the Baltic with a powerful naval force. Denmark and Sweden made vain preparations to guard the passage of the Sound and defend the approaches to Copenhagen. On the 2nd of April was fought the terrible battle of Copenhagen, in which England triumphed over all the maritime impediments which had been opposed to her ascendency.

Eleven days previous the imperial palace of St. Petersburg had become the theatre of a catastrophe which alone had changed the aspect of affairs in the North. On the 22nd of March, the Emperor Paul, a monarch equally capricious and violent, and occasionally despotic even to frenzy, was deprived of the throne by the only mode of deposition practicable in a despotic monarchy.

I received by *estafette*, from a foreign banker, the first tragical intelligence of this event. I hurried to the Tuileries and found the First Consul, whose courier had also just arrived, grasping and twisting his dispatch, while he walked about in a hurried manner and with a haggard air. " What ! " said he, " an emperor not in safety in the midst of his guards ! " In order to appease him, some of my colleagues, myself, and the consul Cambacérès, told him that whatever might be the mode of deposition practised in Russia, luckily the south of Europe was a stranger to such treacherous habits and attempts. But none of our arguments appeared to affect him; his sagacity perceived their hollowness in regard to his position and the danger he had run in December. He gave vent to his passion in ejaculations, stampings of the foot, and short fits of rage. I never beheld so striking a scene. To the grief which the result of the battle of Copenhagen had inflicted was now added the poignant mortification which he experienced from the unexpected murder of the Russian potentate, whose friend and ally he had become. Political disappointments thus added additional pangs to his regret. There was an end to the Northern League against England.

The tragical death of Paul I. inspired Bonaparte with melancholy ideas, and aggravated the mistrust and suspicion of his character. He dreamt of nothing but conspiracies in the army; he cashiered and caused to be arrested several general officers, among others Humbert, whom I had some difficulty in saving from his inflexible severity. At the same time an informer caused the intentions of Bernadotte to be suspected, and seriously compromised him. For more than a year Bernadotte commanded the army of the west, and had his headquarters at Rennes. Nothing could be objected to his always discreet and moderate operations. The preceding year, during the campaign of Marengo, he had prevented the disembarkation at Quiberon, and the departments of the west continued to exhibit the most complete submission.

At various intervals advantage had been taken of some republican speeches made by him in his état-major, to excite the distrust of the First Consul against him. All of a sudden he was unexpectedly recalled, and fell into disgrace. All that can be made out—for the accusation was sent directly to the First Consul's cabinet—was that the accuser pointed out one Colonel Simon as having imprudently divulged a plan of military insurrection against the chief magistrate; a plan perfectly chimerical, since the design was to march to Paris in order to depose the First Consul. It was supposed that there was reality in this pretended plot, and that it was not unconnected; that it was linked with a republican conspiracy, at the head of which Bernadotte was naturally placed, and which extended its ramifications through the entire army. There were several arrests, and the whole staff of Bernadotte was disorganised, but without much noise; above all, Bonaparte wished to avoid publicity. "Europe," said he, "ought to think that there are no more conspiracies against me." I maintained a great reserve about all the particulars which were sent to me concerning an affair which was more military than civil, and which was connected by very slight points of union with my functions. But I gave Bernadotte, whom I forbore to see, some useful directions, for which he expressed his obligations. A little time after, his brother-in-law, Joseph Bonaparte, arranged his reconciliation with the First Consul; it was the second since the 18th Brumaire. In consequence of my advice, Bonaparte made an effort, by well-deserved favours and rewards, to attach so distinguished a statesman and skilful a general to his person.

The vortex of affairs and the progress of foreign politics fortunately imparted a diversion to all these interior intrigues. The new Emperor of Russia, declaring himself for another system, caused, in the first instance, all the English marines who were prisoners to be set at liberty, and a convention signed at St. Petersburg, between Lord St. Helens and the Russian ministers, soon adjusted all differences.

At the same time the Czar gave Count Marckoff full powers to negotiate peace with the First Consul and his allies. It was sufficiently obvious that the cabinets were inclined towards a pacific system. Already England, towards the end of the year 1800 and the beginning of 1801, perceiving itself involved in a new quarrel for the maintenance of its maritime rights, while left to contend single-handed with the power of France, appeared to abjure a system of perpetual war against our Revolution. That political transition was in some degree effected by the resignation of the celebrated Pitt, and by the dissolution of his war ministry. From that time peace between the cabinet of St. James and that of the Tuileries was considered practicable. It was accelerated by the results of two rival expeditions into Portugal and Egypt.

The mission of Lucien to Madrid had also a political object—the declaration of war against Portugal by Spain, at the instigation of the First Consul, who justly regarded Portugal as an English colony. The ascendency of his brother Lucien over the minds of Charles IV. and his queen was without bounds. Everything proceeded in the interests of our politics. At the same time that a Spanish army obtained possession of Alentejo, a French army, under the order of Napoleon's brother-in-law, Leclerc, entered Portugal by way of Salamanca.

In its distress the court of Lisbon endeavoured to find safety by lavishing its treasures on its invaders. It opened direct negotiations with Lucien, and, on the 6th of June, preliminaries of peace were signed at Badajoz, through the operation of a secret subsidy of thirty millions, which were shared between the First Consul's brother and the Prince of Peace. Such was the source of the immense fortune of Lucien. The First Consul, who wished to occupy Lisbon, was at first outrageous, threatening to recall his brother, and not to recognise the stipulation of Badajoz. Talleyrand and I endeavoured to make him feel the ill effects which would result from such a public display. Talleyrand supported his argument in favour of the basis of the treaty by the interest of our alliance with Spain, by the happy position thus supplied us of an approximation with England, who, finding herself excluded from the ports of Portugal, would be anxious to re-enter them; he very adroitly proposed modifications of the treaty. In fine, the sacrifice of the diamonds of the Princess of Brazil, and a gift to the First Consul of ten millions for his private purse, mollified him so much that he suffered the definitive treaty to be concluded at Madrid.

On their side the English had just effected a disembarkation in Egypt, in order to wrest that possession from us; and on the 20th of March General Menou lost the battle of Alexandria. Cairo and the principal cities of Egypt successively fell into the power of Anglo-Turks. At length Menou himself capitulated on the 7th of August, and found himself compelled to evacuate Alexandria. So vanished the magnificent project of the Directory to make a French colony of Egypt, and Bonaparte's still more romantic project of recommencing there the Empire of the East.

The war between England and France having from that time no object worthy the trouble of prolonging the struggle, and each of the two countries being sufficiently consolidated in their government to preclude any hope of change being therein effected by the other, preliminaries of peace were signed at London on the 1st of October between M. Otto and Lord Hawkesbury. The news was received with extraordinary demonstrations of joy by both nations.

No further misunderstanding now existed between Russia and France, the First Consul having neglected nothing to gain the son and successor of Paul I. The Russian plenipotentiary, M. Marckoff, employing his full powers immediately after the preliminaries of London, signed a definitive treaty of peace between the Czar and the First Consul, to be completed by a new treaty of commerce.

This approximation, effected between France and Russia, was a master stroke for the First Consul. The extension of his power both within and without, which he too much abused afterwards, must be dated from that fortunate epoch. It was not, however, without experiencing on the score of his treaty with Russia some opposition in the interior.

When communicated to the Tribunat, where the most obstinate republicans held their sittings, this treaty was sent back to a commission charged to examine it, and report accordingly. In its report it declared that the word *subject* employed in it had

excited surprise, inasmuch as it did not accord with
the idea they entertained of the dignity of French
citizens.   It was requisite to discuss the treaty in
private committee; and there the tribunes did not the
less persevere in pronouncing the word *subject* to be
improper, without, however, pretending that this was a
sufficient motive for rejecting the treaty.

In the privy council, which took place that evening,
we had much difficulty in appeasing the First Consul,
who thought he perceived in the difficulty raised by
the Tribunat an intention to render him unpopular
and shake his power.   I represented to him, with
some energy, after having made a summary of the
state of opinion in the capital, that it was important
to temporise with the remains of the republican spirit
by an apparent deference.   He concluded by yielding
to my reasons.   The councillor of state, Fleurieu, was
dispatched to offer explanation to the Tribunat by a
note from the cabinet of the First Consul, in which
he declared that for a long time the French government had abjured the principles of dictating any kind
of treaty, and that Russia having appeared to desire
the mutual guarantee of the two governments against
troubles interior and exterior, it had been agreed that
neither should grant any kind of protection to the
enemies of the other state; and that it was for the
purpose of stating this that the articles in which
the word subject had been employed were compiled.
Everything now appeared satisfactory, and the treaty
was approved by the legislative body.

It occasioned in the cabinet a more serious incident,
which excited in the highest degree the anger of the

First Consul. In the secret articles of the treaty the two contracting parties mutually promised to arrange the affairs of Germany and Italy by common accord.

It must be well understood how important it was to England to have certain proofs promptly furnished of the existence of this first link of a continental diplomacy which united to her detriment the political interest of the two most powerful empires of Europe, who by that means became arbiters of her excommunication. The secret articles were therefore sold to her for their weight in gold; and her cabinet, always very generous for similar disclosures, paid to the faithless betrayers the sum of sixty thousand pounds sterling. Being shortly apprised of this diplomatic robbery, the First Consul sent for me to the Tuileries, and commenced by accusing at once the police and his ministry of foreign affairs—the police as incapable of preventing or discovering criminal communications with foreigners, the ministry of M. de Talleyrand as trafficking in affairs of state. I supported my defence by instancing the intrigues of all periods which no power could restrain; and when I observed that the suspicions of the First Consul carried him too far, I did not hesitate to tell him that I had reason to believe, according to information given me, that the state secret had been stolen by M. R. L., confidential secretary of M. de Talleyrand, and afterwards sent either directly to England or to M. le Comte d'Antraigues, agent of Louis XVIII., by M. B——, the elder, one of the proprietors of the *Journal des Débats*, a particular friend of M. R. L. I added that I had strong reasons to believe that this individual was a

secret correspondent of foreign powers, but that **at**
all times it was difficult for the police to change data
or simple indications into material proof; that it could
only follow the track.   The first impulse of the Consul
was to order the production of the two accused before
a military commission.   I remonstrated.   On his side
M. de Talleyrand alleged that the secretary of M. de
Marckoff, or even perhaps some clerk of the Russian
office, might be equally suspected of this infidelity; but
there was not a sufficiently long interval from the signature to the publication to permit the surmise that it had
gone to St. Petersburg previous to reaching London.

But, however that may be, M. R. L. received an
order of banishment and went to Hamburg; M. B.,
the elder, was in appearance worse treated; the gendarmes deported him from brigade to brigade to the
isle of Elba.   There his exile was singularly mitigated.

I did not fail in the course of this affair to remind
the First Consul that he had formerly laid it down as
a maxim in *haute diplomatie,* that after the lapse of
forty days there was no longer any secret in Europe
for cabinets directed by statesmen.   It was on this
basis that he afterwards wished to erect his diplomatic
chancery.

In the interim the Marquis of Cornwallis came to
France as plenipotentiary ambassador to negotiate a
definite peace.   He went to Amiens, the spot selected
for the conferences; but the treaty experienced unexpected delays, which did not prevent the First Consul
from industriously pursuing two projects of great importance, one relative to Italy, the other to St. Domingo.
I shall have occasion to speak of the first; as to the

second, the execution of which Bonaparte considered as most urgent, its object was the reconquest of the colony of St. Domingo, over which the armed negroes maintained the authority of masters.

On this matter I did not participate in the views of the privy council, nor of the council of state, where my ancient colleague and friend, M. Malouet, a man of honourable character, had just taken his seat; but he looked at this great affair of St. Domingo with prejudices which impaired the rectitude of his judgment. His plans, chiefly directed against the liberty and power of the negroes, prevailed in part, and were ruined by the awkwardness and unskilfulness of our états-majors. I received from Sonthonax, formerly so celebrated at St. Domingo, some well-written and soundly reasoned memoirs respecting the method to be pursued for resuming our influence; but Sonthonax was himself in so much disgrace that he had no means of getting the First Consul to relish his ideas; he even gave me a formal order to banish him from Paris. Fleurieu, Malouet, and all the colonial party carried the day. It was decided that, after conquest, slavery should be maintained, conformably to the laws and regulations anterior to 1789, and that the trade in blacks and their importation should take place according to the laws existing at that epoch. The result is known; the loss of our armament and the humiliation of our arms.

But the true cause of this disastrous expedition must be sought in the impulses of the First Consul's heart. In this respect Berthier and Duroc knew more than the minister of police. But could I be mistaken for a moment? The First Consul ardently seized the *happy* occasion of sending away a great number of regiments and general officers formed in the school of Moreau, whose reputation pained him, and whose influence with the army, if not a subject of alarm, was at least to him one of vexation and inquietude. He equally comprised in the expedition the general officers whom he judged to be not sufficiently devoted to his person and interest, or whom he considered still attached to republican institutions. The malcontents, who had always more or less favour in public opinion, no longer kept any measures with respect to this subject; and such were the rumours that my police bulletins became frightfully imbued with truth. "Well," said Bonaparte to me one day, "your Jacobins malignantly allege that they are the soldiers and friends of Moreau, whom I am sending to perish at St. Domingo; they are grumbling maniacs. Let them jabber as much as they like. No government could proceed if people were to allow themselves to be impeded by defamation and calumnies. Only endeavour to create for me a better public spirit." "That miracle," I replied, "is reserved for you, and it will not be your first essay in that department."

When everything was ready, the expedition, consisting of twenty-three ships of the line, and twenty-two thousand men, sailed from Brest in order to reduce the colony. There was an assurance of the assent of England, for the peace was not yet concluded.

Before the signature of the definitive treaty, Bonaparte put the second project which had engaged his attention into execution. A council of Cisalpins having been convoked at Lyons, he went there in person in January, 1802, was received with much pomp, opened the council, and got himself elected president, not of the Cisalpine republic, but of the Italian; thus revealing his ulterior views upon the whole of Italy. On the other hand, that same republic, the independence of which was guaranteed by treaty, beheld French troops establishing themselves on her territory instead of evacuating it; it thus became an appanage of France, or rather of Bonaparte's power.

In arrogating to himself the presidency of Italy, he had authorised the rupture of the negotiations; but he was in this respect without any fear, well knowing that the English ministry were not in a condition to resist, and moreover supporting himself by the secret stipulations consented to by Russia. There was so general a persuasion of the necessity of peace in England, and of the impossibility of obtaining better conditions by a protracted contest, that Lord Cornwallis, on the 25th of March, took upon himself to sign the definitive treaty known under the name of the peace of Amiens, which concluded a nine years' war, as bloody as it was destructive.

It was obvious to any statesman that the condition in which Malta was left was the weak part of the treaty. I expressed this opinion frankly in the council; but the public mind was in such a state of intoxication after the signature of the preliminaries that my precaution was considered unseasonable and vexatious. I nevertheless observed, in the debates of the British parliament, that one of the most considerable cabinet ministers of that country viewed in the same light as I did the stipulations relative to the possession of Malta. In general, the new opposition of the old

ministers and their friends considered the peace as an
armed truce, the duration of which was incompatible
with the honour and prosperity of Great Britain.   In
fact, of all her conquests, she only preserved Trinidad
and Ceylon, while France retained all hers.   On our
side, moreover, peace was a triumph for the principles
of our Revolution, which derived stability from the
brilliancy and charm of success.   Besides, it was in
reality a lucky hit for Bonaparte.

But could it be fancied that he would employ it
for the good of France ?   I had seen and known enough
of him to believe that he would employ it in order to
perpetuate and corroborate his authority.   It was also
obvious to me that the enlightened class of the English
nation, and the friends of liberty in France, did not
without regret survey an event which seemed for ever
to consolidate the power of the sword.

I commenced this new era by communicating to
Bonaparte a memoir, which I had taken pains to
make him demand of me, on the subject of the
interior establishment of peace.

After having pointed out therein the shades and
vicissitudes of opinion, and the last agitations of
different parties, I represented that France could in
a few years obtain the same preponderance over
pacific Europe as her victories had given her over
Europe in arms ; that the gratitude and submission
of France applied less to the warrior than to the
restorer of social order ; that, called to preside over
the destinies of thirty millions of Frenchmen, he
ought to make it his study to become their benefactor
and father. rather than consider himself as a dictator

and military chief; that, if decided henceforth to
become the protector of religion, good morals, the
arts, the sciences, all that improves society, he would
be sure by his example to prompt all Frenchmen to
the observance of the laws, decorum, and domestic
virtue; that, in fine, with respect to the exterior relations of France, there was every security, France
having never been either so great or so powerful since
Charlemagne; that she had just established a durable
order of things in Germany and Italy; that she had
disposed of Spain; that she, moreover, had redis-
covered among the Turks that ancient good feeling
which attached them to the French; that, besides,
the auxiliary states established beyond the Rhine and
the Alps as a barrier, expected nothing at his hand
but salutary modifications and reforms; that, in a
word, his glory and the interest of the world required the consolidation of a state of peace which
was also necessary to the well-being of the Republic.

He knew that we sympathised with the development
of his secret views. For more than a year past he
had been prompted by the advice of the consuls
Lebrun and Cambacérès, and the councillor of state,
Portalis, to a design of re-establishing and recalling
all the emigrants into the bosom of their country.
Many projects on this subject had been read in
council. Personally consulted on these great measures,
I immediately admitted that religion could not be
neglected by the government of the First Consul, and
if established by his hands she might afford him
substantial support. But I did not share the opinion
that we ought to come to a concordat with the court

of Rome, to the effect of which there was a project presented. I represented that it was a great political error to introduce into the bosom of a state, where the principles of the Revolution had prevailed, a foreign domination, capable of giving trouble; that the intervention of the head of the Roman Church was at least superfluous; that it would conclude by causing embarrassments and probably disputes; that, moreover, it was reviving in the state that mixture of the spiritual and the temporal which was at once absurd and fatal; that all that was necessary was to proclaim the free exercise of public worship, but securing revenues and salaries for that worship which the majority of Frenchmen professed.

I perceived shortly that this project was nothing more than a stepping-stone to another project of still higher importance, and of which the poet Fontanes had suggested the idea. He had remitted to the First Consul by his sister Eliza, to whom he was attached, an elaborate memoir, which had for its object to induce him to follow the model of Charlemagne in employing great officers and priests for the re-establishment of his empire, and for this purpose to avail himself of the aid of the Roman see, as Pepin and Charlemagne had given the example.

The re-establishment of the empire of Charlemagne had also occurred to my thoughts, with this difference, that the poet Fontanes and his party wished to employ the elements of the *ancien régime* for the purpose of this resurrection, while I maintained that it was requisite to employ the men and the principles of the Revolution. I did not pretend to exclude the old royalists from participation in the government, except in such a proportion as should always leave them in the minority. This project, moreover (and it was that which had most charms for Bonaparte), appéared to me premature in reference to its execution; it required to be matured, prepared, and brought forward with great address. I caused it to be postponed.

But in other respects my system of discretion and delay ill accorded with that impatience and decision of character which distinguished the First Consul. Ever since the month of June in the preceding year (1801) Cardinal Gonsalvi, secretary of state to the court of Rome, had come to Paris by his invitation, and there had drawn the bases of a convention, which the First Consul made known to his council of state on the 10th of August following.

The philosophical party, of which I passed for the protector, had exhibited indocility, and in the council itself had represented that, however powerful the First Consul was, it was necessary to take precautions in effecting the re-establishment of Catholic worship, since they had not only to fear the opposition of the old partisans of philosophical and republican ideas, which were in great numbers among the public authorities, but also that of the chief military men, who manifested great opposition to religious ideas. Yielding to the desire of not losing a part of his popularity by giving too abrupt a shock to prejudices which had their source in the condition of society, the First Consul, in conjunction with his council, consented to delay the re-establishment of the peace of the Church, and to cause it to be preceded by the publication of a maritime peace.

On this occasion I obtained concessions with more facility on the subject of a measure relative to the emigrants. Here my functions placed me in a condition to exercise still greater influence, and therefore my views, embraced in two memoirs, with some slight modifications, prevailed.

The list of the emigrants, which composed nine volumes, exhibited a nomenclature of about 150,000 individuals, out of which number there was no necessity for regulating the lot of more than 80,000 at the utmost. The rest had already returned or perished. I succeeded in obtaining an order that no emigrants should be definitively erased *en masse*, except by an act of amnesty; and that they should remain for ten years under the surveillance of the high police, reserving to myself the right of keeping them at a distance from their ordinary residence. Many categories of emigrants, attached to French princes, and who remained enemies of the government, were finally retained on the list to the number of a thousand persons, of whom five hundred were to be designated in the current era. There was an important exception to the restitution of undisposed of property belonging to erased emigrants; namely, that of woods and forests, comprising four hundred acres; but this exception was nearly delusive with regard to old families. The First Consul, of his own free-will, authorised frequent restitution of plantations, in order to obtain creatures among the restored emigrants.

It had been equally decreed that the promulgation of this law of amnesty should be deferred to a general peace, as well as a project of a law for the establish-

ment of a legion of honour. We at length reached
the epoch so impatiently expected for the display of
these great measures. From the 6th of April, 1802,
the concordat on ecclesiastical affairs, signed on the
preceding 15th of July, was sent for approbation to an
extraordinary assembly of the legislative body. It received the vote of the Tribunat through the organ of
Lucien Bonaparte, who, on his return from Madrid,
had taken his place among the tribunes. On this
occasion he emphatically pronounced an eloquent dis-
course, polished by the poet Fontanes, whose pen had
become devoted to a torrent of new power, which was
about in his case to become a golden Pactolus.

Easter Sunday was selected for the solemn promulgation of the concordat, which was done at the
Tuileries by the First Consul in person, in the first
instance, and repeated throughout the whole of Paris
by the twelve mayors of the capital. A religious
ceremony was got up at Notre Dame, to return
thanks to Heaven, as well for the conclusion of the
treaty of Amiens as of that of the concordat. I had
informed the consuls that they would only be attended
by the generals and officers on service ; a kind of
league having been formed among the superior officers
then in Paris not to assist at the solemnity. An expedient was quickly devised, for it was not safe yet
awhile to employ constraint. Berthier, in his character of war minister, invited all the superior generals
and officers to a splendid military breakfast, at the
conclusion of which he placed himself at the head, and
induced them to go to the Tuileries, in order to pay
their respects to the First Consul. There Bonaparte,

whose cavalcade was ready, desired them to follow him to the metropolitan church, and none of them dared to refuse. Throughout his progress he was saluted by public acclamations.

The re-establishment of Catholicism was followed closely by a Senatus Consultum, granting an amnesty to the emigrants. This act, which was very much cried up, singularly alarmed the acquisitionists of national property. It required all the firmness of the administration, and all the vigilance of my ministry, to obviate the serious inconveniences which might have resulted from collisions between the old and new proprietors. I was seconded by my colleagues of the home department and the council of state, which regulated the jurisprudence of the matter in favour of the interest of the Revolution.

It was obvious that the Revolution was on the defensive, and the Republic without guarantee or security. All the designs of the First Consul tended to transform the government into a monarchy.

The institution of the legion of honour was also at that epoch a subject of alarm and inquietude to the ancient friends of liberty; it was generally regarded as a monarchical plaything, which impaired those principles of equality which had obtained so easy a possession of the public mind. This disposition of public opinion, which I did not allow to remain in the dark, made no impression on the mind of the First Consul, nor on that of his brother Lucien, who was a great promoter of the project. The absurdity was pushed so far as to have it represented on government authority by Rœderer, a salaried orator, as an

institution auxiliary to all republican laws. A strong
and well-argued opposition was found in the Tribunat;
the law was designated as attacking the foundations
of public liberty. But the government had already in
its hands so many elements of power that it was sure
to reduce all opposition to a feeble minority.

I perceived day by day how much easier it was to
get possession of the sources of opinion in the civil
hierarchy than in the military order, where the opposition was not less serious for being less perceptible.
The counter-police of the palace were too active and
too vigilant in this respect; the officers called malcontents were suspended, exiled, or imprisoned. But
the discontent soon degenerated into irritation among
the generals and colonels, who, deeply imbued with
republican ideas, saw clearly that Bonaparte only
trampled on our institutions in order to advance more
freely to absolute power.

For some time past it was notorious that he concerted measures with his partisans for acquiring,
under legitimate pretences, a perpetuity of power. It
was in vain I represented in the council that a fitting
time was not yet come; that public opinion was
not sufficiently mature to estimate the advantages of
monarchical stability; that there would be even a risk
of disgusting the *élite* of the army, and those individuals from whom the First Consul derived his
temporary power; that if he had till now exercised
it to public satisfaction, because he had at the same
time exhibited himself in the character of a moderate
ruler and skilful general, he ought to take care not
to lose the advantages of so splendid a position by

placing himself either in too narrow a defile or on too steep a declivity. But I made very little impression; I was not even long in perceiving that a kind of reserve was maintained towards me, and that, in addition to the deliberations of the privy council, mysterious conferences were held at the house of Cambacérès.

I penetrated into the secret, and, desiring to act as much in favour of the First Consul's interest, as well as that of the state, I imparted, with as much discretion as possible, a particular impulse to my friends who had seats in the senate.

My object was to counteract and invalidate the plans concerted at the house of Cambacérès, and of which I had evil forebodings.

Many of our friends, on the same day, dispersed themselves amongst the most influential and most accredited senators. Then extolling Bonaparte, who, after having established a general peace, was about to re-erect our altars and attempt to heal the last wounds of our civil discords, these wise friends added that the First Consul held the reins of government with a firm hand, that his administration was irreproachable, and that it appertained to the senate to fulfil the general wish by prolonging the supreme power beyond the ten years of his magistracy; that this act of national gratitude would have the double advantage of imparting more weight to the senate and more stability to the government. Our friends took special care to have it thought that they were the organs of the desires of the First Consul; and the success at first surpassed our hopes.

On the 8th of May the conservative senate assembled, and wishing, in the name of the French people, to testify its gratitude to the consuls of the Republic, issued the Senatus Consultum which re-elected citizen Bonaparte First Consul for ten years beyond the ten years fixed by Article 34 of the additional Act of the 13th of December, 1799. A message immediately communicated this decree to the First Consul, the legislative body, and the Tribunat.

It would have been necessary to have witnessed, as I did, all the indications which the First Consul gave of distaste and constraint to conceive an idea of them. His partisans were in consternation. The reply to the message was couched in ambiguous terms; it was insinuated that the senate dispensed the public remuneration with too niggardly a hand; a tone of hypocritical sentiment reigned throughout; and this prophetic phrase was remarked: " Fortune has smiled upon the Republic, but fortune is fickle; and how many men have there been loaded with her favours who have lived too long by several years ! "

It was nearly the same language as Augustus employed in a similar situation. But the ten extra years added by the senate to his actual power could not satisfy the impatient ambition of the First Consul. He saw nothing in this act of prolongation than a first step in order to assist him in more rapidly ascending the summit of power. Resolved on seizing it with the same ardour as on the field of battle, he two days after, that is to say, on the 10th of May, urged the two other consuls, whom the constitution invested with no authority, to institute a decree purporting that the French people should be consulted on this question: "Shall Napoleon Bonaparte be consul for life?" The reading of this decree, and of the letter of the First Consul to the senate, was going on when I arrived to take my seat. I must confess, in my turn, that it was requisite for me to employ all my energy to restrain the feelings by which I was agitated during the reading. I perceived that all was over, but that it was still necessary to make a stand in order to moderate, if possible, the rapid invasion of a power henceforward divested of counterpoise.

This act of fraudulent intrusion caused at first among the primary authorities a rather unfavourable impression. But already the springs of action were prepared.

In a short time the senate, the legislative body, and the Tribunat were canvassed with a venal success. It was demonstrated to the senate that what it had done was considerably behind what was expected of it; it was proved to the legislative body and the Tribunat that the First Consul, in wishing the French people to be consulted, did no more than pay due homage to the sovereignty of the French people, to that grand principle which the Revolution had so solemnly consecrated, and which had survived so many political hurricanes. The captious arguments obtruded by the confidants and hirelings obtained the adherents of the majority; to those who objected it was thought sufficient to say, "Let us wait, the nation will definitively decide."

While the registers devoted to the inscription of

the public votes were ridiculously opened in the secretariates of all the departments of government, in the offices of all the tribunals, of all the mayors, and of all the public functionaries, there happened a serious incident which transpired, notwithstanding all the care that was taken to suppress the particulars. At a dinner, at which were assembled some twenty discontented officers, along with some old republicans and violent patriots, the ambitious projects of the First Consul were brought upon the *tapis* without compromise. When their spirits had once become elevated by the fumes of wine, some of the parties went so far as to say that it was indispensable to make the new Cæsar a participator in the same destiny as the old, not at the senate, where there were nothing but subjected and slavish spirits, but in the middle of the army, at a grand parade at the Tuileries. So great was the excitement that a colonel of the 12th regiment of hussars, Fournier Sarlovèse, famous at that time as a good shot, affirmed that he would pledge himself not to miss Bonaparte at fifty paces' distance. Such was at least the imprudent proposal that L., another of the guests, maintained he had heard on the same evening, and went immediately to denounce to his friend, General Menou, with the intention of obtaining access by his means to the First Consul; for Menou, since his return from Egypt, was in high favour. In fact, he himself took the informer to the Tuileries, and arrived there at the same moment in which Bonaparte was about to enter his carriage to go to the opera. The First Consul heard the accusation, gave orders to his military police, and immediately proceeded to his box at the theatre. He was there informed that Colonel Fournier was at that time in the pit. The order was instantly given to his aide-de-camp, Junot, to arrest and carry him before me, as a person accused of conspiracy against the external and internal safety of the state.

Apprised beforehand of the imprudent and blamable intemperance of language of five or six weak heads, heated by wine, by recollections of liberty, by the open or tacit approbation of some twenty guests, I interrogated and reprimanded the colonel. I listened to the expression of his repentance, while I did not disguise that his affair might become extremely serious after an examination of his papers. He assured me that he feared nothing on that head.

I thought at first of hushing up the matter, by reducing the rigour of the First Consul into a simple military correction. But here an accident occurred to aggravate the offence. The colonel passed the night at the prefecture, and the next day police agents conducted him to his own house, in order to assist in the examination of his papers. Although there was no indication of any meditated attempt, the idea that verses, couplets, directed against Bonaparte might be found there came into his head. What was he to do? Without permitting his design to be suspected, he locked his keepers in his room, and made his escape. The rage of the First Consul may be conceived. Luckily it had to vent itself against the stupidity of the agents of the prefecture, as I, on my side, had the evening before given him irrefragable proof that the indiscretion of the military dinner had come to my knowledge. Nothing could have excused me if so culpable a conversation, carried on before so large a number of assembled persons, had come to the ears of the chief magistrate without the head of the police first obtaining intelligence of it. I carried to him the papers of the colonel whose hiding-place I undertook to find; and I entreated him, after the examination, not to give the affair the importance of a conspiracy, as it would be doubly impolitic, first with regard to the army, and next with reference to the First Consul's position, contrasted as it was with that of the whole nation convoked to give its suffrage on the question of the consulship for life. As I had undertaken, the colonel was discovered and arrested, but with a military display which to me appeared ridiculous. The *chef d'escadron*, Donnadieu, since become a general, and the same who is now called a celebrated one, was simultaneously arrested, and sent with Colonel Fournier to a dungeon in the Temple. Thanks to my representations, the catastrophe was not tragical; it was only distinguished by deprivations, exile, and disgrace, accompanied by recompense to the informer.

The First Consul only pursued the object of his ambition with more fervour. All the solicitude of the ministry was, during six weeks, devoted to collecting and transcribing the registers in which the suffrages for the consulship for life were inscribed. Got up by a special committee, the *procès-verbal* exhibited 3,568,185 votes in the affirmative, and only 9,074 in the negative. On the 2nd of August a Senatus Consultum, called organic, conferred the perpetual power on the First Consul Bonaparte. Very little importance was attached to the manner in which this proceeding was managed. The greater part of the citizens who had voted in favour of investing him with the chief magistracy for life considered themselves as re-establishing the monarchical system in France, and with it stability and repose.   The senate believed, or feigned to believe, that Napoleon was obeying the popular will, and that sufficient guarantees had been given in his reply to the message of the first body in the state.   " Liberty," said the First Consul, " equality, the prosperity of France, shall be secured.   Satisfied," he added, with a tone of inspiration, "of being elected by the order of that power from whence all emanates, to restore order, justice, and equality on the earth."

Without reference to this concluding passage, the vulgar might really believe him born to command the universe, so singular were the ways by which his fortune had arrived at the highest point of elevation, and so much capacity did he demonstrate in governing men with *éclat*.   Perhaps more fortunate than Alexander and Cæsar, he might have reached and embraced the great chimera of universal power if his passions had not obscured his views, and if the thirst for tyrannical domination had not concluded by revolting the popular mind.

All was not yet accomplished in this quackery of the consulship for life ; and on the 6th of August, an organic Senatus Consultum of the constitution of the year XIII. made its appearance from the workshop of the two journeymen consuls, elaborated by the familiars of the cabinet, and proposed *in the name of the government.*

Since the French enthusiastically adopted the government to be in future comprised in the person of the First Consul, he took care not to give them time to cool; he was, moreover, persuaded that his authority would never be entirely established while there remained in the state a power which did not directly emanate from himself.

Such was the spirit of the Senatus Consultum of the 6th of August imposed on the senate. It may be considered as a fifth constitution, by which Bonaparte became master of the majority of votes in the senate, as well for the elections as for the deliberations, reserving to the senators, henceforward under his thumb, the right of changing the public institutions by means of organic Senatus Consulta; reducing the Tribunat to a nullity by diminishing one-half of the members by dismission, by depriving the legislative body of the right of approving, and by concentrating all the powers of government in his single will. Moreover, the council of state was recognised as a constituted authority; finally, the Consul for life caused himself to be invested with the noblest prerogative of sovereign authority—the right of pardoning. He recompensed the services and the docility of the two consuls, his acolytes, by also investing them for life with their consular functions. Such was the fifth constitution, extorted from a people as full of levity as want of reflection, which possessed very few correct ideas respecting political and social organisation, and which proceeded, without pausing, from a Republic to an Empire. One step alone remained to be taken, but who could prevent it.

In my own secret mind I saw nothing in this result but an ill-formed and dangerous piece of workmanship, and 1 expressed that opinion without disguise. I said to the First Consul himself that he had just declared himself the head of a transitory monarchy, which, according to my view, had no other basis but his victories and the sword.

On the 15th of August, the anniversary of his birth, solemn prayers were offered up to God, for having, in his ineffable bounty, granted to France an individual capable of consenting to bear the burden of supreme power for his whole life.

The Senatus Consultum of the 6th of August also conferred on the First Consul the faculty of presiding over the senate. Compelled to employ it, and still more to sound the public feeling with regard to him, he went in great pomp, on the 21st, to the Luxembourg, accompanied by his two colleagues, his ministers, his council of state, and a brilliant escort. Troops under arms and in handsome uniform lined both sides of the street from the Tuileries to the palace of the Luxembourg. Having taking his place, the First Consul received the oath of all the senators. M. de Talleyrand then read a report on the subject of the indemnities to be granted to the different princes of Germany, and moreover presented several projects of Senatus Consulta, among others, that which re-united to France the isle of Elba, since become so famous as the first place of exile to the very individual who then was reputed the man of destiny. What a consideration! What an association!

The procession, in going and returning, was not

saluted by any acclamations, nor any sign of approbation on the part of the people, notwithstanding the
demonstrations and salutations made by the First
Consul, and especially his brothers, to the crowd
assembled behind the soldiers which lined the way.
This melancholy silence, and the kind of ostentation
which some of the citizens exhibited, of not wishing to
show themselves at the procession of the chief magistrate, deeply wounded the First Consul. Perhaps on
this occasion he recalled to mind the well-known
maxim : " The silence of the people is a lesson to
kings ; " a maxim which that very evening was
placarded and read next day at the Tuileries and
in some of the public squares.

As he did not fail to impute this chilling reception
to the *maladresse* of administration, and the little zeal
of his friends, I reminded him that he had ordered
me to prepare nothing factitious, and I added, " Notwithstanding the fusion of the Gauls with the French,
we always remain the same people; we always remain
like those ancient Gauls who were represented as
incapable of bearing either liberty or oppression."
" What do you mean ? " he asked with animation.
" I mean to say that the Parisians have imagined
they perceived, in the last modifications of government, the total loss of liberty, and too obvious a
tendency towards absolute power." " I should not,"
replied he, " have been able to govern six weeks in
this pacific vacuum, if, instead of becoming the
master, I had only remained the image of authority."
" But, be at once paternal, affable, strong, and just,
and you will easily reconquer what you appear to

have lost." "There is an oddity or caprice in public opinion; I shall be able to improve it," he said to me as he turned his back.

I had a secret presentiment that my dismissal was not far off; I no longer doubted of it after this last interview. Moreover, a knowledge of the manœuvres of my enemies could not have escaped me. I had powerful ones who incessantly watched for an opportunity to overthrow me. My opposition to the last measures furnished them with a pretext. I had not only Lucien and Joseph against me, but I had also their sister Eliza, a woman at once haughty, nervous, passionate, dissolute, and devoured by the double hysterics[1] of love and ambition. She was influenced, as has been seen, by the poet Fontanes, in whom she was wrapped up, and to whom she, at that time, opened all the gates of favour and fortune. Timid and cautious in policy, Fontanes himself never acted except under the influence of a coterie, pretending to the title of religious and monarchical; this coterie controlled a portion of the journals, and had its own romantic author, making a poem of Christianity and a jargon of the French tongue. Proud of his success, of his favour, and of his small literary senate, Fontanes was inflated to the last degree in being able to intro-

---

[1] In the first edition the printer had thought it better to substitute the word *hochet* for that of *hoquet*, which appeared to him improper in the sense in which Fouché employs it. This alteration was not happy; we have replaced the word *hoquet*, a very singular expression beyond a doubt, but which is, doubtless, that used by the Duke of Otranto. It is explained elsewhere by the species of convulsive hiccups by which the sister of Bonaparte was really afflicted.—*Note by the French Editor.*

duce to the illustrious imitator of Charlemagne the literary novices whose flights he superintended, and who thought that they, as well as he, had a call to reconstitute society with the *débris* of monarchy.

This Celadon of literature, an author as elegant as pure, did not dare to attack me in front ; but in clandestine memoirs which he remitted to the First Consul, he cried down all the liberal doctrines and institutions, endeavouring to render all the men of mark produced by the Revolution suspected, representing them as the inveterate enemies of the unity of power. His theme and object was to restore Charlemagne in Napoleon, in order that the Revolution might be appeased and merged in a great and powerful Empire. This was the chimera of the day, or rather such was known to be the hobby of the First Consul and his intimate friends. On this account all aspirers after places, favours, and fortune did not fail to model their plans and views on this basis, with more or less exaggeration and extravagance. Towards this period also appeared in the department of fabricating secret writings, the pamphleteer F., originally agent of the agents of Louis XVIII., afterwards agent for Lucien at London at the time of the preliminaries, whence he had written, in a trenchant and self-sufficient tone, wretched balderdash respecting the springs and operation of a government which he was not in a condition to comprehend. Pensioned for some reports, which reached me anonymously from the cabinet, he grew bold, and profiting by the favour of Lavalette, the postmaster, he caused the first essays of a correspondence, which afterwards became more regular, to be conveyed to the First Consul. Assuming the airs of office, he descanted, right or wrong, on Charlemagne, on Louis XIV., on the social order, talking of reconstruction, unity of power, the monarchy—all things, be it remembered, quite incompatible with the Jacobins, even with those whom he called, with an assumed air of capacity, the *hommes forts* of the Revolution. This officious correspondent, while scraping together the reports of the saloons and coffee-houses, fabricated a thousand tales against me and the general police, of which he made a bugbear : such, no doubt, were his instructions.

At length, all the materials being ready and the occasion being favourable—Duroc and Savary having been adroitly sounded—it was resolved, in an assembly at Morfontaine, Joseph's residence, that in the next family council, at which Cambacérès and Lebrun should assist, a memoir should be read, in which, without attacking me personally, an effort should be made to prove that, since the establishment of the consulate for life and the general peace, the ministry of police was a useless and dangerous power; useless against the royalists, who, now disarmed and subjected, only required to rally round the government; dangerous as being of republican institution, and forming the mock thunder of incurable anarchists who found therein pay and protection. From thence it was inferred that it would be impolitic to leave so great a power in the hands of a single man ; that it was consigning to his mercy the whole machine of government. The project of Rœderer, the factotum of Joseph, came next, the object of which was to concentrate the functions of the police in the minister of justice; namely, in the hands of Regnier, under the name of grand judge.

When I was informed of this hotch-potch, and before the decree of the consuls was signed, I could not help telling my friends that I was superseded by a *grosse bête;* and it was true. The dull and heavy Regnier was never called by any other name from that time but that of the *gros juge.*

I did nothing to parry the blow, so prepared was I for it. Accordingly my confidence and tranquillity astonished the First Consul, who, at the end of my final task, said to me: " M. Fouché, you have well served the government, which will not confine itself to the rewards which it has just conferred upon you; for from this time you will constitute a portion of the first body of the state. It is with regret that I part with a man of your merit; but it has been indispensable to prove to Europe that I have frankly united with the pacific system, and that I confidently repose on the love of Frenchmen. In the new arrangement which I have just decreed the police will henceforward be no more than a branch of the ministry of justice; and that will be no sufficient field for you. But be assured that I will neither renounce your counsels nor your services—there is no dismissal in this case; and do not suffer yourself to be annoyed by the idle gossip of the saloons of the Faubourg Saint-Germain, nor by that of the pot-houses where the old orators of the clubs assemble, at whom we have so often laughed together."

After thanking him for the testimonials of satisfaction which he deigned to give me, I did not dissemble that the changes which he had thought fit to decide on had by no means taken me by surprise. "What! you had some idea of it?" exclaimed he. "Without being precisely sure," I replied, "I had prepared myself for it, in consequence of certain hints and whisperings which reached my ears."

I begged him to believe that no personal interest entered into the composition of my regret; that I was only moved by the extreme solicitude which I had always felt for his person and government; that these sentiments induced me to beg permission to send him in writing my last reflections on the present condition of affairs. "Communicate to me all you wish, citizen senator," he rejoined; "all that comes from you will always attract my notice."

I requested and obtained an audience for the next day, in which I proposed to furnish him with a detailed statement of the state of the secret funds belonging to my department.

I went immediately to compile my closing report, for which I had already provided notes. It was brief and nervous. I began by representing to the First Consul that to my view nothing was less certain than the continuance of peace, a circumstance which I endeavoured to prove by laying open the germs of more than one future war. I added that, in such a state of things, and while public opinion was not favourable to the encroachments of power, it would be impolitic to divest the supreme magistracy of the security afforded by a vigilant police: that, far from slumbering in imprudent security at a moment when the permanence of the executive authority had been abruptly decided, it was expedient to conciliate public opinion, and attach all parties to the new order of things; that this could not be effected except by abjuring all kinds of prejudices and distastes against particular men; that while disapproving the measures which had prevailed in the council, I had always expressed myself with a view to the interest of the First Consul, as those of his most devoted and intimate servants may also have done; that our intentions were in all cases the same, but our views and measures were different; that if there was a perseverance in erroneous views, the issue would be without intending it an intolerable oppression or a counter-revolution; that it was more especially indispensable to avoid transmitting the public affairs to the mercy of imprudent hands, or of a coterie of political eunuchs, who, at the first shock, would surrender the state to royalists and foreigners; that it was in bold opinions and in new-created interest that a substantial support was to be looked for; that the support of the army would not suffice to maintain a power too colossal not to excite the greatest alarm in Europe; that too much solicitude could not be shown not to commit the new destinies of France to the chances of new wars, which would of necessity flow from the armed truce in which the respective powers at present reposed; that, before re-entering the arena, it was requisite to be assured of the affection of the nation, and to rally round the government, not disturbers, anarchists, and counter-revolutionists, but straightforward men of character, who would find no security nor well-being for themselves except by maintaining it; that they were to be found among the men of 1789, and all the discreet friends of liberty, who, detesting the excesses of the Revolution, looked to the establishment of a strong and moderate government; and, in fine, that in the precarious situation in which France and Europe then were, the chief of the state could not retain his sword in the scabbard and resign himself to a satisfactory security except when surrounded by his friends, and preserved by them. Then came the application of my views and my system to the different parties which divided us, parties whose passions and colours, it is true, became weaker and weaker every day, but whom a shock, an imprudence, repeated faults, and a new war, might awaken and bring into collision.

The next day I remitted to him this memoir, which was in some sort my political testament; he received it with an affected affability. I next brought under his notice a detailed account of my secret management; and seeing with surprise that I had an enormous reserve of near two millions four hundred thousand francs, " Citizen senator," said he to me, " I shall be more generous and equitable than Sieyes was in respect to that poor devil Roger Ducos, in appropriating to himself the amount of the funds of the expiring Directory : keep the half of the sum which you consigned to me; it is not too much as a mark of my personal and private satisfaction; the other half will go into the fund of my private police, which, in conformity with your sagacious advice, will receive a new impulse, and on the subject of which I must entreat you to furnish me often with your ideas."

Affected by this conduct, I thanked the First Consul for thus raising me to the level of the best remunerated men of his government (he had just conferred upon me the senatorship of Aix); and I protested that I should always remain devoted to the interest of his glory.

I was sincerely persuaded then, as I am now, that in suppressing the general police he had no other object than to disembarrass himself of an institution which, being incapable of saving what he had himself overthrown, appeared to him more formidable than useful; it was the instrument which he at that time feared more than the hands which controlled it. But he had not the less yielded to an intrigue, by suffering himself to be deluded on the score of the motives alleged against me by my adversaries. In one word, Bonaparte, secured by the general peace against the machinations of the royalists, imagined that he had no longer any other enemies than those of the Revolution; and as he was incessantly told that these men were attached to a department of government, which, dating its birth from the Revolution, protected its interest and defended its doctrines, he abolished it by that means, hoping to remain the arbiter of the mode in which he should from that time please to exercise his power.

I returned into private life with a feeling of content and domestic happiness, the sweets of which I had accustomed myself to taste in the midst of the greatest affairs. On the other hand, I found myself in so superior a condition of fortune and consideration that I felt myself to be neither injured nor fallen. My enemies were disconcerted by it. I even acquired in the senate a marked influence on the most honourable of my colleagues, but I was in no way tempted to abuse it; I even abstained from turning it to profit, for I was aware that there were many eyes upon me. I passed happy days and nights on my estate of Pont Carré, seldom coming to Paris. In the autumn of 1802, when it pleased the First Consul to give me a public mark of favour and confidence, I was called upon to constitute a part of a commission charged with holding a conference with the deputies of the different Swiss cantons, a country too near France not to influence it by a powerful interference. By its geographical position Switzerland appeared destined to be the bulwark of that most accessible part of France, which possesses no other military frontiers than its passes; and, if I may so say, no other sentinels than its peasantry. Under this point of view, the political situation of Switzerland had two more claims on the attention of the First Consul, since he had not a little contributed, after the peace of Campo Formio, to induce the Directory to invade and occupy it in a military manner. His experience, and the comprehension of his views, caused him to perceive that this once it was expedient to avoid the same errors and the same excesses. His measures were much more adroit and skilful.

The independence of Switzerland had just been recognised by the treaty of Lunéville. This treaty secured to her the right of providing herself with such a government as best suited her. She thought herself indebted to the First Consul for her independence;

and he fully expected that the Swiss would make an abusive exercise of their emancipation. In fact, they were torn to pieces by two opposite factions; namely, the unionist, or democratic party, which desired a republic one and indivisible; and the federalist party, or the men of the old aristocracy, who demanded the ancient institutions. The unionist party was engendered by the French Revolution; the other was that of the *ancien régime*, and it leant secretly towards Austria; between these two factions the moderate or neutral party balanced. Abandoned to themselves during the year 1802, the unionists and the federalists came to blows and civil war, each party by turns secretly encouraged by our minister Verninac, in conformity with the instructions of the cabinet of the Tuileries, the policy of which tended to a *dénouement* skilfully calculated, and on that account inevitable. The federalist party having got the upper hand, the unionists threw themselves into the arms of France. This was what the First Consul expected. He suddenly caused his aide-de-camp Rapp to make his appearance, as the bearer of a proclamation, in which he spoke in the tone of a master rather than a mediator, ordering all the parties to lay down their arms, and causing a military occupation of Switzerland by a *corps d'armée* under the orders of General Ney. In yielding to force, the last federal Diet yielded none of its rights. On that account the confederated cantons were treated as conquered countries; and Bonaparte was seen to proceed to his task of mediator as if he were going to a conquest which was the prize of his achievements. In this manner the last efforts of the

Swiss to recover their ancient laws and government became abortive.

The delegates of the two parties had their rendezvous at Paris, in order to implore the powerful interposition of the mediator. Thirty-six deputies of the unionists proceeded there. The federalists were more dilatory, so much repugnance had they to a proceeding which they regarded as a humiliation; their delegates nevertheless arrived, to the number of fifteen, and the whole were assembled at Paris in the month of December. It was then that the First Consul nominated the commission charged with the function of conferring with them, and maturing such an act of mediation as should terminate the troubles of Switzerland. This commission, over which the senator Barthélemi presided, was composed of two senators, the president and myself being therein comprised, and of the two councillors of state, Rœderer and Demeunier. The choice of the president could not have been more happy. As well as the senator Barthélemi, I was assailed by the worthy Swiss, who resorted to us as if we composed an Areopagus. It was in vain that I told them that all ulterior decision would depend on the will of the First Consul, of which we were only the reporters; they persisted in attributing to me in particular a great influence; my closet and my *salon* were never empty.

The conferences opened; and in the first sitting, held on the 10th of December, our president read to the delegates a letter in which the First Consul disclosed to them his intention. "Nature," said he, "has made your state federative; the attempt to vanquish it would not be wise." This oracle was a thunderbolt for the unionist party; it was quite upset by it. However, to moderate the triumph of the federalists, who already conceived that the ancient order of things was about to revive, the consular letter added: "A renunciation of all privileges is your primary want, and your first duty." Thus there was an end of the ancient aristocracy. The close of the letter contained the express declaration that France and the Italian republic would never permit the establishment in Switzerland of a system tending to favour the interests of the enemies of Italy and France.

I immediately proposed that the *consulta* should nominate a commission of five members, with whom the consular commission and the First Consul himself might confer. The next day, 12th of December, Bonaparte had a conference, in our presence, with the committee of the *consulta*, in which his intentions were more clearly expressed. A third party immediately formed itself, which concluded by supplanting the unionists and the federalists, whom we had determined to neutralise. A tolerably strong opposition of views and interests gave place to very animated discussions, which, sometimes interrupted and sometimes resumed, were protracted till the 24th of January, 1803. That day the First Consul put a stop to them, in causing the *consulta* to be called upon to name commissioners who should receive from his hand the act of mediation which he had just completed (in conformity with our reports and views), an act on which they would be permitted to offer their opinions. Convoked to a new conference, which lasted nearly eight hours, the Swiss commissioners obtained different modifications in the project of the constitution; and, on the 19th of February, received from the hand of the First Consul, in a solemn sitting, the act of mediation which was to govern their country. This act imposed a new federative compact on Switzerland; and, moreover, decided the particular constitution of each canton. The next morning, the *consulta* having been dismissed, the consular commission, of which I composed a part, closed it sittings and its *procès verbaux*.

Thus finished the interference of the French government with the internal affairs of Switzerland.

It would be difficult, I imagine, to conceive a transitory *régime* more conformable with the real wants of its inhabitants. Besides, never did Bonaparte less abuse his vast preponderance; and Switzerland is, without contradiction, of all states, near or distant, over which he has exerted his influence, that to which he exhibited most leniency in his authority during the fifteen years of his ascendency and glory. In order to pay a proper tribute to truth, I will add that the act of mediation in Switzerland was impregnated as much as possible with the conciliatory and characteristically moderate spirit of my colleague Barthélemi; and I dare affirm on my side that I seconded his views to the utmost of my capacity and power. I had on this subject many particular conferences with the First Consul.

But how little did his conduct with reference to the rest of Europe resemble his moderate policy towards our neighbours the Swiss!

Everything had also been matured in order to strike a powerful blow at the Germanic confederation, the demolition of which was about to be set on foot.

The affair of the indemnities to be given to those members of the Germanic body who, either entirely or in part, had been deprived of their estates and possessions, as well by various cessions as by the reunion of the left bank of the Rhine to France, had been sent back to an extraordinary deputation of the Empire. The extraordinary commission was opened at Ratisbon in the summer of 1801, under the mediation of France and Russia. Its operations awakened all our intriguers in diplomacy; they composed a mine of it, which they exploded with an audacity which at first revolted the chief magistrate, but which he could not repress in consequence of the great number of high personages connected with it. He was, besides, naturally indulgent to all exactions which pressed upon foreign nations. In this important affair our influence predominated over the Russian. The extraordinary commission did not give in its report, after its forty-sixth sitting, till the 23rd of February, 1803, at the very epoch when the Swiss mediation terminated. The activity of intriguers, and the disgraceful proceedings which occurred during this long interval, especially in proportion as it approached its term, may be conceived from this: When complaints arrived that great rogueries had been detected, everything was imputed to the management of the public offices, where there were nothing but subordinate agents, while the whole culpability really was derived from certain cabinets and certain *boudoirs* where indemnities and principalities were put up for sale. Although I was no longer in office, it was always to me that complaints and disclosures with regard to denials of justice were transmitted; it was obstinately concluded that I still retained my influence and the ear of the master.

But it was not on the side of Germany, already fallen into obvious decay, that the tempest which was about to bring back upon us the scourges of war and revolutions matured its elements; it was beyond the straits of Calais. What I had foreseen was realised by a series of irresistible causes. The enthusiasm which the peace of Amiens had excited in England was not of long duration. The English cabinet, on its guard, and placing little reliance on the sincerity of the First Consul, delayed, under certain pretexts, to give up its possession of the Cape of Good Hope, Malta, and Alexandria in Egypt. But this only referred to political relations; Bonaparte was in that respect less assiduous than with reference to the maintenance of his personal authority, which, in the English papers continued to be attacked with a virulence to which he could not become accustomed. His police was then so feeble that it was soon seen to struggle without dignity, and without success, against the press and the intrigues of the English. To every memorial presented against the invectives of the London journalists, the ministers of Great Britain replied that it was one consequence of the liberty of the press; that they were themselves exposed to it; and that there was no recourse against such an abuse but the law. Blinded by his anger, and ill-advised, the First Consul fell into the snare; he committed himself with the pamphleteer Peltier,[1] who was only sentenced to a fine, in order

[1] Author of the " Ambigu," and a multitude of very witty pamphlets against Bonaparte and his family.

to triumph with more effect over his adversary. A subscription was instantly set on foot by the most influential classes in England, to put him in a condition to carry on a paper war against Bonaparte, before which the *Moniteur* and the *Argus* turned pale.

Hence the resentment which Bonaparte felt against England. "Every wind which blows," said he, "from that direction brings nothing but contempt and hatred against my person." From that time he concluded that the peace could not benefit him; that it would not leave him sufficient facility to aggrandise his dominion externally, and would impede the extension of his internal power; that, moreover, our daily relations with England modified our political ideas and revived our thoughts of liberty. From that moment he resolved to deprive us of all connection with a free people. The grossest invectives against the government and institutions of England soiled our public journals, which assumed a surly and wrathful character. Possessing neither a superior police nor public spirit, the First Consul had recourse to the artifices of his minister of foreign affairs, in order to give a false colour to French opinion. Heavy clouds now obscured the peace, which had become problematical, but to which Bonaparte still clung involuntarily through a kind of presentiment of fatal catastrophes.

Beyond La Manche everything was becoming hostile, and the complaints against the First Consul were explicitly expressed. He was reproached with the incorporation of Piedmont and the isle of Elba; he was accused of having disposed of Tuscany and kept Parma; of having imposed new laws on the Ligurian and

Helvetian republics; of having united in his own person the government of the Italian republic; of treating Holland like a French province; of collecting considerable forces on the shores of Brittany, under the pretext of a new expedition to St. Domingo; of having stationed another corps the importance of which was was quite out of proportion with its avowed object—that of taking possession of Louisiana—at the mouth of the Meuse; in conclusion, of having sent officers of artillery and engineers in the guise of commercial agents to explore the harbours and ship-roads of Great Britain, in order, in this manner, to prepare, in the midst of peace, for a clandestine invasion of the shores of England.

The only complaint which the First Consul could adduce against the English was comprised in their refusal to give up Malta. But they replied that political changes effected since the treaty of Amiens rendered that restitution impossible without some preliminary arrangements.

It is certain that sufficient circumspection was not employed in the political operations directed against England. If Bonaparte had desired the maintenance of peace, he would sedulously have avoided giving umbrage and inquietude to that power, on the score of its Indian possessions, and would have abstained from applauding the braggadocio of the mission of Sebastiani into Syria and Turkey. His imprudent interview with Lord Whitworth accelerated the rupture. I foresaw from that time that he would quickly pass from a certain degree of moderation as chief of the government to acts of provocation.

Such was the decree of the 22nd of May, 1803, ordering the arrest of all Englishmen who were on business or on their travels in France. There had never been till then an example of such a violence against the rights of nations. How could M. de Talley-rand lend himself to become the principal instrument of so outrageous an act—he who had always given express assurance to the English residing in Paris that they would, after the departure of their ambassador, enjoy the protection of the government to as great an extent as during his stay? If he had had the courage to resign, what would have become of Napoleon without a superior police, and without a minister capable of counterpoising the politics of Europe? How many other complaints should we then have had to express, how many other accusations to exhibit on the subject of more monstrous co-operations! I thought myself lucky at that time to be no longer in office. Who can answer for himself? I also might have yielded like another; but at all events I should have recorded my resistance, and made a protest of my disapprobation.

Without more delay Bonaparte took possession of the electorate of Hanover, and ordered the blockade of the Elbe and Weser. All his thoughts were directed towards the execution of his great project for invading the enemy's shores. The cliffs of Ostend, of Dunkirk, and Boulogne were covered with camps; the squadrons at Toulon, Rochfort, and Brest were fitted out; our docks were crowded with pinnaces, praams, sloops, and gunboats. England on her side took her measures of defence; the force of her navy

was raised to four hundred and sixty-nine ships of
war, and a flotilla of eight hundred vessels guarded
her coasts ; all her national population rushed to
arms ; camps were erected on the heights of Dover
and in the counties of Sussex and Kent; the two
armies were only separated by the Channel, and the
enemy's flotilla came and insulted ours, under the
protection of a coast lined with cannon.

In this manner formidable preparations on both
sides indicated the revival of the maritime war, which
was a prelude more or less proximate of a universal
war.	A more serious political motive had accelerated
the rupture on the part of England.	The cabinet of
London had early notice that Bonaparte was preparing, in the silence of his closet, all the necessary
steps for getting himself declared Emperor, and for
reviving the empire of Charlemagne.

Ever since my retreat from public affairs the First
Consul was persuaded that the opposition which he
would experience to his coronation would be very
feeble, republican ideas having fallen into discredit.
All the reports that came from Paris agreed on this
point, that he would soon encircle his head with the
diadem of kings.	That which particularly awakened
the notice of the cabinet of London was the proposal
made to the house of Bourbon to transfer to the
First Consul their rights to the throne of France.
Not daring to make the proposal directly himself, he
availed himself for the purpose of this negotiation of
the Prussian cabinet, which he moulded as he pleased.
The minister Haugwitz employed M. de Meyer, president of the regency of Warsaw, who offered to

Louis XVIII. indemnities and a magnificent establishment in Italy.   But, nobly inspired, the King made
this well-known admirable reply: "I know not what
may be the designs of Providence respecting my family
and myself; but I know the obligations which He has
imposed upon me by the rank to which He has pleased
to call me.   As a Christian, I will fulfil these obligations
to my last breath; as a son of St. Louis, I shall, from
his example, know how to respect myself, even in
chains; as a successor of Francis I., I at least desire
the ability to say with him, 'We have lost everything
but our honour.'"   All the French princes concurred
with this noble declaration.   I have expatiated on this
fact, because it serves to explain what I have to say
on the subject of the conspiracy of Georges and
Moreau, and of the murder of the Duke d'Enghien.

The ill success of the overture to the princes having
retarded the development of Bonaparte's plan, the rest
of the year (1803) passed in expectation.   An air was
assumed of being exclusively occupied with preparations for invasion.   But a double danger appeared
imminent at London; and there the conspiracy of
Georges Cadoudal was devised, upon the sole foundation of discontent in Moreau, who was known to be in
opposition to Bonaparte.   There was not the least idea
of harmonising and uniting the two extreme parties—
the armed royalists on the one hand and the in-
pendent patriots on the other.   To cement such an
alliance was beyond the power of the agents who interfered in it.   Intriguers could only conduct it to a
false result.   The discovery of a solitary branch of the
conspiracy rendered the whole abortive.   When Réal

had received the first disclosures of Querelle, who was sentenced to death, and had given an account of them, the First Consul, in the first instance, refused to give them credit. I was consulted, and I perceived traces of a plot which it was necessary to penetrate and follow. I could from that moment have caused the re-establishment of the police administration and resumed the reins of it myself, but I took care not to do so, and eluded it. I yet awhile saw nothing clear in the horizon. I admitted with candour that the *gros-juge* was incapable of detecting and transacting an affair of so much moment; but I cried up Desmarets, chief of the secret division, and Réal, councillor of state, as two excellent bloodhounds and well-trained explorers. I said that Réal, having had the good fortune to make the discovery, it was proper to give him the confidential employment of accomplishing his work. He was put at the head of an extraordinary commission, with *carte blanche*, and he was permitted to call in the aid of the military power, Murat having been appointed governor of Paris.

Proceeding from discovery to discovery, Pichegru was next arrested, and afterwards Moreau and Georges. Bonaparte recognised in the nature of this conspiracy, and especially in the implication of Moreau, a stroke of fortune which secured to him possession of the Empire; he thought that it would be sufficient to characterise Moreau as a conspirator in order to denationalise him. This mistake, and the assassination of the Duke d'Enghien, very nearly caused his ruin.

I was one of the first to obtain a knowledge of the mission of Caulaincourt and Ordener to the banks of

the Rhine; but when I was informed that the telegraph
had just announced the arrest of the prince, and that
an order to transfer him from Strasburg to Paris was
given, I foresaw the catastrophe, and I trembled for
the life of the noble victim. I hurried to Malmaison,
where the First Consul then was; it was the 29th
Ventôse (20th of March, 1804). I arrived there at
nine o'clock in the morning, and I found him in a
state of agitation, walking by himself in the park. I
entreated permission to say a word to him about the
great event of the day. "I see," said he, "what
brings you; I am about this day to strike a great and
necessary blow." I represented to him that France
and Europe would be roused against him, if he did
not supply undeniable proof that the duke had conspired against his person at Ettenheim. "What necessity is there for proof?" he exclaimed. "Is he not
a Bourbon, and the most dangerous of all of them."
I persisted in offering arguments of policy calculated
to silence the reasons of state. But all in vain; he
concluded by impatiently telling me, "Have not you
and your friends told me a thousand times that I should
conclude by becoming the General Monk of France, and
by restoring the Bourbons? Very well! there will no
longer be any way of retreating. What stronger
guarantee can I give to the Revolution, which you
have cemented by the blood of a king? It is besides
indispensable to bring things to a conclusion; I am
surrounded by plots; I must imprint terror or perish."
In saying these last words, which left nothing more
to hope, he had approached the castle. I saw M. de
Talleyrand arrive, and a moment after the two consuls

Cambacérès and Lebrun.   I regained my carriage, and re-entered my own house in a state of consternation.

The next day I learned that after my departure a council had been held, and that Savary had proceeded at night to the execution of the unfortunate victim; atrocious circumstances were quoted. Savary had revenged himself, it was reported, of having missed his prey in Normandy, where he had flattered himself with having ensnared, by means of the network of the conspiracy of Georges, the Duke de Berri and the Count d'Artois, whom he would have more willingly sacrificed than the Duke d'Enghien.[1]   Réal assured me that he was so little prepared for the nocturnal execution that he had departed in the morning to go to the prince at Vincennes, expecting to conduct him to Malmaison, and conceiving that the First Consul would finish the affair in a magnanimous manner.   But a *coup d'état* appeared indispensable to impress Europe with terror, and eradicate all the germs of conspiracy against his person.

Indignation, which I had foreseen, broke out in the most sanguinary manner. I was not the person who hesitated to express himself with the least restraint respecting this violence against the rights of nations and humanity. "It is more than a crime," I said, "it is a political fault"; words which I record because they have been repeatedly attributed to others.

---

[1] Without seeking to exonerate M. the Duke de Rovigo, who has so inefficiently justified himself from participation in the murder of the Duke d'Enghien, we will just observe that Fouché labours here under a little suspicion of partiality; he did not like M. de Rovigo, who was invested subsequently with his post as minister of police.—*Note by the French Editor.*

The trial of Moreau created a momentary diversion, but by giving birth to a danger more real in consequence of public excitement and indignation. Moreau appeared to the eyes of all as a victim to the jealousy and ambition of Bonaparte. The general tendency of the public mind gave reason for fearing that his condemnation would induce an insurrection and defection of the army. His cause became that of the greater part of the generals. Lecourbe, Dessoles, Macdonald, Masséna, and several others, spoke out with a menacing fidelity and energy. Moncey declared that he could not even answer for the gendarmerie. A great crisis was at hand, and Bonaparte remained shut up in the castle of St. Cloud, as if it were a fortress. I presented myself to him, two hours after having addressed him in writing, in order to point out the abyss which yawned at his feet. He affected a firmness which at the bottom of his heart he did not possess.

"I am not of opinion," said I to him, "that Moreau should be sacrificed, and I do not approve of violent measures in this case at all; it is necessary to temporise, for violence has too great an affinity to weakness, and an act of clemency on your part will produce a stronger effect than scaffolds."

Having lent an attentive ear to my exposition of the danger of his situation, he promised me to pardon Moreau by commuting the pain of death into a simple exile. Was he sincere? I knew that Moreau was urged to abstract himself from justice by making an appeal to the soldiers, whose disposition in his favour were exaggerated. But better counsels and his own instinct prevailed so as to retain him within just bounds. All the efforts of Bonaparte and of his partisans to get Moreau condemned to death failed. The issue of the trial having disconcerted the First Consul, he caused me to be sent for to St. Cloud, and there I was instructed to take upon myself the direct management of this delicate affair, and bring about a peaceable issue. I, in the first instance, saw the wife of Moreau, and exerted myself to appease her profound and vivid feelings of resentment. I afterwards saw Moreau, and it was easy for me to get him to consent to his ostracism, by exhibiting to him the perspective of danger, from a detention of two years, which would place him, in a manner, in the power of his enemy. To say the truth, there was as much danger for one as the other: Moreau might be assassinated or liberated. He followed my advice, and took the road to Cadiz, in order to pass from thence into the United States.

The next day I was received and thanked at St. Cloud, in terms which gave me reason to presage the approaching return of very brilliant favour. I had also given to Bonaparte advice to make himself master of the crisis, and cause himself to be proclaimed Emperor, in order to terminate all our uncertainties, by the foundation of a new dynasty. I knew that his resolution was taken. Would it not have been absurd on the part of the men of the Revolution to compromise everything in order to defend our principles, while we had nothing further to do but enjoy the reality ? Bonaparte was then the only man in a position to maintain us in the possession of our

property, our distinctions, and our employments. He
profited by all his advantages, and even before the
dénouement of the affair of Moreau, a suborned tribune
made a motion to confer the title of Emperor and the
imperial hereditary power upon Napoleon Bonaparte,
and to instil into the organisation of the constituted
authorities the modifications which the establishment
of the Empire might exact, with the proviso of preserving in their integrity the equality, the liberty, and
the rights of the people.

The members of the legislative body assembled,
with M. de Fontanes at their head, in order to give
in their adhesion to the vote of the Tribunat. On
the 16th of May three orators of the council of state
having carried a project of a Senatus Consultum to
the senate, the report was sent to a commission, and
adopted on the same day. It was thus Napoleon
himself, who in virtue of the initiative conferred upon
him, proposed to the senate his promotion to the imperial dignity. The senate, of which I composed a
part, went in a body to St. Cloud, and the Senatus
Consultum was proclaimed at the very moment by
Napoleon in person. He pledged himself, during the
two years which would follow his accession, to take
an oath in the presence of the great officers of the
Empire and his ministers, to respect, and cause to
be respected, the equality of our rights, political and
civil liberty, the irrevocability of the national property;
not to raise any impost, nor establish any tax, except
by virtue of the law. Whose fault was it that the
Empire from its establishment was not a real constitutional monarchy? I do not pretend to set myself

against the public body of which I composed a part at that period, but I found at that time very few materials for a national opposition.

The title of Emperor and the imperial power was hereditary in the family of Bonaparte from male to male, and by order of primogeniture. Having no issue male, Napoleon might adopt the children or grandchildren of his brothers; and in that case his adopted sons were to enter into the line of direct descent.

This arrangement had an object, which could not escape the attention of whomsoever was acquainted with the domestic situation of Napoleon. It was singular; and it would require the pen of a Suetonius to describe it. I will not make the attempt; but it is necessary to touch upon it for the sake of the truth and utility of history.

For a long time Napoleon was convinced, notwithstanding the artifices of Josephine, that she would never give him any progeny. This situation was calculated sooner or later to tire the patience of the founder of a great empire, in all the vigour of his age. Josephine therefore found herself between two rocks: infidelity and divorce. Her anxieties and alarms had increased since his accession to the consulship for life, which she knew was only a stepping-stone to the Empire. In the interim, mortified by her sterility, she conceived a plan for substituting her daughter Hortense in the affection of her husband, who already, in a sensual point of view, was escaping from her, and who, in the hope of seeing himself born again in a son, might break the knot which united him to her; it would not have been without pain. On one side, habit; on the other, the amiable temper of Josephine, and a kind of superstition, seemed to secure to her for ever the attachment, or at least the attentions, of Napoleon; but the great subject for inquietude and anxiety did not the less exist. The alternative naturally presented itself to the mind of Josephine; she was even little impeded in the execution of her plan.

Hortense, when young, had felt a great dislike to the husband of her mother; she indeed detested him; but by degrees, time, age, and the halo of glory which surrounded Napoleon, and his attentions to Josephine, induced Hortense to pass from the extreme of anti-pathy to adoration. Without being handsome, she was witty, sparkling, replete with graces and talents. She pleased; and the liking became so animated on both sides that it was sufficient for Josephine to affect the air of being maternally pleased, and afterwards to shut her eyes upon the matter, in order to secure her do-mestic triumph. The mother and daughter reigned at the same time in the heart of this haughty man. When, according to the mother's views, the tree began to bear fruit, it was necessary to think of masking, by a sudden marriage, an intrigue which already began to reveal itself to the eyes of the courtiers. Hortense would have willingly given her hand to Duroc; but Napoleon, looking to the future, and calculating from that time the possibility of an adoption, wished to concentrate in his own family, by a double incest, the intrigue to which he was about to be indebted for all the charms of pater-nity. Thence the union of his brother Louis and Hor-tense—a melancholy union, which ended in rending the veil of deception.

Meantime the wishes of all parties, with the exception of those of the new husband, were at first auspiciously fulfilled. Hortense gave birth to a son, who took the name of Napoleon, and on whom Napoleon lavished marks of tenderness, of which he was not believed susceptible. This child came forward in the most charming manner, and by its features alone doubly interested Napoleon at the period of his accession to the Empire. No doubt he designed him from that time in his heart as his adopted son.

His elevation to the imperial dignity met, in all quarters, with the most chilling reception; there were public banquets without animation and without gaiety. Napoleon had not waited for the formality of the sanction of the people to hear himself saluted with the name of Emperor, and to receive the oaths of the senate, which was now becoming nothing but the passive instrument of his will. It was in the army alone that he wished to strike deeply the roots of his government; and, accordingly, he hastened to confer the dignity of marshal of the Empire, either on those of his generals who were most devoted to him or on those who had been opposed to him, but whom it would have been impolitic to exclude. By the side of the names of Berthier, Murat, Lannes, Bessières, Davoust, Soult, Lefèvre, on whom he could most calculate, were seen the names of Jourdan, Masséna, Bernadotte, Ney, Brune, and Augereau, more republican than monarchical. As to Pérignon, Serrurier, Kellermann, and Mortier, they were only there in order to make weight and to complete the eighteen columns of the Empire, whose selection was ratified by public opinion.

Murat

Engraved by Ch. Geoffroy after painting by E. Charpentier

There was more difficulty in getting up a court, in re-establishing levees and evening parties, in special presentations, and in creating an imperial household of persons elevated by the Revolution, and of others selected from the old families whom it had despoiled. It was quite right to employ nobles and emigrants; the affairs of the household naturally devolved on them. A little ridicule at first attached itself to these trans-migrations, but the world soon got familiarised with the change.

It was very obvious, however, that everything was strained and forced, and that there was more skill employed in organising the military government. The civil government was as yet no more than a sketch. The elevation of Cambacérès and Lebrun—the first in the character of arch-chancellor, the second in that of arch-treasurer—added nothing to the counterpoise of the public councils. The institution of a council of state as an integral part and superior authority in the constitution had the appearance of being a means of centralisation, rather than the elaboration of discussions and enlightenment. Among the min-isters, M. de Talleyrand alone exhibited himself in a condition to exercise the influence of perspicuity; but that was only with regard to foreign relations. With regard to the interior, an important spring was deficient—that of the general police, which might have rallied the past round the present, and guaranteed the security of the Empire. Napoleon himself perceived the void, and, by an imperial decree of the 10th of July, re-established me at the head of the police, at the same time investing me with stronger functions than those which I had possessed before the absurd fusion of the police with the department of justice.

I here begin to perceive that I must limit the range of my excursion and condense my narrative, for there still remains for me the task of expatiating over a lapse of six years fertile in memorable events. This framework is immense ; and that is an additional reason to set aside all that is unworthy of history, in order not to sketch or fill up anything but what is worthy of the graving tool ; but nothing essential shall be omitted.

Two years before the decree of my re-appointment, I had been sent for to St. Cloud, in order to have a special conference in Napoleon's cabinet. On that occasion I obtained, if I may so express myself, my own conditions, in causing the basis which completed the new organisation of my ministry to be invested with the imperial sanction.

Réal had aspired to the post as a recompense for his zeal in tracing the conspiracy of Georges ; but, though a skilful explorer and a good *chef de division*, he was neither of energy nor calibre sufficient to give motion to such a machine. But if he did not get the post, he was amply recompensed in cash down, to the charms of which he was not insensible ; and he was besides one of the four councillors of state who were united with me in the administrative department, in order to correspond with the departmental prefects. The three other councillors were Pelet de la Lozère, a creature of Cambacérès ; Miot, a creature of Joseph Bonaparte ; and Dubois, prefect of police. These four councillors assembled once a week in my closet to give me an account of all the affairs appertaining to their functions, and take my opinion thereon. I by that means disembarrassed myself of a multitude of tiresome details, reserving to myself the duty of alone regulating the superior police, the secret division of which had remained under the direction of Desmarets, an individual of a supple and crafty character, but of narrow views.

It was to the central focus of my cabinet that all the great affairs of state, of which I grasped the strings, finally converged. It will not be doubted that I had salaried spies in all ranks and all orders; I had them of both sexes, hired at the rate of a thousand or two thousand francs per month, according to their importance and their services. I received their reports directly in writing, having a conventional mark. Every three months I communicated my list to the Emperor, in order that there might be no double employment, and also in order that the nature of the service, occasionally permanent, often temporary, might be rewarded either by places or remunerations.

As to the department of foreign police, it had two essential objects; namely, to watch friendly powers and counteract hostile governments. In both cases it was composed of individuals purchased or pensioned, and commissioned to reside near each government or in each principal town, independent of numerous secret agents sent into all countries, either by the ·minister of foreign affairs or by the Emperor himself.

I also had my foreign spies. It was in my department also that the foreign gazettes prohibited to the perusal of the French people, and transcripts of which were sent to me, were treasured up. By that means I held in my hands the most important strings of foreign politics, and I discharged, in conjunction with the chief of the government, a task capable of controlling or balancing that of the minister charged with the function of foreign relations.

I was thus far from limiting my duties to espionage. All the state prisons were under my control, as well as the gendarmerie. The delivery and the *visa* of passports belonged to me. To me was assigned the duty of overlooking amnestied individuals and foreigners. I established general commissariats in the principal towns of the kingdom, which extended the network of the police over the whole of France, and especially our frontiers.

My police acquired so high a renown that the world went so far as to pretend that I had, among my secret agents, three nobles of the *ancien régime*, distinguished by princely titles,[1] and who daily communicated to me the result of their observations.

I confess that such an establishment was expensive; it swallowed up several millions, the funds of which were secretly provided from taxes laid upon gambling and prostitution and from the granting of passports. Notwithstanding all that has been said against gambling, reflecting and decided minds must allow that in the actual state of society the legal converting of vice into profit is a necessary evil. A proof that all the odium attendant upon the measure is not to be attributed exclusively to the republican governments, is that at

---

[1] The Prince de L——, the Prince de C——, and the Prince de M——.

the present day gambling taxes form part of the budget of the old government now re-established. Since it was an unavoidable evil, it became necessary to employ severe regulations, that the disorder might at least be under control. Under the Empire, the establishment of which cost nearly four hundred millions of francs, since there were thirty families to be provided with dignities and honours, it became necessary to organise the gambling-houses upon a much larger scale, for the produce of them was not solely destined to reward my moving phalanxes of spies. I nominated as superintendent-general of the gambling-houses in France, Perrein the elder, who already farmed them, and who, after the coronation, extended his privilege over all the chief towns of the Empire, upon condition of paying fourteen millions yearly, independent of three thousand francs daily to the minister of the police. All, however, did not remain in his hands.

All these elements of an immense power did not reach my cabinet there to expire without utility. As I was informed of all, it became my duty to centre in myself the public complaints, in order to make known to the head of the government the uneasiness and misfortunes of the state.

I will not therefore dissemble that it was in my power to act upon the fear or terror which either more or less constantly agitated the possessor of unlimited power. The great searcher into the state, I could complain, censure, and condemn for the whole of France. In this point of view, what evils have I not prevented? If I found myself unable to reduce, as was my wish, the general police to a mere scarecrow, or rather to a benevolent institution, I have at least the satisfaction of being able to assert that I have done more good than ill; that is to say, that I have avoided more evil than it was permitted me to do, having almost always to struggle with the prejudices, the passions, and the furious transports of the chief of the state.

In my second ministry I succeeded much more by the force of informations and of apprehension than by restraint and the employment of coercive measures. I revived the ancient police maxim—that three persons could not meet and speak indiscreetly upon public affairs without its coming the next day to the ears of the minister of police. Certain it is that I had the address to make it universally believed that wherever four persons assembled, there, in my pay, were eyes to see and ears to hear. Such a belief, no doubt, tended to general corruption and debasement; but, on the other hand, what evils, what wretchedness, what tears has it prevented! Such then was this vast and terrific machine called the general police of the Empire. It may easily be conceived that, without neglecting the details, I was chiefly engaged upon its *ensemble* and its results.

The Empire had just been hastily established under such fearful auspices, and the public spirit was so ill-disposed and hostile, that I considered it my duty to advise the Emperor to make a diversion, to travel, for the purpose of removing these malevolent and slanderous dispositions against his person, his family, and his new court, more than ever exposed to the malicious taunts of the Parisians.

He acquiesced, and went first to Boulogne, where he caused himself, so to speak, to be raised on the shield by the troops encamped in the neighbourhood. From Boulogne he proceeded to Aix-la-Chapelle, where he received the ambassadors from several powers, who all, with the exception of England, Russia, and Sweden, hastened to acknowledge him.

Then passing rapidly through the United Provinces, and arriving at Mayence, he was visited there by a great number of German princes; he returned to St. Cloud about the end of autumn. The political state of Europe required more management than harshness. One act of passion and rage on the part of the Emperor had nearly ruined all. He caused Sir George Rumbold, the English minister, to be arrested at Hamburg by a detachment of soldiers; his papers were likewise seized, and himself conducted to Paris, and committed to the Temple. This fresh violation of the rights of nations roused the whole of Europe. Both M. de Talleyrand and myself trembled lest the fate of the Duke d'Enghien should be in reserve for Sir George; and we did all in our power to rescue him from a summary sentence. The papers of Sir George had fallen into my hands, and I carefully palliated all that might have been the subject of a serious charge. The interference of Prussia, whom we secretly urged, completed what we had so happily begun. Sir George Rumbold was liberated upon the condition of never again setting foot in Hamburg, and of henceforth keeping himself at a distance of fifty leagues from the French territory; conditions proposed by myself.

I could do nothing against sudden and unexpected

resolves, and I had then no means left me of eluding or opposing those dark acts which, trampling upon the forms of justice, were exercised by a direct order emanating from the cabinet, and committed to sub-alterns over whom I had no official control. I was myself more or less exposed to the malevolence of the prefect of police. At the time of the first affair of General Mallet, he accused me to the Emperor of being desirous of secretly protecting Mallet, of having given Masséna a hint of accusations which were hanging over him, and of having suppressed papers which implicated him. Plots were talked of which had their ramifications in the army and in the high police. I satisfied the Emperor that the whole amounted to having put Masséna upon his guard against the insinuations of certain pamphlets and malicious intriguers.

Many important privy councils were held at St. Cloud, their two principal objects being to obtain the sanction of the Pope's presence at the Emperor's coronation, and to detach Russia from an alliance with England, which would have formed the nucleus of a third coalition, the germs of which we perceived in the political horizon.

The Pope was the first to swallow the bait, so imperious appeared to him the interests of religion; and so striking in his eyes was the parallel of the present times with those of Léon and Etienne, of Pepin and Charlemagne. We knew that the King of Sweden, after the murder of the Duke d'Enghien, was traversing Germany to raise up enemies against us. Snares were laid for him at every step, and at Munich he narrowly escaped being carried off. Russia appeared to me to present greater difficulties; she had vainly offered her mediation for the maintenance of peace between France and Great Britain. The murder of the Duke d'Enghien had changed its coolness into extreme indignation. On the 7th of May the Russian minister had dispatched a note to the Diet of Ratisbon, by which the Empire was requested to demand such reparations as the violation of its territory demanded. The cabinet of St. Petersburg had just satisfied herself of the falsehood of the assertions, according to which the Emperor of Germany and the King of Prussia had fully authorised the French government to cause to be seized, in Germany, the rebels who had deprived themselves of the protection of the law of nations. In short, the Czar showed himself ill-disposed towards us, and inclined for war, which would have overthrown all the plans which the Emperor meditated against Great Britain. To regain Russia, it was proposed to employ the intrigues of courtiers and courtesans; this resource appeared to me perfectly ridiculous, and I affirmed in the council that its success was impossible. "What!" replied the Emperor, "is it a veteran of the Revolution who borrows so pusillanimous an expression? What, sir, is it for you to advance that anything is impossible? you who, during fifteen years, have seen brought to pass events which were with justice thought to be impossible. The man who has seen Louis XVI. place his neck under the guillotine; who has seen the Archduchess of Austria, Queen of France, mend her own stockings and shoes, while in daily expectation of mounting the scaffold; he, in short, who sees himself a minister when I am Emperor of the French; such a man should never permit the word *impossible* to escape his lips." I saw clearly that I owed this severe raillery to my disapprobation of the murder of the Duke d'Enghien, of which they did not fail to inform the Emperor, and I replied, without being disconcerted, " I indeed ought to have recollected that your Majesty has taught us the word *impossible* is not French."

This he immediately proved to us in a most striking manner, by forcing the Sovereign Pontiff from his papal palace, during a winter of extreme severity, to anoint his head with the sacred unction. Pius VII. arrived at Fontainebleau on the 25th of November; and eight days after, on the eve of the coronation, the senate came to present the Emperor with three million five hundred thousand votes in favour of his elevation to the imperial power. In his speech the vice-president, François de Neufchâteau, still spoke of the Republic, which appeared pure derision. At the ceremony of the coronation (Napoleon himself placed the crown upon his head), the acclamations, at first extremely few, were afterwards reinforced by the multitude of officials who were summoned from all parts of France to be present at the coronation.

But upon returning to his palace Napoleon found cold and silent spectators, as when he visited the metropolis. Both in my reports and in my private conferences I pointed out to him how much he still stood in need of friends in the capital, and how essential it was to bury in oblivion the actions imputed to him.

We soon perceived he meditated a great diversion. When he mentioned in council his idea of going to be crowned King of Italy, we all told him he would provoke a new continental war. "I must have battles and triumphs," replied he. And yet he did not relax his preparations for invasion. One day, upon my objecting to him that he could not make war at the same time against England and against Europe, he replied, "I may fail by sea, but not by land; besides, I shall be able to strike the blow before the old coalition machines are ready. The *têtes à perruque* understand nothing about it, and the kings have neither activity nor decision of character. I do not fear old Europe.

His coronation at Milan was the repetition of his coronation in France. In order to show himself to his new subjects, he traversed his kingdom of Italy. Upon seeing the magnificent city of Genoa and its picturesque environs, he exclaimed, "This is, indeed, worth a war!" His conduct throughout was admirable; he paid particular attention to the Piedmontese, especially to their nobility, for whom he had a decided predilection.

Upon his return to the coast of Boulogne, redoubling his preparations, he kept his army ready to cross the strait. But success was so dependent upon the execution of so vast a plan, that it was scarcely possible for it not to be deranged, either by circumstances or unforeseen chances. To make the French fleets, composed of vessels of the line, assist in the disembarkation of the army was no easy task. It was under the protection of fifty men-of-war, which having sailed from Brest, Rochfort, L'Orient, Toulon, and Cadiz, were to rendezvous at Martinique, and then make sail with all expedition for Boulogne, that the disembarkation of a hundred and forty thousand infantry and ten thousand

cavalry was to be effected. The landing once accomplished, the taking of London appeared certain. Napoleon was persuaded that, master of that capital, and
the English army beaten and dispersed, he should be
able to raise in London itself a popular party, which
would overthrow the oligarchy and destroy the government. All our secret information showed the feasibility
of it. But, alas! he lost himself in his maritime plans,
thinking that he could move our naval squadrons with
the same precision as that with which his armies
manœuvred before him.

On the other hand, neither he nor his minister of
marine, Decrès, who enjoyed his utmost confidence,
knew how to form, or where to find, a naval officer intrepid enough to conduct so prodigious an operation.
Decrès persuaded himself that Admiral Villeneuve, his
friend, was adequate to the task; and he was the cause
of the fatal event which completed the ruin of our navy.
Nothing less was required of Villeneuve than to unite
to his twenty vessels the squadrons of Ferrol and Vigo,
in order to raise the blockade of Brest; there, joining
his own fleet with that of Gantheaume, amounting to
twenty-one vessels, making a total of sixty-three French
and Spanish vessels, he was to sail for Boulogne, according to instructions.

When it was known that he had just re-entered
Cadiz, instead of accomplishing his glorious mission,
the Emperor was for several days highly exasperated
at the disappointment. No longer master of himself,
he ordered the minister to have Villeneuve called before
a council of inquiry, and nominated Rosily as his successor. He afterwards wished to embark the army

on board the flotilla, in spite of the opposition of Bruix ; ill-treating this brave admiral so grossly as to oblige him to place his hand upon his sword—a lamentable scene, which caused the disgrace of Bruix, and no longer left any hope of the enterprise.

It might, however, be said that Fortune, while she prevented Napoleon from triumphing upon an element which was hostile to him, prepared for him still greater triumphs on the continent by opening an immense career of glory for him, and of humiliation for Europe. It was chiefly in the dilatoriness and blunders of the different cabinets, however, that he found his greatest strength.

No observations of the ministry, nor any efforts of my agents, had as yet been able to make him give up his fixed resolutions against England. He however knew that since the month of January, 1804, the Austrian minister, Count Stadion, had endeavoured to arouse the demon of coalitions in a memorial addressed to the cabinet of London, a copy of which had been procured. Napoleon also was not ignorant that Pitt had immediately instructed the English legation in Russia to inform the cabinet of St. Petersburg of it, who, since the affair of the German secularisations, was upon cool terms with France. The murder of the Duke d'Enghien kindled the fire which had hitherto smouldered under the ashes. To the note of the Russian minister at Ratisbon, Napoleon had replied by an insulting one, addressed to the *chargé d'affaires*, D'Oubril, recalling the tragical death of a father to the sensibility of his august son. D'Oubril was censured by his court for having received it.

I had just been recalled into the ministry when the
note in answer arrived from the Russian government;
it required the evacuation of the kingdom of Naples,
an indemnity to the King of Sardinia, and the evacuation of the north of Germany. "This," said I to
the Emperor, "is equivalent to a declaration of war."
"No," replied he, "not yet; they mean nothing by
it; there is only that madman, the King of Sweden,
who is really in understanding with England against
me. Besides, they can do nothing without Austria;
and you know that at Vienna I have a party which
outweighs the English one." But are you not appre-
hensive," said I to him, "that this party may slip
through your fingers?" "With God's help and that
of my armies," replied he, "I have no reason to fear
anyone!"—words which he afterwards took care to
insert in the *Moniteur*.

Whether cabinet mystery concealed from us the sub-
sequent transactions, or whether Napoleon studiously
kept his ministers in the dark, it was not till the
month of July that we were informed of the *traité de
concert* signed at St. Petersburg on the 11th of April.
The Archduke Charles had already resigned the helm
of affairs at Vienna, and Austria began its preparations.
This was well known, and yet the good understanding
between France and her appeared unshaken. M. de
Talleyrand strove hard to convince the Count de
Cobentzel that the Emperor's preponderance in Italy
ought not to inspire any apprehensions. Austria first
offered herself as a mediatrix between the courts of
St. Petersburg and Paris; but the Emperor declined her
interference. Informed, however, that military prepara-

tions were in great activity at Vienna, he caused it to
be signified to that court, on the 15th of August, that
he considered them as forming a diversion in favour
of Great Britain, which would oblige him to defer the
execution of his plans against that country, and he
insisted that Austria should reduce its troops to the
peace establishment.

The court of Vienna, finding further dissimulation
impracticable, published, on the 18th, an order which,
on the contrary, placed its troops on a war footing.
By its note of the 13th of September it developed a
succession of complaints against the inroads upon existing treaties, and upon the dependence of the Italian,
Swiss, and Batavian republics, and particularly objected
to the uniting the sovereignty of Italy and of France
in the person of Napoleon. All these communications
were shrouded with the veil of discreet diplomacy, and
the public, who had been solely occupied with the projected invasion of England, saw with astonishment in
the *Moniteur* of the 21st of September the announce-
ment of the invasion of Bavaria by Austria, without
any rupture or previous declaration of war.

What a fortunate diversion for the French Emperor!
It saved his maritime honour, and probably preserved
him from a disaster which would have destroyed both
himself and his nascent Empire. The army hastened
to abandon the Boulogne coast. It was a magnificent
one, and felt the highest enthusiasm at quitting a state
of irksome inaction to march on towards the Rhine.

The European league had for its object the uniting
against France five or, at least, four hundred thousand
men; namely, two hundred and fifty thousand Austrians,

one hundred and fifteen thousand Russians, and thirty-five thousand British. It was with these united forces that the allied cabinets flattered themselves they should be able to obtain the evacuation of Hanover and the north of Germany, the independence of Holland and Switzerland, the re-establishment of the King of Sardinia, and the evacuation of Italy. The real object was the destruction of the new Empire before it had attained all its vigour.

It must be owned that Napoleon did not think himself justified in resting his sole dependence upon his excellent troops. He recollected the saying of Machiavelli: that a prudent prince will be both a fox and a lion at the same time.[1] After having well studied his new field of battle (for it was the first time he made war in Germany), he told us we should soon see that the campaigns of Moreau were nothing in comparison with his. In fact, he acted admirably, in order to corrupt Mack, who permitted himself to be paralysed in Ulm. All the Emperor's spies were more easily purchased than may be conceived, the greater number having already been gained over in Italy, where they in no small degree contributed to the disasters of Alvenzi and Wurmser. Here everything was effected upon a grander scale, and almost all the Austrian staff-officers were virtually gained over (*enfoncés*). I had remitted to Savary, who was intrusted with the management of the espionage at the grand headquarters, all my secret notes upon Germany, and, with his hands full, he worked quickly and successfully, assisted by

[1] In his book, " Of the Prince," chap. xviii.—*Note by the Editor.*

the famous Schulmeister, a very Proteus in subordination and the mysteries of espionage.

All the breaches being once made, to effect the prodigies of Ulm, the bridge of Vienna and Austerlitz was mere play to the valour of our troops and the skill of our manœuvres. Upon the approach of these grand battles, the Emperor Alexander ran blindly into the snare; had he delayed only for a fortnight, Prussia, already urged, would have entered the league.

Thus Napoleon by a single blow destroyed the concerted plans of the continental powers. But this glorious campaign was not without its reverse side of the medal; I mean the disaster of Trafalgar, which, by the ruin of our navy, completed the security of Great Britain. It was a few days after the capitulation of Ulm, and upon the Vienna road, that Napoleon received the dispatch containing the first intelligence of this misfortune. Berthier has since related to me that while seated at the same table with Napoleon, he read the fatal paper, but, not daring to present it to him, he pushed it gradually with his elbows under his eyes. Scarcely had Napoleon glanced through its contents than he started up full of rage, exclaiming, " I cannot be everywhere ! " His agitation was extreme, and Berthier despaired of tranquillising him. Napoleon took his vengeance upon England in the plains of Austerlitz, keeping by this means the Russians at a distance, paralysing the Prussians, and dictating severe conditions to Austria.

Occupied with war and diplomatic intrigues, it was scarcely possible for him, in the midst of his soldiers, to enter into all the details of the administration of the Empire. The council governed in his absence; and, by the importance of my functions, I found myself in some sort first minister; at least no person was independent of me. But it entered into the Emperor's views to make it believed that even in his camp he knew all, saw all, and provided for all. His official correspondents at Paris were eager to address to him, dressed up in fine phrases, all the trifling facts which they gleaned from every refuse of my bulletins of police. Napoleon was above all desirous that people might be simple enough to believe that the interior of the country enjoyed a mild government and a liberality which gained every heart. It was for this reason that during the same campaign he affected to rebuke me, by means of the *Moniteur* and his bulletins, for having refused Collin d'Harleville permission to print one of his pamphlets. "Where should we be," cried he, hypocritically, "if the permission of a censor were necessary in France for making our sentiments known in print?" I, who knew him, only saw in this peevishness an indirect hint for me to hasten my organisation of the censorship and my appointment of censors. A still more serious expression of ill-humour took place upon his return to Paris on the 26th of January, after the peace of Presburg. It first showed itself at the Tuileries in a burst of displeasure which fell upon several functionaries, and especially upon the venerable Barbé-Marbois; the cause was some difficulty in the payments of the bank at the commencement of hostilities. This embarrassment he had himself caused by carrying off from the vaults of the bank more than fifty millions.

Placed upon the backs of King Philip's mules, these millions had powerfully contributed to the prodigious success of this unexpected campaign. But are we not still too near these events for us to remove the veil from before them without inconvenience?

The peace of Presburg rendered Bonaparte master of the whole of Germany and Italy, and he soon seized the kingdom of Naples. Being upon bad terms with the court of Rome, he immediately commenced to harass the Pope, who had so lately crossed over the Alps to give him the holy unction. This glorious peace produced another very important result—the erection of the electorates of Bavaria and Würtemberg into kingdoms, and the marriage of the King of Bavaria's daughter with Eugène Beauharnais, Napoleon's adopted son. Such was the first link in those alliances which at last ruined Bonaparte, who was already less interested in his own glory than infatuated with the wish of distributing crowns, and of mingling his blood with that of the old dynasties which he was continually opposing. At home, the battle of Austerlitz and the peace reconciled Bonaparte with public opinion—all eyes began to be dazzled by the splendour of his victories.

I congratulated him upon this happy improvement in the public mind. " Sire," said I to him, " Austerlitz has destroyed the old aristocracy; the Faubourg St. Germain can no longer form conspiracies." He was delighted at it, and owned to me that in battle, in the greatest dangers, and even in the midst of deserts, he had always in view the good opinion of Paris, and especially of the Faubourg St. Germain. He was

Alexander the Great constantly directing his thoughts towards Athens.

The old nobility were, therefore, now seen besieging the Tuileries, as well as my saloon, and soliciting, nay begging, for appointments. The old republicans reproached me with protecting the nobles. This did not, however, make me change my plan. I had besides a grand object in view, that of extinguishing and converting all party spirit into an undivided interest in the government. Much severity, qualified by mildness, had pacified the departments of the west, so long agitated by civil war. We could now affirm that neither Vendeans nor Chouans any longer existed. The disaffected as well as the emigrants wandered in small numbers through England. Many of the old chiefs had made a sincere submission; few held out. All secret organisations and dangerous intrigues were at an end. The royalist association of Bordeaux, one of the firmest, was broken up. All the agents of the Bourbons in the interior had either been successively gained over or had become known, from M. Hyde de Neuville and the Chevalier de Coigny to Talon and M. Royer-Collard. Some emissaries, suspected of hostile intentions, had been severely dealt with, among whom was the Baron de la Rochefoucauld, who died in a state prison. As to old Talon, arrested by Savary upon his estate at Gâtinais, in consequence of an *ex officio* accusation, he at first experienced such brutal treatment that I informed the Emperor of it. Savary was reprimanded. Talon's daughter, a most interesting girl,[1] excited general sympathy, and contributed in a great

Now the Countess du Cayla.—*Note by the Editor.*

degree to alleviate her father's fate; she herself saved some important papers. I heartily interested myself in affording relief to the victims of the royal cause as well as to the martyrs of republican sentiments. Such a system on my part at first astonished everyone; but it afterwards procured me crowds of partisans. I really appeared likely to succeed in converting the police, an instrument of inquisitorial power and severity, into one of mildness and indulgence. But a malicious spirit interfered; I was continually beset by jealousy, envy, and intrigue on the one side, and on the other by the want of confidence and the mistrust of my master.

Finding itself supported, the counter-revolutionary faction, under the mask of a religious and anti-philo-sophical society, adopted the system of traducing and removing all who had taken part in the Revolution, and of completely surrounding the Emperor. For this purpose, and with the view of commanding public opinion, it got possession of the journals and of literature in general. Affecting to defend taste and the belles-lettres, it carried on a mortal war against the Revolution, whether in the pamphlets of Geoffroi, or in the columns of the *Mercure*. While invoking the grand era of a temperate monarchy, it at the same time was working for a power without control and without limits. As to Napoleon, he attached no political importance, as an organ, to any paper but the *Moniteur*, thinking he had made it the power and soul of his government, as well as his medium of communication with public opinion both at home and abroad. Finding himself more or less imitated in this respect by other governments, he thought himself certain of this moral engine.

I was appointed regulator of the public mind, and of the journals which were its organs; and I had even bureaux for this business. Some persons, however, did not fail to observe that this was placing too much power and strength in my hands. The *Journal des Débats* was accordingly removed from my control, and placed under that of one of my personal enemies.[1] They thought to console me in some degree for this by permitting me to snatch the *Mercure* from the hands of the counter-revolutionary faction. But the system of depriving me of the journals was not less acted upon in the cabinet, and I was soon reduced to the *Publiciste* of Suard and the *Décade Philosophique* of Ginguené.

The influence of Fontanes having continually increased since his advancement to the presidency of the legislative body, he used his utmost to introduce his friends into the avenues of power. His devoted writer, M. Molé, the inheritor of a name illustrious in the parliamentary annals, produced his " Essais de Morale et de Politique," a most injudicious apology for despotism as it is exercised in Morocco. Fontanes passed great eulogiums upon this essay in the *Journal des Débats;* I complained of it. The Emperor publicly blamed Fontanes, who excused himself by his desire of encouraging such *distinguished talents in so distinguished a name.* It was upon this occasion that the Emperor said to him, " In God's name, M. de Fontanes, leave us at least the republic of letters ! '

But the game was now played; the young adept of the imperial orator was almost immediately named

---

[1] Doubtless M. Fiévée.—*Note by the Editor.*

auditor of the council of state, then *maître des requêtes*, and minister *in petto*.

It must be also confessed that the Emperor willingly permitted himself to be smitten by the charm of the names of the old *régime;* he likewise allowed himself to be seduced by the magic of the eloquence of Fontanes, who panegyrised him with dignity, whilst so many others only offered him gross and vulgar flattery. Some idea may be formed of the disposition of the public, and the tendency of literature at this period, from the fact that this very year there appeared a history of La Vendée, in which the Vendeans were represented as heroes, and the republicans as incendiaries and cut-throats. Nor was this all: this history, considered as impartial, and cried up as possessing the greatest interest, was eagerly purchased, and, in fact, became the rage of the day. All the Revolution party were highly indignant at it. I was obliged to interfere, in order to apply an antidote capable of counteracting the assertions of this historian of stage-coach plunderers (*détrousseurs de diligences*).[1]

In the meantime the consequences and political advantages of Austerlitz and Presburg were proving to be immense. First, by an imperial decree, Joseph Bonaparte was proclaimed king of the Two Sicilies, the *Moniteur* having previously announced that the dynasty then upon the throne had ceased to reign. Almost immediately afterwards Louis Bonaparte was proclaimed King of Holland—a crown, no doubt, to

[1] Fouché, no doubt, here alludes to the pamphlet of M. de Vauban, which was published at that time by the police to counterbalance the effect produced by the history of the war of La Vendée.—*Note by the Editor.*

be envied, but one which could not make up for his domestic troubles. Murat had the Grand Duchy of Berg. The principalities of Lucca and Guastalla were given as presents, one to Eliza, the other to Paulina. The Duchy of Plaisance fell to Lebrun's share; that of Parma to Cambacérès; and, at a later period, the principality of Neufchâtel was given to Berthier. In a privy council Napoleon had announced to us that he intended to dispose of his conquests in a sovereign manner by creating grandees of the Empire and a new nobility. Shall I confess that when, in a fuller council, he proposed the question, whether the establishment of hereditary titles was contrary to the principles of equality which almost all of us professed, we replied in the negative? In fact, the Empire, being a new monarchy, the creation of grand officers, of grand dignitaries, and the supply of a new nobility appeared indispensable to us. Besides, the object was to reconcile ancient France with modern France, and to cause all remains of feudality to disappear, by attaching the ideas of nobility to services rendered the state.

On the 30th of March appeared an imperial decree, which Napoleon was satisfied with communicating to the senate, and which erected into duchies, grand fiefs of the Empire, Dalmatia, Istria, Friuli, Cadora, Belluno, Conegliano, Trevisa, Feltre, Bassano, Vicenza, Padua, and Rovigo, Napoleon reserving to himself the conferring the investiture with right of succession. It is for contemporaries to judge who were among the small number of the elect.

Created Prince of Benevento, the minister Talley-

rand possessed that principality as a fief immediately
dependent upon the imperial crown.

I had also a handsome prize in this lottery, and
was not long before I ranked myself, under the title
of Duke of Otranto, among the chief feudatories of
the Empire.

Till now, all fusion or amalgamation of the old
nobility with the chiefs of the Revolution would have
called down the reprobation of public opinion. But
the creation of new titles and of a national nobility
effaced the line of demarcation, and gave rise to a
new system of manners among the higher classes.

An event of greater importance, the dissolution of
the Germanic body, was also the consequence of the
prodigious extension of the Empire. In July appeared
the treaty of the Confederation of the Rhine. Fourteen German princes declared their separation from
the Germanic body, and their new confederation under
the protection of the French Emperor. This new
federative act, drawn up with much ability, was
especially designed to isolate Prussia, and to fix still
firmer the yoke imposed upon the Germans.

This, and the disagreements which arose between
France and Prussia, had the effect of unmasking Russia,
whose policy had for some time appeared equivocal.
She refused to ratify the treaty of peace recently
concluded, alleging that her envoy had exceeded his
instructions. In her tergiversations we only saw an
artifice for gaining time.

Since the decease of William Pitt, whose death had
been occasioned by grief at the disasters of the last
coalition, England negotiated under the auspices of

Charles Fox, who had succeeded to the direction of affairs. Much was expected from a minister who had constantly reprobated the coalitions formed for the purpose of re-establishing in France the old dynasty.

In the meantime the war with Prussia broke out, a war which had been in preparation since the battle of Austerlitz, and which was less occasioned by the counsels of the cabinet than by the compilers of secret memoirs. They began by representing the Prussian monarchy as about to fall by a breath, like a house built with cards. I have read several of these memoirs, one, amongst others, very artfully written by Mont-gaillard, who was then in high pay. I can affirm that for the last three months this war was already prepared like a *coup de théâtre;* all the chances and casualties were calculated, considered, and provided against with the greatest exactness.

I considered it ill-becoming the dignity of crowned heads to see a cabinet so ill regulated. The Prussian monarchy, whose safeguard it should have been, depended upon the cunning of some intriguers and the energy of a few subsidised persons who were the very puppets of our will. Jena! history will one day develop thy secret causes.

The delirium caused by the wonderful results of the Prussian campaign completed the intoxication of France. She prided herself upon having been saluted with the name of the great nation by her Emperor, who had triumphed over the genius and the work of Frederic; and Napoleon believed himself the son of destiny, called to break every sceptre. Peace, and even a truce with England, was no longer thought of; the rupture of the negotiations, the death of Charles Fox, the departure of Lord Lauderdale, and the arrogance of the victor, were events rapidly succeeding each other. The idea of destroying the power of England, the sole obstacle to universal monarchy, now became his fixed resolve. It was with this view he established the *continental* system, the first decree concerning which was dated from Berlin. Napoleon was convinced that, by depriving England of all the outlets for its manufactures, he should reduce it to poverty, and that it must then submit to its fate. He not only thought of subjecting it, but also of effecting its destruction.

Little acted upon by delusion, and enabled to see and observe all, I foresaw the misfortunes which would sooner or later fall upon the people. It was still worse when the lists were to be entered against the Russians. The battle of Eylau, of which I had detailed accounts, made me tremble. There everything had been disputed to the last extremity. It was no longer the puppets which fell, as at Ulm, Austerlitz, and Jena. The sight was equally grand and terrible; corps was opposed to corps, at a distance of three hundred leagues from the Rhine. I seized my pen, and wrote to Napoleon nearly in the same terms I had used before Marengo, but with more explicitness, for the circumstances were more complicated. I told him that we were sure of maintaining tranquillity in France, that Austria could not stir, that England hesitated to unite herself with Russia, whose cabinet appeared to be vacillating; but that the loss of a battle between the Vistula and the Niemen would compromise all, that the Berlin decree was subversive of too many interests, and that, in making war upon kings, care should be taken not to push the people to extremities. I entreated him, in terms the most urgent, to employ all his genius, all his powers of destruction and policy, to bring about a quick and glorious peace, like all those for which we had been indebted to his good fortune. He understood me ; but one more victory was necessary.

From the time of the victory of Eylau he evinced real discretion and ability ; so strong in conception, so energetic in character, and pursuing his object, that of overcoming the Russian cabinet, with unceasing perseverance. Nothing of consequence escaped him ; his eye was everywhere. Many intrigues were formed against him on the continent, but without success. Agents were dispatched from London to tamper with Paris, to tamper even with myself.

Only imagine the English cabinet falling into the snares of our police, even after the mystification of Drake and Spencer Smith ; only imagine Lord Howick, minister of state for foreign affairs, dispatching an emissary to me with secret instructions, and the bearer of a letter for me inclosed in the knob of a cane. This minister requested of me two blank passports for two agents intrusted to open a secret negotiation with me. But his emissary having imprudently placed confidence in the agent of the prefecture, Perlet, the vile instrument of the whole plot, the bamboo of Vitel was opened, and the missive being discovered, together with the secret, nothing could save the life of the unfortunate young man.

It was impossible but that such a circumstance should produce some distrust in the mind of Napoleon ;

he must at least have supposed that the idea in foreign countries was that I was capable of being acted upon, and that I was a man who would listen to all, and take advantage of all, provided I could secure my own safety. Nor was this the only overture of this kind, for such was the blindness of the men composing the cabinet of St. James, in the interests of the counter-revolution, that they persuaded themselves I was not averse to work in favour of the Bourbons, and to betray Bonaparte. This was wholly founded upon the opinion generally disseminated, that, instead of persecuting the royalists in the interior, I, on the contrary, sought to guarantee and protect them; that, besides, any person was always welcome when he applied personally to me for every kind of information and confidence. So much was this the case that, a few months after the death of Vitel, having taken up from off my desk a sealed letter marked *private*, I opened it, and found it so urgent that I granted a private audience to the person who requested it for the next day.

This letter was signed by a borrowed name, but one well known among the emigrants, and I really thought that the subscriber was the person who was desirous of an interview. But what was my surprise, when this person, full of confidence, gifted with a language the most persuasive, and displaying manners the most elegant, owned his artifice, and dared to avow before me that he was an agent of the Bourbons and the envoy of the English cabinet! In an animated and rapid manner, he demonstrated to me the fragility of Napoleon's power, his approaching decline (it was at the commencement of the Spanish war), and his inevitable fall. He then concluded by conjuring me, by the welfare of France and the peace of the world, to join the good cause, to save the nation from the abyss ——. All possible guarantees were offered me. And who was this man? Count Daché, formerly captain in the royal navy. "Unfortunate man!" said I to him, "you have introduced yourself into my cabinet by means of a subterfuge." "Yes," cried he, "my life is in your hands, and, if it be necessary, I shall willingly sacrifice it for my God and my king." "No," rejoined I, "you are seated on my hearth, and I will not violate the hospitality due to misfortune; for as a man, though not as a magistrate, I can pardon the excess of your error and your deluded conduct. I allow you twenty-four hours to leave Paris; but I declare to you that, at the expiration of that time, strict orders will be given for your discovery and apprehension. I know whence you come; I know your chain of correspondence; therefore reflect well that this is only a truce of twenty-four hours; and even I shall not be able to save you in this short space of time if your secret and your conduct be known to any but myself." He assured me that not a soul had the least idea of it, neither abroad nor in France; and that those even who had received him upon the coast were ignorant of his having hazarded himself as far as Paris. "Well," said I to him, "I give you twenty-four hours; go."

I should have been deficient in my duty had I not informed the Emperor of what had passed. The only variation which I allowed myself was the supposition of a safe-conduct previously obtained from me by Count

Daché, under pretext of important information he was desirous of making to me alone. This was indispensable, for I was certain that Napoleon would have disapproved of my generosity, and would even have perceived something suspicious in it. Independently of the police orders, he himself gave some extremely rigorous ones, so much he feared his enemies' energy and decision. The whole of the police were set in motion against the unfortunate count, and such was their perseverance that at the moment of re-embarking for London, on the coast of Calvados, he perished by a dreadful death, having been betrayed by a woman, whose name is now an object of execration among the former friends of the ill-fated count.

It may easily be conceived that so hazardous and perilous a mission was neither given nor executed immediately after the negotiations and the treaty of Tilsit, the glorious result of the victory of Friedland.

I have now to characterise this grand epoch of Napoleon's political life. The event was calculated to fascinate all minds. The old aristocracy was completely humbled by it. " Why is he not a legitimate ? " said the Faubourg St. Germain; " Alexander and Napoleon approach each other, the war ceases, and a hundred millions of men enjoy repose and tranquillity." This trickery gained credit, and it was not perceived that the duumvirate of Tilsit was but a pretended treaty of a division of the world between two potentates and two empires, which, once in contact, must end by clashing against each other.

In the secret treaty Alexander and Napoleon shared between them the continental world : all the South

was abandoned to Napoleon, already master of Italy
and arbiter of Germany, pushing his advanced post
as far as the Vistula, and making Dantzig one of the
most formidable arsenals.

Upon his return to St. Cloud, on the 27th of July,
he received the most insipid and extravagant adulations
from all the principal authorities. Every day I perceived the change which infatuation wrought in this
great character. He became more and more reserved
with his ministers. Eight days after his return he
made some remarkable changes in the ministry. The
portfolio of war was intrusted to General Clarke,
since Duke de Feltre, and that of the interior to
Cretet, at that time a simple councillor of state;
Berthier was made vice-constable. But what caused
the greatest astonishment was to see the portfolio of
foreign affairs given into the hands of Champagny,
since Duke de Cadore. To deprive M. de Talleyrand
of this department was a sign of disgrace, which was,
however, disguised by conferring favours purely honorary. M. de Talleyrand was promoted to be vice-
grand Elector, which did not fail to furnish subject
matter for the punsters. It is certain that a disagreement of opinion upon the projects relative to
Spain was the principal cause of his disgrace; but
this important subject had as yet only been treated of
in a confidential manner between the Emperor and him.
At this period the question had never been agitated in
the council; at least, in my presence. But I penetrated
the mystery before even the secret treaty of Fontainebleau, which was executed towards the end of
October. Like that of Presburg, the treaty of Tilsit was

signalised by the previous erection of a new kingdom
conferred upon Jerome, in the very heart of Germany.
The new king was installed in it under the direction of
preceptors assigned him by his brother, who reserved
to himself the supremacy in the political guidance of
of the new tributary monarch.

About this time was known the success of the attack
upon Copenhagen by the English, which was the first
blow given to the secret stipulations of Tilsit, in virtue
of which the navy of Denmark was placed at the disposal of France.   Since the catastrophe of Paul I., I
never saw Napoleon abandon himself to more violent
transports.   What most struck him, in this vigorous
enterprise, was the promptness of the resolution of the
English ministry.   He suspected a fresh infidelity in
the cabinet and charged me to discover if it was connected with the mortification attendant upon a recent
disgrace.   I again represented to him how difficult it
was in so mysterious a labyrinth to discover anything
except by instinct or conjecture.   " The traitors," said I,
" must voluntarily betray themselves, for the police never
know but what is told them, and that which chance
discovers is little indeed."   Upon this subject I had a
truly historical conference with a personage who has
survived, and who still survives all ; but my present
situation does not permit me to disclose the particulars of it.

Home affairs were conducted upon a system anala-
gous to that pursued abroad, and which began to develop
itself.   On the 18th of September the remains of the
Tribunat were at length suppressed ; not that the small
minority of the tribunes could offer any hostility, but

because it entered into the Emperor's plans not to allow the previous discussion of the laws; these were only in future to be presented by commissioners.

Here opens the memorable year of 1808, the period of a new era, in which Napoleon's star began to wax dim. I had at length a confidential communication of the real object which had induced him to enter into the secret treaty of Fontainebleau, and to determine upon the invasion of Portugal. Napoleon announced to me that the Bourbons of Spain and the house of Braganza would shortly cease to reign. "Leaving Portugal out of the question," said I to him, "which is truly an English colony, with respect to Spain, you have no cause for complaint; those Bourbons are, and will be as long as you wish it, your most humble prefects. Besides, are you not mistaken with respect to the character of the people of the Peninsula? Take care; you have, it is true, many partisans there, but only because they consider you as a great and powerful potentate, as a friend and an ally. If you declare without any cause against the reigning family; if, favoured by domestic dissensions, you realise the fable of the oyster and the lawyers, you must declare against the majority of the population. Besides, you ought to know that the Spaniards are not a cold, phlegmatic people like the Germans; they are attached to their manners, their government, and old customs. The mass of the nation is not to be estimated by the heads of society, who are, as everywhere else, corrupted and possessed of but little patriotism. Once more, take care you do not transform a tributary kingdom into a new Vendée." "What is it you say?" replied he; "every reflecting

person in Spain despises the government. The Prince
of the Peace, a true mayor of the palace, is detested
by the nation.   He is a scoundrel who will himself
open the gates of Spain for me.   As to the rabble,
whom you have mentioned, who are still under the
influence of monks and priests, a few cannon-shot will
quickly disperse them. You have seen warlike Prussia,
that heritage of the great Frederic, fall before my arms
like a heap of rubbish.   Well, you will see Spain surrender itself into my hands without knowing it, and
afterward applaud itself.   I have there an immense
party.   I have resolved to continue in my own dynasty
the family system of Louis XIV., uniting Spain to the
destinies of France.   I am desirous of availing myself
of the only opportunity afforded me by fortune of re-
generating Spain, of detaching it entirely from England,
and of uniting it inseparably to my system.   Reflect
that the sun never sets on the immense inheritance of
Charles V., and that I shall have the Empire of both
worlds."

I found that it was a design resolved upon, that all
the counsels of reason would avail nothing, and that
the torrent must be left to take its course.   However,
I thought it my duty to add that I entreated his
Majesty to consider in his wisdom whether all that
was taking place was not a *ruse de guerre;* whether the
North were not anxious to embroil him with the South
as a useful diversion, and with the ultimate view of
reuniting with England at a convenient opportunity, in
order to place the Empire between two fires.   " You
are," cried he, "a true minister of police, who mis-
trusts everything and believes in nothing good.   I am

sure of Alexander, who is very sincere. I now exercise over him a kind of charm, independently of the
guarantee offered me by those about him, of whom I
am equally certain." Here Napoleon related to me all
the trifling nonsense which I had heard from his suite
respecting the interview at Tilsit and the sudden predilection of the Russian court for the Emperor and
his people. He did not omit the flattery by means
of which he believed he had captivated the Grand
Duke Constantine himself, who, it is said, was not
displeased at being told that he was the best-dressed
prince in Europe, and had the finest thighs in the
world.

These confidential effusions were not useless to me.
Seeing Napoleon in good-humour, I again spoke to
him in favour of several persons for whom I particularly interested myself, and who all received valuable
employments. He began to be more satisfied with
the Faubourg St. Germain, and approving my liberal
mode of directing the police as respected the old aristocracy, he told me that there were near Bordeaux[1]
two families whom I regarded as disaffected and dangerous, but he wished them not to be molested; that
is, that they should be watched, but without any
species of inquisition. "You have often told me,"
added Napoleon, "that you ought to be like me, the
mediator between the old and new order of things:
that is your office; for that, in fact, is my policy in

---

[1] Apparently the families Donnissan and Larochejaquelein,
united by the marriage of the Marquis de Larochejaquelein, who
died in 1815, with the widow of the Marquis de Lescure, daughter
of the Marchioness de Donnissan; they then inhabited the Château of Citran, in Médoc.

the interior. But as to the exterior, do not meddle with that; leave me to act; and, above all, do not be anxious to defend the Pope: it would be too ridiculous on your part. Leave that care to M. de Talleyrand, who is indebted to him for being now a secular, and possessing a beautiful wife in lawful wedlock." I began to laugh, and taking up my portfolio, made way for the minister of the marine. What Napoleon had just said to me about the Pope alluded to his disputes with the Holy See, which began in 1805, and were daily growing more serious.

The entrance of our troops into Rome coincided with the invasion of the Peninsula. Pius VII. almost immediately issued a brief, in which he threatened Napoleon that he would direct his spiritual weapons against him: no doubt they were much blunted, but they would nevertheless have their effect upon many minds. In my eyes these disputes appeared the more impolitic, inasmuch as they could not fail to alienate a great part of the people of Italy, and, among ourselves, to favour the *petite église*, which we had annoyed for a long time, and which began to avail itself of these disputes to make common cause with the Pope against the government. But Napoleon only proceeded to extremities against the head of the Church that he might have a pretext for seizing Rome and despoiling it of its temporalities: this was one branch of his vast plan of a universal monarchy and of the reorganisation of Europe. I would willingly have seconded him, but I saw with regret that he set out with false premises, and that opinion already commenced to arm itself against him. How, in fact, was it possible to proceed thus to universal conquest, without having at least the people on one's side? Before imprudently saying that his dynasty, which was but the dynasty of yesterday, should soon be the most ancient of Europe, he ought to have understood the art of separating kings from their people, and for that purpose, not have abandoned principles without which he himself could not exist.

This affair of Rome was now eclipsed by the events which took place at Madrid and Bayonne, where Napoleon arrived on the 15th of April, with his court and suite. Spain was already invaded; and, under the mask of friendship, the French had taken possession of the principal fortresses in the north.

Having seized Spain, and full of hopes, Napoleon now prepared to appropriate to himself the treasures of the New World, which five or six adventurers came to offer him as the infallible result of their intrigues. All the machinery of this vast plot was prepared; a perfect understanding prevailed from the château of Marrac to Madrid, Lisbon, Cadiz, Buenos Ayres, and Mexico. Napoleon was followed by his private establishment of political imposture: his Duke of Rovigo, Savary, his Archbishop of Malines, the Abbé Pradt, his Prince Pignatelli, and many other tools more or less active of his diplomatic frauds. The ex-minister, Talleyrand, was also in his suite, but more as a passive observer than an agent.

I had warned Napoleon, on the eve of his departure, that public opinion was becoming irritated by the anxiety of expectation; and that the talk of the day had already reached a height far above the power of my three hundred regulators of Paris to suppress.

Insurrection at Madrid

Engraved by Paul Girardet after picture by Karl Girardet

This was still worse when events developed themselves; when by stratagem and perfidy all the family of Spain found itself caught in the Bayonne nets; when the Madrid massacre of the 2nd of May took place; and when the rising of nearly an entire nation had set almost the whole of the Peninsula in a conflagration. All was known and ascertained in Paris, notwithstanding the incredible efforts of all the police establishments to intercept or prevent the knowledge of public events. Never in the whole course of my two ministries did I see so decided a reprobation of the insatiable ambition and Machiavellism of the head of the state. This convinced me that in an important crisis truth would assert all its rights and regain all its empire. I received from Bayonne two or three very harsh letters respecting the bad state of the public mind, for which I seemed to be in some degree considered as responsible; my bulletins were a sufficient answer. Towards the end of July, after the capitulation of Baylen, it became impossible to restrain it. The counter-police and the Emperor's private correspondents took the alarm; they even deceived themselves so far as to put him on his guard against the symptoms of a conspiracy totally imaginary in Paris. The Emperor quitted Bayonne in all haste, after several violent fits of rage, which were metamorphosed in the saloons of the Chaussée d'Antin and the Faubourg St. Germain into an attack of fever. Traversing La Vendée, he returned to St. Cloud by the Loire.

I expected some severe observations upon my first audience, and was consequently on my guard. "You have been too indulgent, Duke d'Otranto," were his

first words. " How is it that you have permitted so
many nests of babblers and slanderers to be formed
in Paris?" "Sire, when everyone is implicated, what
is to be done? Besides, the police cannot penetrate
into the interior of families and the confidences of
friendship." "But foreigners have excited disaffection
in Paris." "No, Sire, the public discontent has been
confined to itself; old passions have been revived, and
in this respect there has been much expression of discontent. But nations cannot be aroused without
arousing the passions. It would be impolitic, imprudent even, to exasperate the public mind by unseasonable severity. This disturbance has likewise been
exaggerated to your Majesty; it will be appeased as
so many others have been; all will depend upon this
Spanish business and the attitude assumed by continental Europe. Your Majesty has surmounted difficulties much more serious and crises much more
important." It was then that, striding up and down
his cabinet, he again spoke to me of the Spanish war
as a mere skirmish, which scarcely deserved a few
cannon shot; at the same time flying into a rage
against Murat, Moncey, and especially Dupont, whose
capitulation he stigmatised with the term infamous,
declaring that he would make an example in the army.
" I will conduct this war of peasants and monks," continued he, "myself, and I hope to thrash the English
soundly. I will immediately come to an understanding with the Emperor Alexander for the ratification
of the treaties and the preservation of the tranquillity
of Europe. In three months I will reconduct my
brother to Madrid, and in four I myself will enter

Lisbon if the English dare to set foot there. I will punish this rabble, and will drive out the English." All was henceforth conducted upon this plan of operations. Confidential agents and couriers were dispatched to St. Petersburg. The favourable answer was not long delayed. The town of Erfurt was chosen for the interview of the two Emperors. Nothing could be more auspicious than this interview, where, at the end of September, the Czar came to fraternise with Napoleon. These two formidable arbiters of the continent passed eighteen days together in the greatest intimacy, in the midst of fêtes and amusements. Recourse was also had to a diplomatic mummery sent to the King of England, for the apparent purpose of obtaining his being a party to the general peace. I had given the Emperor, before his departure, information that ought to have undeceived him. But what do I say? He, perhaps, believed no more than myself in the possibility of a peace with which he would not have known what to do.

Erfurt brought back opinion. At the opening of the legislative corps, on the 26th of October, Napoleon, on his return, declared himself to be indissolubly united with the Emperor Alexander both for peace and war. " Soon," said he, " my eagles shall hover over the towers of Lisbon."

But this circumstance revealed to reflecting minds his weakness in a national war, which he dared not prosecute without a support in Europe, which might escape him. It was no longer Napoleon acting by himself. His embarrassments became serious from the time of his declaring war against the people.

Spain, the gulf in which Napoleon was about to plunge, raised in me many gloomy forebodings; I saw in it a centre of resistance, supported by England, and which might offer to our continental enemies favourable opportunities of again assailing our political existence. It was melancholy to reflect that, by an imprudent enterprise, the solidity of our conquests, and even our existence as a nation, had become a matter of doubt. By continually braving new dangers, Napoleon, our founder, might fall either by ball or bullet, or sink under the knife of the fanatic. It was but too true that all our power centred in a single man, who without posterity required of Providence at least twenty years to complete and consolidate his work. If he were taken from us before this term, he would not even have, like Alexander the Macedonian, his own lieutenants for the inheritors of his power and glory, nor for the guarantee of our existence. Thus this vast and formidable Empire, created as if by enchantment, had nothing but a fragile foundation, which might vanish on the wings of death. The hands which had assisted in its elevation were too weak to support it without a living stay. If the serious circumstances in which we were placed gave rise to these reflections in my mind, the peculiar situation of the Emperor added to them the greatest degree of solicitude and anxiety.

The charm of his domestic habits was broken ; death had carried off that infant who, at the same time his nephew and adopted son, had by his birth drawn so close the ties which bound him to Josephine through Hortense, and to Hortense through Josephine. "I recognise myself," said he, "in this child ! " And he already indulged the fond idea that he would succeed him. How often on the terrace of St. Cloud, after his breakfast, has he been seen contemplating with transport this tender offset, whose disposition and manners were so engaging; and, disengaging himself from the cares of the Empire, join in its infantine games! Did he evince ever so little determination, ever so trifling a predilection for the noise of the drum, for arms and the glorious circumstance of war, Napoleon would cry out with enthusiasm: "This boy will be worthy to succeed me—he may even surpass me!" At the very moment such high destinies were preparing for him, this beautiful child, a victim to the croup, was snatched away from him. Thus was snapped the reed on which the great man had been fain to lean.

Never did I see Napoleon a prey to deeper and more concentrated grief; never did I see Josephine and her daughter in more agonising affliction : they appeared to find in it a mournful presentiment of a futurity without happiness and without hope. The courtiers themselves sympathised with them in a misfortune so severe ; as for myself, I saw broken the link of the perpetuity of the Empire.

It would ill have become me to have kept within my own breast the suggestions of my foresight ; but in order to make them known to Napoleon, I waited till time should have in some manner alleviated his grief. With him, besides, the pains of the heart were subordinate to the cares of empire, to the highest combinations of policy and war. What greater diversion could he have ? But already distractions of a different kind and more efficacious consolations had

soothed his regrets and broken the monotony of his
habits : officiously encouraged by his confidant Duroc,
he had given himself up, not to the love of women,
but to the physical enjoyment of their charms.   Two
ladies of the court have been mentioned as being
honoured with his stolen embraces, and who were just
replaced by the beautiful Italian, Charlotte Gaz——
born Brind——.   Napoleon, captivated by her beauty,
had conferred a recent favour upon her.   It was also
known that, being freed from the restraints of com-
mon-place domesticity, he no longer had the same
room nor the same bed as Josephine.   This kind of
nuptial separation had taken place in consequence of
a violent altercation caused by the jealousy of his
wife,[1] and since then he had refused to resume the
domestic chain.   As to Josephine, her torments were
much less occasioned by a wounded heart than by the
thorns of unquiet apprehensions.   She was alarmed at
the consequences of the sudden loss of Hortense's son,
of the neglect of her daughter, and the abandonment
of herself.   She foresaw the future, and was in despair
at her sterility.

The concurrence of these circumstances both political
and domestic, and the fear of one day seeing their
Emperor, when age approached, follow the traces of a
Sardanapalus, suggested to me the idea of endeavouring
to give a future prospect to a magnificent Empire of
which I was one of the chief guardians.   In a confidential memoir, which I read to him myself, I represented to him the necessity of dissolving his marriage;

[1] In 1805, at the camp of Boulogne, according to the "Mémorial
de Sainte Hélène."—*Note by the Editor.*

of immediately forming, as Emperor, a new alliance more suitable and more happy; and of giving an heir to the throne on which Providence had placed him. My conclusion was the natural consequence of the strongest and most solid arguments which the necessities of the state could suggest.

Without declaring anything positive upon this serious and important subject, Napoleon let me perceive that, in a political point of view, the dissolution of his marriage was already determined in his mind, but that he was not yet as decided respecting the alliance he intended to form; that, on the other hand, he was singularly attached, both by habit and a kind of superstition, to Josephine; and that the most painful step for him would be to inform her of the divorce. The whole of this communication was made in a few significant monosyllables and two or three almost enigmatical phrases; but these were sufficient for me. Urged by an excess of zeal, I resolved to effect the breach, and prepare Josephine for this great sacrifice demanded by the solidity of the Empire and the Emperor's happiness.

Such an overture required some preliminaries. I waited for an opportunity; it presented itself one Sunday at Fontainebleau, upon returning from mass. There, detaining Josephine in the recess of a window, I gave, with all verbal precautions, and all possible delicacy, the first hint of a separation, which I represented to her as the most sublime and at the same time as the most inevitable of sacrifices. She coloured at first; then turned pale; her lips began to swell, and I perceived over her whole frame symptoms which caused me to apprehend a nervous attack, or some other physical convulsion. It was only in a stammering voice that she questioned me, to know if I had been ordered to make her this melancholy communication. I told her I had had no order, but that I foresaw the necessities of the future; and, hastening by some general reflection to break off so painful a conversation, I pretended to have an engagement with one of my colleagues, and quitted her. I learnt the next day that there had been much grief and disagreement in the interior of the palace; that a very passionate but affecting explanation had taken place between Josephine and Napoleon, who had disowned me; and that this woman, naturally so mild, so good, and being besides under more than one kind of obligation to me, had earnestly solicited as a favour my dismissal for having preferred the welfare of France to her personal interests and to the gratification of her vanity. Although he protested that I had spoken without orders, the Emperor refused to *dismiss* me—for that was the word—and he pacified Josephine as well as he could by alleging on my behalf political pretexts. It was evident to me that, if he had not already secretly determined upon his divorce, he would have sacrificed me, instead of contenting himself with a mere disavowal of my conduct. But Josephine was his dupe; she had not strength of mind sufficient to prevent her flattering herself with vain illusions; she thought she could obviate all by wretched artifices. Who would believe it? She proposed to the Emperor one of those political frauds which would have been the derision of all Europe, offering to carry on the deception of a fictitious pregnancy. Certain that she would have recourse to this, I had trumpeted forth the possibility of this trick by means of my agents, so that the Emperor had only to show her my police bulletins to get rid of her importunities.

Greater events made a powerful diversion. On the 4th of November Napoleon in person opened the second campaign of the Peninsula, after having drawn from Germany eighty thousand veterans. After kindling an immense conflagration, he hastened to extinguish it by rivers of blood. But what could he do against a whole people in arms, and revolutionised? Besides, all was now to inspire him with suspicion and inquietude; he went even so far as to persuade himself that a centre of resistance was forming in Paris, of which M. de Talleyrand and I were the secret promoters.

After learning that one hundred and twenty-five black balls, being one-third of opposers to his will, had just astonished the legislative body, he was so shocked and alarmed at it that he had thought fit to dispatch from Valladolid, on the 4th of December, an official note, explanatory of the essence of the imperial government, and the place which he was pleased to assign the legislature in it. " Our misfortunes," said he, " have partly arisen from those exaggerated ideas which have induced a body of men to believe themselves the representatives of the nation ; it would be a chimerical and even criminal pretension to wish to represent the nation before the Emperor. The legislative body should be called the legislative council, since it has not the power of making laws, not having the power of proposing them. In the order of the constitutional hierarchy, the first representative of the nation is the

Emperor, and his ministers the organs of his decisions.   All would fall again into anarchy if other
constitutional ideas should interfere and pervert those
of our monarchical constitution."

These oracles of absolute power would but have
exasperated the public mind under a weak and capricious prince ; but Napoleon had continually the
sword in his hand, and victory still followed his steps.
Thus all succumbed ; and the mere ascendency of
his power sufficed to dissipate every germ of legal
opposition.   When it was known that he had just
entered Madrid as an irritated conqueror, and that he
was determined to surprise and drive the English
army before him, the war was supposed to be finished,
and I thus instructed my active agents.   But, suddenly
leaving the English and abandoning the war to his
lieutenants, the Emperor returned amongst us in a
sudden and unexpected manner ; whether, as those
about him assured me, that he was alarmed at the
information that a band of Spanish fanatics had sworn
to assassinate him (I believed it, and had on my side
given the same advice), or whether he was still acted
upon by the fixed idea of a coalition in Paris against
his authority.   I think both these motives united had
their weight with him, but they were disguised by
referring the urgency of his sudden return to the preparations of Austria.   Napoleon had still three or four
months good, and he knew as well as I that if Austria
did make a stir she was not yet ready.

At my first audience he sounded me upon the
affair of the legislative body and his imperial rebuke.
I saw him coming round, and I replied that it was

very well; that it was thus monarchs should govern; that if any body whatsoever arrogated to itself alone the right of representing him, the sovereign, the only thing to be done would be to dissolve it; and that if Louis XVI. had acted so, that unhappy prince might still have lived and reigned. Fixing upon me eyes full of astonishment: "What, Duke d'Otranto!" said he to me, after a moment's silence; "if I recollect right, however, you are one of those who sent Louis XVI. to the scaffold!" "Yes, Sire," I replied, without hesitation, "and that was the first service I have had the happiness of rendering your Majesty."

Summoning to his aid all the strength of his genius and character to surmount the aggression of Austria, he arranged his plans, and hastened to execute them with the utmost promptitude. Some apprehensions were entertained that he might be forced, or else surprised, in the defiles of the Black Mountains, for his forces were not strong, and he would have been reduced to act on the defensive had he permitted the concentration of the Austrian masses to be effected. Tann, Abensberg, Eckmühl, and Ratisbon witnessed the rapid triumph of our arms, and signalised the happy commencement of a campaign the more serious from our carrying on, contrary to the rules of sound policy, two wars at once.

The preparations made by Schill in Prussia revealed to us all the danger. This Prussian major, raising the standard of revolt, had just been brought forward by the Schneiders and the Steins, the chiefs of the *illuminati;* it was a weak effort upon the part of Prussia. The inhabitants of the northern part of

Germany were very near rising, in imitation of the people of the Peninsula. Hemmed in by two national wars, Napoleon would have fallen four years sooner. This circumstance caused me to make serious reflections upon the fragility of an Empire which had no other support than arms and no other stimulus than an unbridled ambition.

We breathed again after the occupation of Vienna; but Schill was still active in Saxony, and the inhabitants of Vienna showed much irritation. Several insurrections took place in this capital of Austria. Soon the first reports upon the battle of Essling arrived to renew our alarms and increase our uneasiness; these reports were succeeded by confidential communications, almost all afflicting. Not only Lannes, the only remaining friend of Napoleon who dared to tell him the truth, had fallen gloriously, but we had also eight thousand men killed, eighteen thousand wounded, among whom were three generals, and above five hundred officers of all ranks. If, after losses so serious, the army was saved, it owed its preservation not to Napoleon, but to the coolness of Masséna.

Our perplexity in Paris may be easily conceived, as well as what efforts and address were necessary to throw a veil over this severe check, which might be followed by more than one disaster! As to Napoleon, he declared himself, in his bulletins, to have been victorious, and to account for not following up his victory he accused, in rather a trivial manner, *General Danube*, the best officer in the Austrian service. In fact, it was impossible to account for the want of activity in the archduke, after so many losses on our side, and when we could only find refuge in the isle of Lobau. In proportion to the impudence of the bulletin, the greater were the commentaries upon it.

The numerous enemies which Napoleon had in France, whether among the republicans or the royalists, again began to show themselves. The Faubourg St. Germain resumed its hostility, and even some conspiracies were on foot in La Vendée. All those parties openly flattered themselves that the affair of Essling would prove a fatal blow to the Emperor.

The events upon the Danube had created so much interest that scarcely any attention was bestowed upon those taking place at Rome. It was reserved for us— for us philosophers, the offspring of the eighteenth century and adepts of incredulity—it was reserved for us, I say, to deplore as impolitic the usurpation of the patrimony of St. Peter and the persecution of the head of the Church by him even whom we had chosen for our perpetual dictator. A decree of Napoleon's towards the end of May had ordered the annexation of the Roman states to the French Empire. What was the consequence? The venerable Pontiff, riveted to the papal throne, finding himself disarmed, despoiled, and having only at his command spiritual weapons, issued bulls of excommunication against Napoleon and his coadjutors. All this would have only excited ridicule had the people remained indifferent, if public indignation had not rekindled expiring faith in favour of the unyielding pontiff of the Christians. Then it was that, after sustaining a species of siege in his palace, Pius VII. was forcibly torn from it and carried from Rome, to be confined in Savona. Napoleon was aware

how averse I was to these outrages; therefore I was
not intrusted with the direction of them. The principal instruments against the Pope were Murat, Salicetti, Miollis, and Radet. I had to go great lengths
when the Pope had arrived in Piedmont to prevent his
being forced to cross the Alps. It would have been
upon me that they would willingly have thrown the
responsibility of the last scenes of this persecution,
which appeared to all so odious and unjust.

In spite of the reserve of the government and the
silence of its agents, all public interest was directed
upon Pius VII., who in the eyes of Europe was considered as an illustrious and affecting victim of the
greedy ambition of the Emperor. A prisoner at
Savona, Pius VII. was despoiled of all his external
honours and shut out from all communication with the
cardinals, as well as deprived of all means of issuing
bulls and assembling a council. What food for the
petite église, for the turbulence of some priests, and for
the hatred of some devotees! I immediately foresaw
that all these leavens would reproduce the secret associations we had with so much difficulty suppressed. In
fact, Napoleon, by undoing all that he had hitherto
done to calm and conciliate the minds of the people,
disposed them in the end to withdraw themselves from
his power, and even to ally themselves to his enemies,
as soon as they had the courage to show themselves
in force. But this extraordinary man had not yet lost
any of his warlike vigour; his courage and genius
raised him above all his errors. My correspondence
and bulletins, which he received every day at Vienna,
did not dissimulate the truth of things nor the unhappy

state of the public mind. "A month will change all this," he wrote me. "I am very easy, you are so too," were his very words. I had never accumulated on my head so much power and so much responsibility. The colossal ministry of the police and *per interim* the portfolio of the interior were both intrusted to me. But I was reassured, for never had the encouragement of the Emperor been so positive nor his confidence greater. I was near the apogee of ministerial power; but in politics the apogee often conducts to the Tarpeian rock.

The horizon underwent a sudden change. The battle of Wagram fought and gained forty-five days after the loss of the battle of Essling, the armistice of Znaïm agreed to six days after the battle of Wagram, and the death of Schill, brought us back days of serenity and of fairer promise.

But in the interval the English appeared in Escaut with a formidable expedition, which, had it been more ably conducted, might have brought back success to our enemies, and given Austria time to rally.

I perceived the danger. Invested during the Emperor's absence with a great part of his power, by the union of the two ministries, I instilled energy into the council, of which I was the life, and caused it to pass several strong measures. No time was to be lost: Belgium was to be saved. The disposable troops would not have been sufficient to preserve this important part of the Empire. I caused it to be decreed, with the Emperor's concurrence, that at Paris and in several of the northern departments there should be an immediate and extraordinary levy of national guards.

Upon this occasion I addressed to all the mayors of Paris a circular containing the following phrase: " Let us prove to Europe that if the genius of Napoleon can shed lustre around France, his presence is not necessary to repel the enemy."

Who would have believed it ? Both this phrase and the measure which preceded it gave umbrage to Napoleon, who, by a letter addressed to Cambacérès, ordered the levy in Paris to be at once suspended; and for the present nothing was done but appointing officers.

I did not at first suspect the real motive of this suspension for the capital, the more so as elsewhere the levy, operating without any obstacle, and with the utmost rapidity, gave us about forty thousand men, ready equipped and full of ardour. Nothing could so much embarrass the measures I had caused to be adopted, and the execution of which I had superintended with so much zeal and care. It had been a long time since France had given a spectacle of such a burst of patriotism. During her journey to the waters of Spa, the Emperor's mother had been so much struck with it that she herself even congratulated me upon it.

But it was necessary to appoint a commander-in-chief to this national auxiliary force, which was to rendezvous under the walls of Antwerp. I was in doubt upon whom to fix, when Bernadotte unexpectedly arrived from Wagram. The very day, when I had scarcely heard of his arrival, I proposed him to the minister of war, the Duke de Feltre, who lost no time in giving him his commission.

The Battle of Wagram

Engraved by Paul Girardet after painting by H. Vernet

What was my surprise the next day, when Bernadotte informed me, in the overflowings of friendship
and confidence, that having commanded the left at
Wagram, and the Saxons who composed part of it
having been routed, the Emperor, under this pretext,
had deprived him of the command, and sent him back
to Paris; that his wing had, however, behaved well at
the close of the battle; but that he had not been less
censured at headquarters for having, in an order of
the day, addressed to his soldiers a kind of commenda-
tory proclamation; that he imputed this new disgrace
to the malevolent reports made to the Emperor; that
many complaints were made of Savary, who had charge
of the secret police of the army; that Lannes, after
having had the most violent scenes with him, could
alone restrain him; but that since the death of that
hero, the influence of Savary had become unlimited;
that he watched for opportunities of irritating the Emperor against certain generals who were the objects of
his dislike; that he even proceeded to impute to them
connections with the secret society of the Philadelphians,
which he converted into a scarecrow for the Emperor,
by supposing, upon vague surmises, that it had dangerous ramifications in the army.

For these reasons Bernadotte testified some repugnance to accept the commission of commander-in-chief
of the national guards of the Empire, destined for the
defence of Antwerp. I represented to him that, on
the contrary, this was the time to re-establish himself
in the Emperor's confidence; that I had already several
times contributed to reconcile them, and to do away
with any misunderstanding between them; that, with

the high rank he held, if he refused to fulfil the commission conferred upon him by the minister at war, he
would appear to assume the air of a discontented person,
and to refuse an opportunity of rendering fresh services
to his country; that in case of need, we ought to serve
the Emperor in spite of himself, and that by thus doing
his duty he devoted himself to his country. He understood me, and, after other confidential communications,
he set off for Antwerp.

The success attendant upon this movement is
well known; it was general throughout our northern
provinces, and the English dared not attempt a
landing. So happy a result, joined to the judicious
conduct of Bernadotte, compelled Napoleon to keep
his suspicions and discontent to himself; but in
reality he never pardoned either Bernadotte or me
for this eminent service, and our intimacy became
more than ever an object of suspicion with him.

Other private information which reached me from
the army perfectly coincided with what I had learnt
from Bernadotte respecting the Philadelphians, whose
secret organisation commenced during the perpetual
consulship. The members did not affect secrecy;
their object was to restore to France the liberty of
which Napoleon had deprived it by the re-establishment of the nobility, and by his concordat. They
regretted Bonaparte the First Consul, and considered
the despotism of Napoleon as Emperor insupportable.
The suspected existence of this association had already
caused the arrest and continued detention of Malet,
Guidal, Gindre, Picquerel, and Lahorie; more recently,
the brave Oudet, colonel of the ninth regiment of the

line, was suspected of having been raised to the presidency of the Philadelphians. A vile accusation having designated him as such, the fate of this unfortunate officer was as follows: Having been appointed on the day preceding the battle of Wagram chief of brigade, he was the evening after the action decoyed during the darkness of the night into an ambuscade, where he fell under the fire of a troop supposed to be gendarmes; the following day he was found stretched out lifeless, with twenty-two officers of his party killed around him. This circumstance made much noise at Schönbrunn, at Vienna, and at all the état-majors of the army, without, however, any means of fathoming so horrible a mystery.

Since the armistice, however, difficulties were being slowly removed; the ratification of the new treaty of peace with Austria did not arrive; but every letter represented it as certain. We were expecting to receive momentary intelligence of its conclusion, when I learnt that the Emperor, while reviewing his guard at Schönbrunn, had narrowly escaped the dagger of an assassin. Rapp had just time to seize him, Berthier having thrown himself before the Emperor. He was a young man of Erfurt, hardly seventeen years of age, and solely excited by patriotic fanaticism; a long sharp knife was found upon him, with which he intended to execute his purpose. He confessed his design, and was shot.

The treaty of Vienna was signed a few days after (the 14th of October); Napoleon, the conqueror and pacificator, returned almost immediately to his capital. It was from his own mouth that we learnt what serious difficulties he had had to surmount, and how determined and strong had been the opposition of Austria.

I had several conferences with Napoleon at Fontainebleau before his entry into Paris, and I found him much exasperated against the Faubourg St. Germain, which had resumed its satirical and sarcastic habits. I could not avoid informing the Emperor that after the battle of Essling, as after the Bayonne affair, the wits of the Faubourg had spread the ridiculous report that he had been struck with mental alienation. Napoleon was extremely incensed at this, and he spoke to me of adopting severe measures with creatures " who," he said, " wound me with one hand and solicit with the other." I dissuaded him from it. " It is proverbial," I said to him; " the Seine flows; the Faubourg intrigues, solicits, spends, and calumniates; it is in the nature of things. Who has been more slandered than Julius Cæsar ? I will, besides, assure your Majesty that among this party there will be no Cassius or Brutus found. On the other hand, do not the worst reports proceed from your Majesty's ante-chambers ? Are they not propagated by persons forming part of your establishment and of your government ? Before measures of severity could be adopted, a council of ten must be appointed; the doors, the walls, and the chimneys must be interrogated. It is the part of a great man to despise the gabble of insolence and to stifle it under a mass of glory and renown." He acquiesced. I knew that, after the battle of Wagram, he had hesitated whether he should dismember the Austrian monarchy; that he had several plans upon this subject; that he had even boasted he would soon distribute

crowns to some of the archdukes whom he supposed
discontented or blinded by ambition; but that, arrested
by the fear of awakening the suspicions of Russia and
of raising the people of Austria, whose affection for
Francis II. could not be called in question, he had
had time to appreciate another difficulty in the execution of his plan. It required the military occupation
of the whole of Germany, which would not have permitted him to put an end to the Peninsular War, which
now claimed all his attention.

The moment appeared to me favourable to make
him acquainted with the whole truth. I represented
to him, in a confidential report upon our actual situation, how necessary it had become to put a stop to a
system of policy which tended to estrange from us the
people; and I first entreated him to accomplish the
work of peace, either by sounding England or offering
her reasonable propositions; adding that he had never
been in a better situation to make himself listened to;
that nothing equalled the power of his arms, and that
now there was no longer any doubt respecting the
firmness of his connections with the two most powerful
potentates of Europe next himself; that by showing
himself moderate in his demands with respect to Portugal, and disposed, on the other hand, to evacuate
Prussia, he could not fail to obtain peace, and secure
his dynasty in Italy, Madrid, Westphalia, and Holland;
that these should be the limits of his ambition and of
a lasting glory; that it was already a splendid destiny
to have re-created the Empire of Charlemagne, but
that it became necessary to give this Empire guarantees
for the future; that for this purpose it became urgent,

as I had before represented to him, to dissolve his marriage with Josephine, and to form another union, demanded by state reasons as much as by the most important political considerations, for, in seeing himself renewed, he at the same time insured existence to the Empire; that it was for him alone to determine whether it would be preferable to form a family alliance with one of the two great northern courts, either Russia or Austria, or to isolate himself in his power, and honour his own country by sharing the diadem with a Frenchwoman rich in her fecundity and her virtues; but that the plan suggested by the want of social stability and monarchical permanence would be destroyed to its foundations if not supported by a general peace; that I insisted strongly upon this point, begging him to let me know his intentions upon the two principal views of my report and my conclusions.

I only obtained a tacit assent, the only answer I had been accustomed to hope for upon serious subjects, which were considered out of my province. But I saw that the dissolution of the marriage was settled for at no very distant period, Cambacérès having been authorised to confer with me respecting it. I instantly had the rumour set afoot in the saloons, and it was everywhere whispered that Josephine, plunged in security, had not the least hint of it, so much was she admired and pitied.

I also perceived that the Emperor, whether from pride or policy, was inclined to unite himself to one of the old courts of Europe, and that the previous divorce was intended to induce them to make overtures, or prepare them to receive them.

The show of power was not however neglected. Napoleon, having in absolute dependence upon himself the kings whom he had made, sent for them to his court, and on the 3rd of December required them to be present in the metropolitan church to hear the "Te Deum" sung in commemoration of his victories and of the anniversary of his coronation.

Upon quitting Notre Dame he proceeded to open the sittings of the legislative corps; there, in a presumptuous speech, he expressed himself in these terms: "When I shall appear on the other side of the Pyrenees, the frighted leopard shall seek the ocean to avoid shame, defeat, and death."

It was with these lofty images he endeavoured to palliate the difficulties of the Spanish war, deceiving himself, perhaps; for, with regard to this contest, he had never had but very incorrect ideas.

The next day, during a *tête-à-tête* dinner with Josephine, he informed her of his resolution. Josephine fainted. It required all the rhetoric of Cambacérès, and all the tenderness of her son Eugene, both to calm her excitement and dispose her to resignation.

On the 15th of December the dissolution of the marriage was proceeded with according to the form; and all being adjusted, an officer of the guard was commissioned to escort Josephine to Malmaison, whilst the Emperor on his side went to the grand Trianon to pass a few days there in retirement. The chancery was now fully instructed to open a parallel negotiation with the two courts of St. Petersburg and Vienna. In the first, the grand duchess, sister to the Czar, was the desired object; and in Austria, the

Archduchess Maria Louisa, daughter of the Emperor
Francis. Russia was first sounded. It was said that
in the council the Emperor Alexander was favourable
to the union, but that there was a difference of
opinion in the imperial Russian family.

That which took place at Vienna, almost simultaneously, deserves the mention of a few preliminaries
to which I was not altogether a stranger.

One of the foremost men in the annals of polite-
ness and gallantry at the court of Louis XVI. was
undoubtedly Count Louis de Narbonne. Some persons had been pleased to increase his celebrity by
deducing from the striking resemblance of his features
to Louis XVI. an inference implying some great mystery as to his birth. He had also himself laboured
to add to his reputation by his perfect amiability of
disposition, his intimate *liaison* with the most extraordinary woman of the age, Madame de Staël, and,
in short, by the easy and courteous manner in which
he exercised in the war department a constitutional
ministry in the decline of the monarchy. Forced to
emigrate, and exposed to the shafts of the ultra-re-
publicans and the ultra-royalists, he was at first
neglected upon his re-entering France; at a later
period, however, I gave him a reception full of that
warmth with which the patriots of 1789, who had a
wish to conciliate royalty with liberty, had inspired
me. To accomplished manners he joined a brilliant
and ready wit, and often even a correctness and
depth of observation. At length he was with me
daily; and such was the charm of his conversation
that it afforded me, in the midst of the most fatiguing

labours, the sweetest relaxation. All that M. de Narbonne requested of me on behalf of his friends and connections I granted him. I spoke of him to the Emperor. I had some difficulty in overcoming his repugnance to him; he was distrustful of his former connection with Madame de Staël, whom Napoleon regarded as an implacable enemy. I, however, persisted, and the Emperor at length allowed him to be presented. Napoleon was immediately struck with him, and first attached him to his person as *officier d'ordonnance*. General Narbonne followed him in the campaign of Austria, during which he was appointed governor of Trieste, with a political mission, of which I had intelligence.

Upon the Emperor's return, and when the affair of the marriage was brought on the *tapis*, I named him as the fittest person for adroitly sounding the intentions of the court of Austria. It would have been contrary to all propriety and custom for Napoleon to have taken any decided step before positively ascertaining the determination of the Emperor Alexander; therefore the instructions delivered to the Count de Narbonne merely authorised him to act in his own name, and as a private individual, with all the delicacy and ability requisite in an affair of such high importance. He arrived at Vienna in the month of January, 1810, his only apparent object being to pass through it on his way to return to France through Germany. There, opening his batteries, he first saw M. de Metternich, and was afterwards introduced to the Emperor Francis.

The question of the marriage of the Emperor at

that time interested all Europe, and naturally became
one of the subjects of his conversation with the Emperor
of Austria.   M. de Narbonne did not fail to observe that
the greatest sovereigns of Europe courted the alliance
of Napoleon.   The Emperor of Austria immediately expressed his surprise that the court of the Tuileries had
overlooked his family, and he said sufficient for M. de
Narbonne to know what he had to depend upon.   He
wrote to me the same day, and, in communicating to
me the hints of the court of Vienna, said that he
thought he might conclude from them that an alliance
with an archduchess would enter into the views of
Austria.   Upon the arrival of the courier, I immediately
hastened to communicate his dispatch to the Emperor.
I never saw him so joyous and happy.   He caused
Prince Schwartzenberg, the Austrian ambassador, to be
sounded ; directing that this delicate negotiation should
be conducted with such circumspection that the ambassador should find himself compromised before he was
aware of it.   The object was, not to offend the Emperor
Alexander by giving him room to suspect that a double
negotiation had been set on foot, and at the same
time of making all Europe suppose that the Emperor
had had the choice of a grand duchess and an archduchess ; as to the Princess of Saxony, that was a
mere matter of form.

On the 1st of February Napoleon summoned at
the Tuileries a grand privy council, composed of the
high dignitaries, great officers, all the ministers, the
presidents of the senate, and the legislative corps, and
those of the sections of the council of state.   We were
in all twenty-five persons.   The council being assembled,

and the deliberations begun, the minister Champagny first communicated the dispatches of Caulaincourt, our ambassador in Russia. From his representation it appeared that the marriage with a Russian princess solely depended upon our allowing her the public exercise of her worship, and permitting for her use the erection of a chapel of the Greek ritual. He then made known the hints and desires of the court of Vienna: thus embarrassment of choice seemed the only difficulty. Opinions were divided. As I was in the secret I abstained from giving mine, and purposely withdrew before the end of the deliberation. Upon the council breaking up, Prince Eugene was commissioned by the Emperor to make formal overtures to Prince Schwartzenberg. The ambassador had received his instructions, and all was arranged without the least difficulty.

Thus Napoleon's marriage with Maria Louisa was proposed, discussed, determined upon in council, and stipulated within twenty-four hours.

The day after the holding of the council a senator, one of my friends, always *au fait* at news,[1] came to inform me that the Emperor had decided for an archduchess. I affected surprise, and at the same time regret, that a Russian princess had not been chosen. "If this be the case," cried I, "I must pack up!" availing myself thus of a pretext to give my friends a hint of my approaching disgrace.

Gifted with what is called tact, I had a secret

[1] A *recueil* of anecdotes, in which this circumstance is related, mentions M. de Sémonville as the person; but Fouché suppresses the name.—*Note by the Editor.*

presentiment that my ministerial power would not long survive the new order of things, which would, doubtless, effect a change in the habits and character of Napoleon. I did not in the least doubt that, having become the ally of the house of Lorraine, and believing himself henceforth certain of the cabinet of Austria, and consequently of having it in his power to subject ancient Europe to his will, he would think himself in a situation to get rid of his minister of police, as had already been the case after the peace of Amiens. I was also firmly convinced that he would never pardon my having of myself raised an army, forced the English to re-embark, and saved Belgium. I knew, in fact, that since that time my intimacy with General Bernadotte had been an object of suspicion with him.

The more he indulged within himself dispositions inimical to me, the more I was persuaded of their existence. They revealed themselves upon my proposing to him to set at liberty, on the approaching occasion of the celebration of his nuptials, a part of the prisoners of state, at the same time relieving others from surveillance. Instead of complying with my wish, he exclaimed with an affectation of humanity against the deplorable despotism exercised by the police, telling me that he thought of putting an end to it. Two days afterwards he sent me the sketch of a report drawn up in my name, and of an imperial decree, which, instead of one state prison, established six,[1] ordering besides that henceforth no one could be arrested but in virtue

[1] Vincennes, Saumur, Ham, Landskrona, Pierre-Châtel, and Fenestrelle.—*Note by the Editor.*

of a decision of the privy council. This was a bitter
scoff, the privy council being nothing else than the will
of the Emperor. The whole was so artfully managed
that I was compelled to present the project to the
council of state, where it was discussed and finally
adopted on the 3rd of March. In this manner did
Napoleon elude putting an end to illegal arrest and
throw upon the police all the odium of arbitrary deten-
tions. He also obliged me to give him a list of individuals under surveillance. Surveillance was a very mild
police measure, which I had invented merely to relieve
from the severities of arbitrary detention the numerous
victims daily hunted down by hired accusers, whom I
had great difficulty to keep within any bounds. This
odious and secret militia was inherent in a system
raised and maintained by the most suspicious and mistrustful man that perhaps ever existed. It was a state
wound. I had sometimes the weakness to imagine
that now, firmly established and at ease, Napoleon
would adopt a system of government more paternal,
and at the same time more conformable to our
manners. Under this point of view the marriage with
an archduchess gave me hopes; but I felt more and
more that the sanction of a general peace was indispensable. Could I not myself contribute to this peace,
as I had co-operated by my impulse to the dissolution of a sterile connection and to the alliance with
Austria? If I succeeded in this object, I might, from
the importance of such a service, triumph over the
prejudices of the Emperor and reconquer his confidence. But England was first to be sounded. I had
the less hesitation, from the change which had taken

place in the composition of the English ministry having given me some just grounds of hope.

The ill-success of the greater part of its operations in this last campaign had excited the displeasure of the English nation, and produced serious dissensions among the ministers. Two among them, Lord Castlereagh and Mr. Canning, had even gone so far as to fight a duel, after having sent in their resignations. The cabinet had hastened to recall from the Spanish embassy the Marquis of Wellesley to succeed Mr. Canning in the place of secretary of state for foreign affairs; and to place at the head of the war department Earl Liverpool, formerly Lord Hawkesbury. I knew that these two ministers indulged lofty but conciliatory views. Besides, the cause of Spanish independence being almost desperate, in consequence of the victory of Ocanna and the occupation of Andalusia, I imagined that I should find the Marquis of Wellesley more open to reasonable overtures; I therefore determined to reconnoitre the ground, and that in virtue of the powers which I had frequently used, of sending agents abroad.

In this mission I employed M. Ouvrard, for two reasons: first, because a political overture at London could scarcely be begun but under the mask of commercial operations; and next, because it was impossible to employ in so delicate an affair a man more broken into business or of a more insinuating and persuasive character. But as M. Ouvrard could not without inconvenience enter into direct relations with the Marquis of Wellesley, I associated with him M. Fagan, an old Irish officer, who, being intrusted with the first dispatches, was to open to him, so to speak, the way to the British minister.

I determined that M. Ouvrard should not set off till after the celebration of the marriage. The entry of the young archduchess into Paris took place on the 1st of April; nothing could be more magnificent or more interesting. The day was beautiful. The expressions of joy from the prodigious crowds assembled were rapturous. The court immediately set off for St. Cloud, where the civil act was gone through, and the next day the nuptial benediction was given to Napoleon and Maria Louisa in one of the saloons of the Louvre, amid numbers of ladies sparkling with jewels and magnificent attire. The fêtes were splendid. But that which was given by Prince Schwartzenberg, in the name of his master, offered a sinister omen. The dancing-room, built in the garden of his hotel, took fire, and in an instant the saloon was in a blaze; many persons perished, among others the Princess Schwartzenberg, wife to the ambassador's brother. The unfortunate conclusion of this fête, given to celebrate the alliance of two nations, did not fail to be compared to the catastrophe which had marked the fêtes on the occasion of the marriage of Louis XVI. and Marie Antoinette; the most unfortunate presages were drawn from it. Napoleon himself was struck with it. As I had given the prefecture all the requisite orders, and as that office had been specially charged with this part of the public surveillance, it was upon that, or at least upon the prefect of police, that the Emperor's resentment fell. He disgraced Dubois; and, unfortunately, a public disaster was necessary to remove a

man who had so often misdirected the moral end of
the police. At court and in the city the order of the
day was henceforth to please the young Empress,
who, without a rival, captivated Napoleon. It was
even on his side a kind of childishness. I knew
that an opportunity was being sought of finding fault
with the police touching the sale of certain works
upon the Revolution, which might have hurt the
Empress. I gave orders for their seizure;[1] but such
was the cupidity of the agents of the prefecture,
that these very works were clandestinely sold by
those even whose duty it was to send them to the
mill. Towards the end of April the Emperor set off
with the Empress to visit Middleburg and Flessingue;
he also went to Breda. This journey was fatal to me.

[1] The police, in virtue of an order from the Duke of Otranto,
made the most severe search, forbade and seized all works upon
the Revolution which were written with a bias towards royalty.
The editor of "Irma," having published a large portion of those
works which recalled to the memory of the French nation the royal
family of the Bourbons, was the chief object of the inquisitorial
visits of the police. Thus this last search in his warehouses
continued for two days; almost all his books were confiscated;
he was himself seized and conducted to the prefecture. One
work only was partly the cause of this excessive severity; it
had been published a long time; it was the history of the
iniquitous trials of Louis XVI., the Queen, Madame Elizabeth,
and the Duke of Orleans. The work contained passages of the
highest importance, such as secret interrogatories, secret declara-
tions, decrees, and other unknown pieces, extracted from the
journals of the revolutionary tribunals, and which had never
seen the light. This work alone cost the editor more than
thirty domiciliary visits without their ever being able to seize
the entire edition, only some isolated copies being taken. In
spite of all these searches and visits the work was constantly
sold, and people even hid themselves in order to read it.—*Note
by the Editor.*

The Emperor, struck with my reflections upon the
necessity of a general peace, had endeavoured, without
my knowledge, to open secret negotiations with the
new English minister, through the medium of a
commercial house at Amsterdam. From this resulted
a double negotiation and double propositions, which
surprised the Marquis of Wellesley extremely. Both
the Emperor's agents and mine being equally suspected met with a similar refusal. The Emperor,
surprised at so sudden and unexpected a conclusion,
in order to discover the cause, employed his foreign
agents and counter-police. At first he had only vague
informations; but he was soon enabled to judge that
his negotiation had been crossed by other agents,
whose mission he was unacquainted with. His suspicions at first fell on M. de Talleyrand; but, upon
his return, having received fresh information, he
discovered that M. Ouvrard had made overtures,
drawn up without his knowledge, to the Marquis of
Wellesley; and, as M. Ouvrard was known to be
connected with me, it was inferred that I had given
him his instructions. On the 2nd of June, being at
St. Cloud, the Emperor asked me in full council
what M. Ouvrard had gone to England for? "To
ascertain for me the sentiments of the new ministry
relative to peace, in conformity to the idea I had
the honour to submit to your Majesty before your
marriage." "So," replied the Emperor, "you make
war and peace without my being a party." He left
us, and gave orders to Savary to arrest M. Ouvrard,
and to conduct him to Vincennes; at the same time
I was forbidden to have any communication with the

prisoner. The next day, the portfolio of the police
was given to Savary. It was this time a real disgrace.

I should certainly have made a prediction rather
premature, by recalling the words of the prophet :
" In forty days Nineveh shall be destroyed ; " but I
might have predicted with confidence that in less
than four years the Empire of Napoleon would no
longer exist.

END OF VOL. I.

Lightning Source UK Ltd.
Milton Keynes UK
20 August 2009

142897UK00001B/4/A